OPERATION VIJAY

The Ultimate Solution

Shrikant Y. Ramani

About the Author

Shrikant Yeshwant Ramani

Com Curso Complementar de Ciencias (Portuguese)

DME, DBIM

BA (HISTORY)

Cdt. Under Officer NCC (C CERT. INFANTRY)

SOME COMMENTS:

The rich documentation provided by Shri Ramani is the need of the hour....This book superbly illustrated with rare military maps, archival documents and photographs needs to be on the shelf of all educated Goans who love their motherland. ....The letter written by Mahatma Gandhi to the Portuguese governor Dr. Jose Bossa and quoted in this book needs to be translated in Konkani and Marathi, framed and displayed in all the schools of Goa for our students to read...We can at least find some answers about our own historic shortcomings and mistakes if we read books like OPERATION VIJAY -the ULTIMATE SOLUTION....

-Dr. Nandkumar Kamat

This book is the right answer for those people who still praise the Portuguese rule in Goa. Today's Goan generation only knows that Indian Government liberated Goa by ordering **OPERATION VIJAY**. The details of this operation planning and what were the reasons why this action had to be undertaken are meticulously given in this book.

-Shri Naguesh Karmali

Besides a couple of typographical errors , the book is fairly well illustrated...I must commend the hard work put in to write this book, the dedication to painstakingly source his information despite his reported frustration at being denied access to information by the authorities...

-Lt. Cdr John Eric Gomes in Herald

This book could become like a document for the future generations and a awakener for youth who are practically unaware about the whole issue.

-Shri Manohar Parrikar
Ex. Chief Minister of Goa

THIS BOOK IS DEDICATED TO

**SONS and DAUGHTERS of this COUNTRY
WHO DEDICATED THEMSELVES to
BREAK
The LAST SHACKLES HOLDING OUR
MOTHERLAND IN BONDAGE**

And

**THE VALIANT ARMED FORCES
WHO LIBERATED
OUR GOA IN SWIFT ACTION DURING
OPERATION VIJAY**

First Edition : 22-09-2008
Revised & update second edition: 2012

© Published by:

BROADWAY PUBLISHING HOUSE

1st Floor, Ashirwad Bldg., Next to Rizvi Towers,
Near Caculo Island, 18th June Road, Panjim, Goa
Tel: 2420677, 6647037, 6647038, Fax: 6647038
Website: ww.bbcbooks.net
Email: bbcbooks@rediffmail.com

The writer can be contacted on shrikantramani@yahoo.co.in

ISBN: 9789380837376

Printed by: Rama Harmalkar, 9326102225
Cover Design by : Sunil Naik 9822115870

Price : ₹ 495/-

PREFACE

Today, I remember in our house in the village the picture of Bharatmata in chains. Who is this sad lady in chains? I used to wonder in my childhood. She was not my mother nor was she my grandmother. I was told that she was Bharatmata, mother of all of us. She was sad because she was not free. People who came from distant lands had enslaved and chained her. I used to look at her from the corner of my eyes, as I did not dare to confront her melancholic eyes.

Years passed and I saw that the British had left. We said that India had attained Independence. After some time we saw that the French had left too but our Goa and Daman and Diu still continued to be under foreign occupation. It was painful to imagine that the last chain was continuing to shackle our beloved country for fourteen long years even after Independence of the rest of the country in 1947.

Today, I am very happy to see that she is free and we all, her children are rejoicing and living as free people.

When Netaji Subhash Chandra Bose was traveling by Japanese submarine to reach Singapore, he told Capt. Teraoka, the Captain of the submarine, to inform him when he was at the southern end of India. After three days journey, Capt. Teraoka told him that they are at such a point wherefrom they will reach Indian coast if they go northwards. Netaji told the captain to surface the submarine, so that he could pray at the feet of his beloved **Motherland.** Despite grave risk the captain brought the submarine to the surface and after paying respects to the **MOTHER INDIA** he could not see, Netaji closed his eyes and sang the lines written by great poet **Bankim Chandra Chattopadhyaya** a century ago:

Tumi Vidya Tumi Dharm
Tumi Hridi Tumi Marma,
Baahute Tumi Maa Shakti,
Hridaye Tumi Maa Bhakti
Twaam Pranaa Sharire,
Mataram Vande, Mataram

(Oh Mother, Thou art the Knowledge,
Thou art the Spirit
Thou art the Heart, Thou art the Essence
Mother Thou art Strength of my Arms
Mother Thou art the Devotion in my Heart
Thou art the Life in my Body
Oh Mother I bow before You)

Let me pray the same lines before I proceed with the writing of this book.

This book dwells on in brief about the different phases of liberation initiatives after Independence and the decision to launch **Operation Vijay as the ultimate solution.**

I have used the material available in Indian as well as Portuguese books and records. I have literally reproduced words and complete sentences from these books. My aim has been, as far as possible, to give complete picture of the incidents which occurred almost half a century ago. Certainly this is not a book of historical fiction.

I hope this book will be of interest to readers and scholars who wish to know about the military solution India was forced to take due to the obduracy of the then Portuguese rulers. Today India and Portugal have established friendly and diplomatic relations. Both are trying to forget the dark pages in their historical past and to learn lessons from history.

With the publication of this book I am happy to have fulfilled a pledge I had taken years ago.

Vande Mataram !

Preface to second edition

I am humbled by the response given by readers and students of history to the first edition published on 22-09-2008.

As desired by the readers I have inserted important pictures and added some additional information connected with this operation, in this edition

I hope the readers will continue to read this book that tells many facets of war of Liberation of Goa, that incidentally is completing 50th year of its liberation.

Shrikant Yeshwant Ramani

Panaji- Goa.
Date : 1-9-2011

ACKNOWLEDGEMENT

First let me thank the Almighty who reminded me every moment about writing this book. A book that emphasizes that the loss of freedom will degrade the human mind and corrodes his self respect which ultimately leads him to servility;

I thank all the persons in the Historical Archives of Goa who helped me in securing all the information I needed. I specially thank Shri A. Yalgi and Shri R.S. Sambrekar who were a source of support in my endeavour;

I thank the staff in the Central Library especially Smt Pia Rodrigues, Smt Lourdes Costa e Rodrigues and Smt Malini Bhide who made my work simpler by providing me with the books I needed from time to time.

I thank my wife Prabha who helped me in completing this work. I could discuss with her the details of this book and get some useful hints;

I thank my son Milind for his help in the preparation of the book, especially in the use of computer features;

I thank Prof. D. S. Bhende for having taken pains to check the manuscript for errors.

I thank the History Division of the Ministry of Defence for their permission for the access to the Reference of the book OPERATION VIJAY, The Liberation of Goa and Other Portuguese Colonies in India;

I thank the authors of all the books mentioned in the BIBLIOGRAPHY, especially those who could not be contacted, as their present addresses were not available.

I thank the Naval Authorities at INS GOMANTAK for permitting me to photograph the memorial to fallen seamen at Angediv during Operation Vijay in 1961.

I thank Shri Rama Harmalkar and his team for extending all out help in bringing out this book.

CONTENTS

ILLUSTRATIONS

CHAPTER I

PORTUGUESE ENCLAVES IN INDIA

The Portuguese set foot on Indian soil on 20th May 1498. They reached Kappad near Kozikode or Calicut on the Malabar Coast on that day. During a period of a century they established many forts and factories in the West as well as East coast of India.[2] For centuries they created major upheavals on Indian soil. They fought with the Muslim rulers of Gujarat for the control of trade in the Gulf of Cambay. They secured a foothold in Diu and Daman after endless conflicts with the rulers of Gujarat.

They were in the Red Sea, Aden, Socotra Archipelago and Ormuz in the Persian Gulf. They had forts at Diu, Daman Tarapore, Bassein, Thana and Mumbai. On the west coast they were at Chaul, Mangalore, Honavar, Cannanor and Cochin.

In the 17th century the Dutch defeated them and dislodged them from the Malabar Coast. In the 18th century the Marathas under Chimnaji Appa, brother of Peshwa Baji Rao, defeated them at Bassein and then forced them to cede Chaul. Thereafter they were left with only Goa, Daman and Diu. The Portuguese continued to call this remnant of their empire along the Indian Ocean as **Estado Portugues da India.**[2]

They first conquered island of Goa in March 1510 from Adil Shah of Bijapur. However the Adil Shahi General Kamal Khan drove them away in a counter attack. Afonso de Albuquerque reconquered it on 25th November 1510 where they remained till the time of Independence of India and thereafter upto 19th December 1961 when they were defeated in the military action and forced to leave Indian soil forever.

The pages that follow describe how independent India tried to persuade them to leave these enclaves peacefully and in a dignified manner. It also tells how Portugal followed a policy of refusal of meeting the aspirations of the people of India. It tells how it changed the nomenclature of Colony to Overseas Province to escape the censure of world opinion. It used the Indian Government policy of non-violence to pin India down and create a stalemate.

The Indian Government finally had to give up its policy of non-violence for the liberation of these enclaves and was forced to order the launching of **Operation Vijay** as an **Ultimate Solution** to liberate these enclaves of **Goa, Daman** and **Diu.**

Land and the people

Goa

Goa extends for 100 kilometres along the western coast of India, its capital being 400 kilometres to the south of Bombay. It is situated between 14 ° 08and 15 ° 48' N, and 73 ° 45' and 74° 24' E.

A crescent shaped territory with an area of 3635 square kilometres, Goa is bounded on the north by Terekhol River, separating it from Sindhudurg district of Maharashtra State. On the east it is bounded by the range of the Western Ghats separating it from the districts of Belgaum and North Kanara of Karnataka state and in the west by the Arabian Sea. Its greatest length from north to south is about 100 kilometres and breadth from east to west is 64 kilometres.

The most distinguishing feature of mountain-studded Goa is the Western Ghats of the Sahyadri range. It skirts a considerable portion of the northeastern and southeastern boundaries and it branches off westwards across the territory into numerous spurs and ridges.

As one enters the territory by rail from the east, one passes through one of the most picturesque slopes of the Western Ghats with a panoramic view of the lush valleys and green hills, covered with forests, through which can be seen the silvery lines of many rivers and rivulets rushing down to level country down below. As one moves on, one finds the unspoiled countryside covered with pretty coconut and betelnut groves, till one reaches the coastal area where the vast blue expanse of the Arabian Sea comes into view.

The highest hill range is Sosogad which is 3827 feet above sea level; others of varying heights are to be found on the north, east and west of which Dudhsagar is perhaps the best known. The beautiful waterfalls emanating from there can be seen from a distance, while passing through the Ghats by train.

Map of Goa

The territory is intersected by numerous rivers, which are generally navigable. Some of the principal rivers are the Terekhol or Arondem, the Chapora, the Mandavi, the Zuari or Rachol. All these rivers run roughly from east to west, the approach from east follows the grain of the country and therefore, leads comparatively easily to the main inhabited area. The approaches from north and south run across the grain of the country and end (from the logistics point of view) at two great river obstacles, which cover the direct approaches to Panjim, the capital, and Velha (Old) Goa. These two rivers are Mandavi and Zuari, which together encircle the island of Goa (Ilhas), being connected on the landward side by a creek. The island is triangular, the apex (called the cabo or cape) being a rocky headland separating the harbour of Goa into two anchorages: Aguada at the mouth of the Mandavi on the north and Mormugao at the mouth of the Zuari on the south.

The climate of Goa is pleasantly warm, the minimum temperature being 14.4° C and the maximum never crossing 36.7° C. The rainy months are from June to September, during which the average rainfall is about 330 cms.

Apart from the beautiful countryside and cities, there are many places of historical interest, ports, ancient and modern temples, mosques and various churches. Old Goa is a city of ruins but some relics of Portuguese architecture dating back to 16-17th centuries still survive. The important ones are: Se' Catedral, Convent of St. Francis, Basilica of Bom Jesus, Church of S. Caetano, Convent of Santa Monica.

The chief Hindu temples are: Shri Manguesh at Mangueshim (Priol), Shri Shantadurga at Kavlem, Shri Ramnath at Ramnathi, Shri Naguesh and Shri Mahalakshmi at Bandoda and Shri Mahalasa at Mardol. There is also Safa Masjid at Ponda built during Adilshahi rule.

At one time, Goa used to be the chief entrepot of trade between the East and the West. It was particularly well known for its flourishing trade in horses with the Persian Gulf. With the passage of time and decline of the Portuguese power due to Dutch attacks, commerce declined and the place lost its importance.

Panjim became the capital of Goa in 1843 although it had been the Portuguese Viceroy's residence since 1759. It is situated on the southern bank of the Mandavi estuary, and seen from the river it presents an imposing sight. It is a beautiful city.

Daman

Daman is situated on the western coast of India and lies on the entrance to the Gulf of Cambay, about 160 kilometres north of Bombay. It is bounded on the north by the river Kolak, on the south by the Kalu River, and on the west by the sea. The eastern frontier touches Gujarat State.

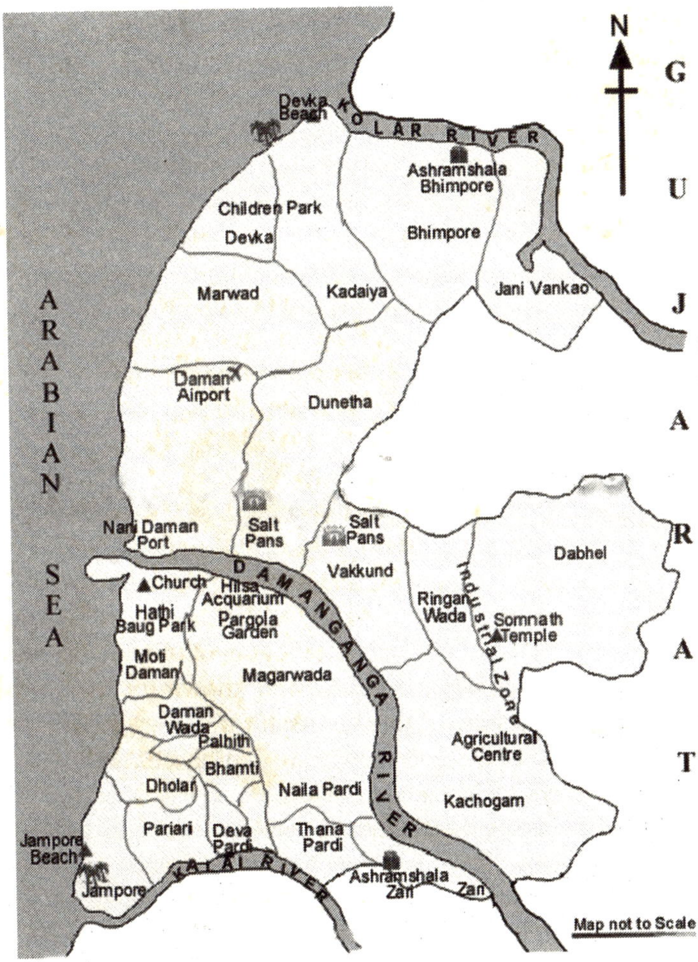

Map of Daman

Before 1954 the settlement was composed of two parts: Daman proper and the detached Pargana of Nagar Haveli to its east, isolated from it by a narrow strip of Indian Territory eight to eleven kilometres in width. Another tiny enclave, Dadra, formed part of the Pargana of Nagar Haveli. From both these enclaves (Dadra and Nagar Haveli) the Portuguese were ousted by freedom fighters in 1954.

The town of Daman lies between 20° 25' N and 72° 53' E and is divided into two distinct parts, called Nani (small) Daman and Moti (big) Daman, each with a fort.

The area of Daman, including the Pargana of Nagar Haveli, was 213 square kilometres, the area of Daman itself being about 60 square kilometres only. The predominant language used was Gujarati, but a few spoke Marathi, Urdu and other miscellaneous languages. Hindus formed the majority of population, followed by Muslims and then Christians. There were a few hundred Parsis, Khojas and Bohras.

The soil of Daman is fertile. Its climate is fairly pleasant throughout the year, except from May to August when it is uncomfortable, due to the summer heat.

Daman was once known for its commerce and trade. In the early 19th century its main trade was opium, which it imported from Karachi and exported to China. Of late it used to import luxury goods and smuggle them across India. This was done with the connivance of the Portuguese administration.

Diu

The Portuguese colony of Diu consisted of some territories on the mainland, the island of Diu and another small island, Panikota, about 19 kilometres to the east. Diu island lies between 20° 43' N and 71° 2' E in western India, and is separated from the southern extremity of Kathiavar peninsula by a narrow tidal creek flowing through considerable swamp. Its extreme length from east to west is about 11 kilometres and its greatest breadth from north to south a little more than 3 kilometres, the entire area of the colony being less than 39 square kilometres. Fishing boats

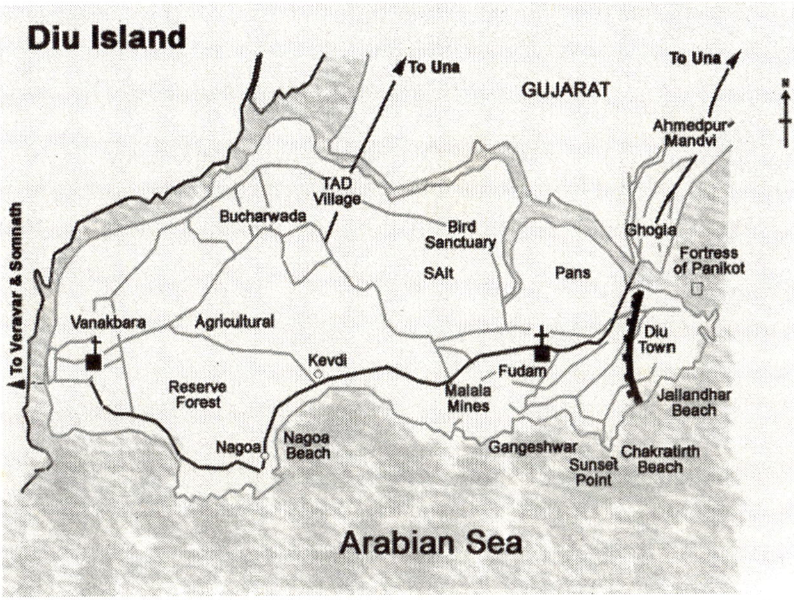

Map of Diu

and small crafts can only cross the narrow channel, which separates the island from the mainland. A sandstone cliff washed by the sea forms the southern face of the island.

Diu has a small but excellent harbour where vessels can safely ride at anchor in two fathoms of water. The elevation is nowhere more than 100 feet. The climate is generally dry and sultry.

The town and citadel of Diu stand on the east end of the island at a distance of 8 kilometres from Navibandar. Besides Diu town there are a few large villages on the island, namely Brancawara, commanding the channel on the west, Nagwa with a small fort on the bay on the south, and two bigger forts: de Passo Seco and de Passo Covo.

More than 96% of the people spoke Gujarati; the rest used miscellaneous languages including Urdu and Marathi.

Diu once enjoyed a flourishing trade with Arabia and the Persian Gulf, which made it a prosperous and wealthy island. In 1529 D. Nuno de Cunha arrived in India to take charge as Governor. He was under royal order to build a fort in Diu, which was under Bahadur Shah, Sultan of Gujarat. He did not succeed despite having a powerful fleet under him. Four years later Sultan Bahadur Shah allowed the Portuguese to build a fort as a token of gratitude for receiving help against the Mogul Emperor Humayun.

The Turks considered the Portuguese their rivals in the gulf trade and tried several times to dislodge them from Diu. The attacks under Malik Ayyaz and Khwaja Saffar form an important part of Gujarat history. The death of Sultan Bahadur Shah at Diu was a cowardly act executed by the Portuguese. He was drowned in a scuffle when he had come to visit Nuno da Cunha[3]

References:

1—BankimChanda Chattopadhyaya quoted in 'NETAJI' by V.S.Walimbe p-439

2—Encyclopedia Britannica

3—Whiteway—The Rise of Portuguese power in India -p247

—Chaube—History of Gujarat kingdom—p275

CHAPTER II

ON THE EVE OF INDIA'S INDEPENDENCE

One of the most significant events in the history of Goa occurred on 18th June, 1946. On this historic day, the first civil disobedience movement against the then 435 years old Portuguese Rule was launched in Goa. For the first time Goan Nationalists and Indian freedom fighters joined hands to wreck the political barrier created by the Portuguese between Indians in Goa and Indians living in the then British India.

Dr. Ram Manohar Lohia, the Indian Socialist leader, took a leading part in this movement. At a public meeting held in Margao on June 18th, 1946 he told the people that it was time they liberated themselves from the Portuguese shackles and moulded their own destiny. He stressed on the methods of economic exploitation the colonial powers used to enrich themselves.

Dr. Lohia was arrested and later released on the Indian border. The rousing reception given to Dr. Lohia by Goans indicated their political consciousness and their desire to integrate with the Mother Country - India.

Masses of Goans began to demonstrate in front of the administrative offices shouting the slogans ***Jai Hind, Jai Goa.*** Their conduct was orderly and peaceful and their method non-violent. The Gandhian movement of non-violence had at last reached Goa. The Portuguese made several attempts to disperse the people but the crowds became larger and larger. The panic stricken police resorted to violence but the Goans still continued chanting the same slogan in defiance of Portuguese authority.

The late Dr. Tristao Braganca e Cunha was the first to offer Satyagraha and court arrest. Dr. Ram Hegde, Purshottam Cacodcar, Adv. Jose Loyola and Laxmicanta Bhembre followed him. The movement continued up to November 1946 in spite of the violence, repressive policies and terrorism of the authorities. About 1,500 people were arrested, beaten and held in detention for various terms. Dr.

T.B.Cunha was sentenced to eight years imprisonment and ordered to be deported. The Portuguese thought that by deporting the Goan leaders to Portugal with savage sentences, they would break down the spirit of the Goan people. But the more oppressive the sentence, the greater was the resistance to Portuguese rule and more the number of arrests.

When Dr. T.B.Cunha was arrested and sentenced in Goa, Mahatma Gandhi was in Sevagram. He was very depressed by the developments in Goa. He stated:

"The Goan authorities are going on merrily with their dehumanizing activities by gagging the people of Goa. The latest instance is that of the "court martial" sentencing of Mr. Braganza Cunha to eight years and deporting him to a far off Portuguese settlement in Africa for the crime daring to assert his elementary right to civil liberty." [4]

The Congress working Committee passed on August 12, 1946 the following resolution, which read:

"The people of these (the Portuguese) possessions have been reduced to poverty and degradation; politically they have practically no rights, and even the most elementary civil liberties are denied them. The Fascist administration of Portugal functions in a peculiarly oppressive way in this small colony. It was once rich and prosperous and now deserted, with its people migrating elsewhere in search of a living."

"Goa has always been, and must inevitably continue to be, part of India. It must share in the freedom of the Indian people". [5]

Gandhiji on Goa

"In a free India, Goa cannot be allowed to exist as a separate entity in opposition to the laws of the Free State"

At the time of the arrest of Dr. Lohia in Goa, Mahatma Gandhi was in New Delhi. When he was manhandled by the Portuguese police and deported, Gandhiji reacted strongly and criticised the action of the Portuguese Government. He immediately issued a statement in support of Goa's struggle for freedom and praised Dr. Lohia for rendering a service to the cause of civil liberty especially to Goans. The statement read:

"The little Portuguese settlement which merely exists on the sufferance of the British Government can ill-afford to ape its bad manners. In free India, Goa cannot be allowed to exist as a separate entity in opposition to the laws of the Free State. The present Portuguese Government will no longer be able to rely on the protection of British arms to isolate and keep under subjugation the inhabitants of Goa against their will. I venture to advise the Portuguese Government of Goa to recognise the sign of the times and come to honourable terms with the inhabitants rather than function on any treaty that might exist between them and the British Government."[6]

Mahatma Gandhi reiterated his assurances to the Goan people:

"To the inhabitants of Goa I will say that they shed fear of the Portuguese Government as the people of the other parts of India have shed fear of the mighty British Government and assert their fundamental rights of civil liberty and all it means. The differences of religion among the inhabitants of Goa should be no bar to common civil life. Religion is for each individual to live. It should never become a bone of contention or quarrel between religious sects." [7]

Dr. Jose Bossa's Objection to Gandhiji's Letter to Goans

In reply to the remarks made by Gandhiji in 'The Harijan' Dr. Bossa, the then Governor-General of Portuguese India, sent a long letter to Gandhiji expressing surprise at his apparent support for the 'recent anarchical agitation'.

He asked in his letter: *"What moral or legal right has a* ***stranger*** *like Dr. Lohia to come and disturb these peaceful people? The Portuguese did not come to India merely for the purpose of domination or economic exploitation, which does not exist, but were guided by the lofty ideal of brotherhood, and therefore always considered the Indians as brothers and never as subjects. Ever since the distant days of Albuquerque, the Portuguese have tried selflessly to free the Indians from the oppressive and iniquitous caste system which, in your own opinion, is a stain on Indian Civilisation, and they have succeeded in this."*[8]

Having thus glorified the past, the Governor-General went on to say that absolute freedom was an unworkable utopia, and assured Gandhiji that the liberties of the Goan people were not threatened except by those agitators who through bribery or compulsion attempted to lead poorer classes astray from a life of peaceful labour.

Gandhiji's Letter to the Governor-General of Portuguese India

(The following is the text of Gandhiji's letter dated 11th August 1946, to H.E. Jose Bossa, Governor General of Portuguese India, in reply to his letter of the 18th July 1946, which has already appeared in the Press).

> Dear friend
>
> It was kind of you to write to me in reply to what I had written in 'Harijan' about Goa affairs. I suppose you know that I have visited Mozambique, Delagoa and Inhabane. I did not notice there any Government for philanthropic purposes. Indeed I was astonished to see the distinction that the Government made between Indians and the Portuguese and between Africans and themselves. Nor does the history of the Portuguese Settlement in India prove the claim set forth by you. Indeed what I see and know of the conditions in Goa, is hardly edifying. That the Indians

in Goa have been speechless is proof, not of the innocence or the philanthropic nature of the Portuguese Government but of the rule of terror. You will forgive me for not subscribing to your statement that there is full liberty in Goa and that the agitation is confined only to a few malcontents.

Every account, received personally by me and seen in the papers here in this part of India, confirms the contrary view. I suppose, the report of the sentence by your Court Martial, of eight years on Dr. Braganza and his contemplated exile to a far off Portuguese settlement, is by itself a striking corroboration of the fact that civil liberty is a rare article in Goa. Why should a law-abiding citizen like Dr. Braganza be considered so dangerous as to be singled out for exile?

Though the politics of Dr. Lohia probably differ from mine, he has commanded my admiration for his having gone to Goa and put his finger on its black spot. Inhabitants of Goa can afford to wait for Independence, until much greater India has regained it. But no person or group can thus remain without civil liberty without losing self-respect. He has lighted a torch, which the inhabitants of Goa cannot, except at their peril, allow to be extinguished. Both you and the inhabitants should feel thankful to the Doctor for lighting that torch. Therefore, your description of him as "stranger" would excite laughter, if it was not so tragic. Surely the truth is that the Portuguese coming from Portugal are strangers, whether they come as philanthropers or as governors exploiting the so-called weaker races of the earth.

You have talked of the abolition of caste distinctions. What I see has happened is that not only no caste distinction has been abolished but at least one more caste, far more terrible than the system "caste" has been added by the Portuguese Rulers.

I therefore, hope that you will revise your views on philanthropy, civil liberty and caste distinctions, withdraw all the African police, declare yourself whole-heartedly for civil liberty and if possible, even let the inhabitants of Goa frame their own Government, and invite from Greater India more experienced Indians to assist the inhabitants and even you in forming such Government.[9]

Yours,
M. K. Gandhi

Mahatma Gandhi's stand on the Goan freedom struggle is revealed in his reply to this letter of the Governor

A close examination of Mahatma Gandhi's statement reveals that Gandhiji was fully aware of the political situation in Goa. He was fully behind the struggle for civil liberties in Goa and did not conceive of Goa as separate from India and Goans as different from the rest of the Indians. He believed that the liberation of Goa was not merely the duty of the Goans but of the entire Indian community.

In early January 1948, when Gandhiji was approached for his advice, he said:

"The Indian Constituent Assembly has accepted the principle of self-determination, so that the Goans would decide their future political status in the Indian Union without interference either by Maharashtra or by Karnataka".

"The Goan freedom fighters should carry on their struggle against the Portuguese and start an intensified Satyagraha movement if they had the requisite forces. They should bravely face imprisonment, beatings and hardships. It did not matter if the Portuguese Government sent Goans to Mozambique and other far-off penal settlements for twenty or twenty-five years. He asked the Goans to do their duty and leave the rest to the Indian Union".

Gandhiji advised that those who believed in violence should not be interfered with or criticized by other workers. They should be left alone to follow their line of action unmolested.

He advised all sincere believers in non-violence to be brave enough to openly work among the masses in Goa, even if in the process they were arrested. They need not necessarily court arrest.

References:

4—Gandhiji in 'The Harijan' dtd 18-08-1946

5—Congress W. Comm. Resolution dtd 12-8-1946

6—Gandhiji in 'The Harijan' dtd 30-06-1946

7—Ibid –The Harijan dtd 30-6-1946

8—Dr. Bossa's letter to Gandhiji dtd 18-07-1946

9—Gandhiji's reply to Governor Bossa in 'The Harijan' dtd 1-08-1946.

CHAPTER III

INDIA ATTAINS INDEPENDENCE

The British Government ultimately decided to grant Independence to **India**. Lord Mountbatten, the new Viceroy was sent to work out the details of the Transfer of Power. After meetings with leaders of the Congress and the Muslim League, INDIA under British Rule was divided into dominions of India and Pakistan. The date of transfer of power was decided to be 15th August, 1947 for the dominions of India and Pakistan.

On that day, only the British India became independent. The Native States and the enclaves under the French and the Portuguese were yet to decide their future in Indian Polity.

*(We are dealing with the Portuguese response regarding their territories of **Goa, Daman and Diu** and the stand taken by **Portugal** in the days to come. We are not discussing the entire situation in the Sub-continent after the formation of Independent India.)*

On 12th August, 1947, the Ambassador of Great Britain in Lisbon sent the following note No 173/20/47 to the *Portuguese Presidente do Conselho and Minister for Foreign Affairs:*

Lisboa, 12th August, 1947

Monsieur le Ministre—On instructions from my Government I have the honour to inform Your Excellency of the formal establishment of the **Dominions of India and Pakistan** with effect from **August 15th**.

I shall continue to represent His Magesty the King, in respect of these Dominions until such time as their two Governments make alternative arrangements with the Portuguese Government for their representation. I am to express the hope that this will be agreeable to the Portuguese Government.[10]

Nigel Ronald

The *Presidente do Conselho, Dr. Salazar* sent the following telegram to the Prime Minister of India

Lisboa, 14th August, 1947

Prompted by the unfailing interest with which for centuries they have followed the destinies of India, the Portuguese Government wish on this notable occasion to extend to Your Excellency their best wishes for the success of the peaceful pursuits and future welfare of the peoples of India.[11]

Oliveira Salazar

The Prime Minister Pandit Nehru thanked him with the following telegram:

I hasten to thank Your Excellency for the kind message that you have sent me on the occasion of the attainment by India of her cherished goal of Sovereign State and take this opportunity to convey to you the assurance of my highest consideration.[12]

Pandit Jawaharlal Nehru

After the exchange of formal greetings, the Portuguese Government asked its Consul in Bombay Mr. Joao de Lucena to seek an appointment of Mr. Nehru who also happened to be the Minister for Foreign Affairs. Dr. Salazar wanted to know the actual position of Mr. Nehru regarding Portuguese India.

Up to this point of time the Ambassador of Great Britain in Lisbon represented India while Lisbon could not directly talk to New- Delhi.

The State of Hydrabad had not joined the Indian Union and was trying its best to become independent. It secretly sent feelers to the Portuguese Government with a proposal to buy Goa and its railway. Portugal though not agreeing with the proposal to sell Goa and its railway gave a counter proposal.

When this matter came to the knowledge of Mr. Nehru, he was naturally upset, more so as there was no official denial from the Portuguese side about Hydrabad's offer.

Post Independence Diplomatic Initiatives

Diplomatic Relations

It was necessary for both Portugal as well as India to establish diplomatic relations. India wanted to engage Portugal in talks about the future of their territories in India. Portugal on the other hand wanted to tell India that these territories are part and parcel of their country. Both felt it prudent to first establish diplomatic relations.

The Indian High Commissioner in London Mr. V. K. Krishna Menon and the Portuguese Ambassador in London Duque de Palmella had series of talks to decide about the modalities to settle this issue. After the meeting of Mr. Menon with the Portuguese Foreign minister Dr. Caeiro de Mota in Paris it was decided to issue a simultaneous announcement on 12th August, 1948 as follows:

"The Governments of India and Portugal, desirous of promoting and strengthening friendship between their respective countries, have decided to exchange diplomatic representatives at the Legation levels"[13]

Portugal appointed Dr. Vasco Vieira Garin as Minister at the Legation in New Delhi. He reached Bombay on 15th January, 1949 and stayed in Bombay for four days as guest of the Governor of the State of Bombay Shri Maharaj Singh.

Mr. Garin presented his credentials to the Governor General of the Dominion H. E. C. Rajagopalachari, on 29th January. Earlier on 25th Pandit Nehru received him. He was with him for about forty minutes. As expected the topic of future of Portuguese territories as well as Padroado problem came for discussion. The meeting occurred in a friendly and happy atmosphere.[14]

On 7th March Dr. Garin visited Sardar Patel, Deputy Prime Minister and Minister of Home Affairs at his residence. The first question asked by Sardar Patel was: "*What does the Portuguese Government think regarding the territories it has in India keeping in mind our desire to integrate them in the Indian Union? To Dr. Garin's by now known answer he retorted: You are talking in this manner but if Portugal had foreign enclaves, in its territory you would have understood our sentiments better*".[15]

On 10th June, 1949, the Indian Foreign office informed the Portuguese Government about the appointment of Parekkat Achuta Menon as the Minister at the Indian Legation in Lisbon. Mr. Menon presented his credentials in August 1949.

Aide Memoire

On 20th February, 1950, Mr. Menon handed over to the Portuguese Foreign Minister, Dr. Caeiro Mota an ***AIDE MEMOIRE***[16] expressing India's stand on Portuguese territories on Indian soil.

1. The Government of India have noted with satisfaction the statement made by His Excellency Dr. Salazar, President of Council, on the 20th October, 1949, that problems relating to Portuguese colonies in India are capable of solution by friendly negotiations and that there is great scope for understanding between India and Portugal on moral and economic grounds. They are particularly gratified to note that with regard to the Padroado the Portuguese Government have entered into negotiations with the Holy See to bring the matter to a speedy and amicable conclusion.

2. Dr. Salazar expressed the hope that establishment of an Indian diplomatic mission in Portugal would help in solving the existing problems between the two countries to mutual satisfaction. The Government of India share this hope and feel the time has come to bring to the notice of the Portuguese Government their views on the Portuguese colonies in India, a subject to which Dr. Salazar made reference in his speech.
3. For over 200 years India was under the domination of European powers. The nationalist movement which, after prolonged but peaceful struggle, succeeded in securing the transfer of power from British to Indian hands was not, in sentiment or purpose, confined to what were formerly British India and Indian states under British suzerainty. It was, within the geographical limits of India, a universal movement and remains so. The historical and cultural unity of India transcends political frontiers such as those that now demarcate the French settlements or the Portuguese colonies. Popular feeling in these territories are for union with the new and free India of the Republic. Any other sentiment would be unnatural; the interruption of India's fundamental unity by a few hundred years of foreign rule over various segments of the country cannot, in the perspective of history, be more than a transient phase. This unity has no parallel in Europe or any part of the world because, though often interrupted, it always remained an aspiration and, again and again, over the course of centuries was effectively restored. The movement for the union of the remaining foreign settlements with the Indian Republic is part of this historical process; it is real and vital, and, as such, seeks urgent satisfaction.
4. The Portuguese Government is no doubt aware that the Government of India and France started negotiations nearly two years ago to find a satisfactory solution of the problem of French Settlements on the Indian mainland. This was the inevitable outcome of Indian independence and the recognition by both India and France of the impact of this historic event upon all parts of India, Princely or French or Portuguese. The negotiations with France have been friendly and both Governments look forward to their early and

successful conclusion. The Government of India now approaches the Portuguese Government with the request for an immediate start of negotiations regarding the future of Portuguese colonies in India. They sincerely hope for a prompt and friendly response. Change is of the essence of history and the key to the maintenance of good relations between nations is adaptability to change. No spirit of aggression or aggrandizement animates India. In seeking a reunion of these colonies with herself, she is asking for nothing more than the fulfillment of a natural urge of tradition and human emotion. What France has recognized as natural and legitimate should not appear to Portugal as unnatural and unreasonable. India ardently desires the friendship of Portugal: the peaceful reunion of what is now Portuguese India with the Indian Republic will provide a lasting foundation for that friendship. Once the principle of reunion has been accepted, ways and means to achieve it can be devised in friendly consultation.

Portugal Reveals Her Mind

The extract of the speech delivered by Dr. Salazar in the library of the National Assembly on 25th November, 1947, clearly reveals the mind of the Portuguese Government[17]. He said: *"The Portuguese India has been however an object of great worries. The fall of the (British) Indian empire and the formation of two big dominions, incorporated at the moment in the British Commonwealth, and independent nations, in the days to come are without doubt great events of our times. It is understood that certainly this fact will have repercussions beyond its frontiers, in the dominions not connected with British Sovereignty."*

"If GOA is geographically India, it is Europe from social, religious and cultural points of view. If they live as the Westerners, Indo-Portuguese and Indians, politically they are all Portuguese citizens meaning thereby that they are members without any

distinction of a civilized community, existing for some centuries. They work not only in places they were born but also in Metropole and throughout the Empire."

"If the new circumstances or longings of the population require increase in their responsibilities, justify changes in the statute or administrative regime it is a problem concerning us and Portuguese India. This is under study and it will have a suitable solution. On the other hand we have to trust the patriotism of our people, whose religious, cultural and even civic heritage cannot be safe unless they are loyal to the State."

In another speech delivered on 20th October, 1949 in the National Assembly, Dr. Salazar said: *"The question of Goa is the most serious and delicate, partly due to the external pressures and partly due to disorientation of our people. I do not refer to the campaign in the Indian Press which is free but irresponsible, but to the statements of people in power who freely continue speaking about the integration of Goa in the Indian Union."*

"India has many, many means to create difficulties and complicate the life in Goa: it has territorial contiguity, economic dependence. Working and economy of our immigrants are the arms it can effectively use against us."

"India is compelled to think around the ideal of geographical unity. It is an ideal and not a right. Goa is integrated in the Portuguese sovereignty for many centuries."

"The Government of India placed before the Portuguese Government its objections to the functioning of Padroado. It felt that it is a political interference in the ecclesiastical matter of a sovereign country by a foreign country. As we understand that the sensitiveness of exercise of this right may hurt it, we are now discussing with the Holy See to find a satisfactory solution agreeable to India."

"Goa has complaints and aspirations which on scrutiny were seen that they could not be satisfied, due to restrictions of ACTO

COLONIAL (Colonial Act) which is a part of the Constitution. The revision in the Constitution will help in finding solution to some of the pending questions. However, these are family problems and are not of such magnitude and gravity in the affairs of our India requiring different directives than the ones left by our ancestors under the Portuguese flag!"

Portugal's Reply to Aide Memoire

The reply[18] handed over to India's Minister in Lisbon by the Portuguese Foreign Minister, on 15th June, 1950 stated clearly the Portuguese response to India's *AIDE MEMOIRE* dated 27th February, 1950. It stated:

"In the above AIDE-MEMOIRE, the Government of India has invited the Portuguese Government to initiate the negotiations regarding the future of "Portuguese Colonies" in Hindustan. All the reasons given are repetitions, expressed in the last sentences in the Aide-Memoire, which talks about reunion of GOA, DAMAN and DIU with the Indian Republic. The negotiations therefore would be only to define the format as to how the Portuguese State of Goa would be integrated in the Indian Union."

"Whenever the Presidente do Conselho has referred to India, and more in details in his speech of 30 October, 1949, he has expressed without reservations not only the desire of Portuguese people but also the goodwill of his Government in finding a mutually acceptable solution to multiple problems which the contiguity of territories, the economic dependence, and the common base of sentiments and culture create between the Portuguese State of India and the Indian Republic. He has confirmed this goodwill time and again and would be confirming in corresponding friendly sentiments with the Republic of India.

"There would not be any logic to change from this base and accept the position that these problems will cease to exist by handing over to India a part of the Portuguese Nation. We do not want to discuss the reasons about the parity with other European countries

as there is no similarity at all with the problems posed to the French Government."

"It will be easily recognized that the aspiration of geographical unity will not have any juridical or moral value. With great difficulty it could be conceived such objective in the development of a peaceful international community.

"We conclude as follows: The Portuguese Government understands purely from the human point of view the reasons put forward by the Government of India, and because of this reason it has not been hurt, though this could be considered as a threat to its national integrity. It continues to desire to maintain and have close friendly relations with the Republic of India, and collaborate confidently with its government in solving all the difficulties or problems arising due to existence of Portuguese territory and population in the Indian peninsula. It wants to show its goodwill and friendly spirit in the matter of the references and questions posed, however it wants to declare loyally that it is a question which cannot be discussed and much less accept· the proposed solutions."

Futility of Diplomatic Relations forTransfer of Territories

The Legation of India in Lisbon presented the following note to the Portuguese Foreign Ministry on 14th January,1953.[19]:

> "It will be recalled that an aide memoire from the Government of India was presented to His Excellency the Foreign Minister of Portugal, in Lisbon, on February 27, 1950 regarding the future of Portuguese possessions in India. It was explained in the aide memoire that the nationalist movement, which culminated in the establishment of a free and independent India had for its objective the achievement of the historical and cultural unity of India, which had throughout the centuries transcended political frontiers such as those demarcating Portuguese and French possessions in India.

This movement for union was part of a historical process, which sought urgent satisfaction. It was suggested accordingly that negotiations might be opened to determine the future of Portuguese possessions in India and that, once the principle of reunion of these possessions with India was accepted, ways and means to achieve it could be devised by friendly consultation between the Governments of Portugal and of India".

"The Portuguese Government did not see their way to agree to this request. It was asserted, on their behalf, that Goa, Daman and Diu were not "colonies", but formed an integral part of Portugal, and that there was no popular sentiment in those territories in favour of re-union with Independent India. These views were set forth in greater detail in a note dated June 15th 1950, in which the Portuguese Government stated that they were unable to discuss and much less accept the solution proposed by the Government of India. The then minister in Portugal expressed deep disappointment at this reply, and stated that the Government of India could not accept this as a final disposition of the question or in any way acquiescence in the continuance of the existing position."

The Portuguese Government's note, referring to the political rights of the inhabitants of the Portuguese possessions in India, described the position as one of enjoyment of liberties and privileges identical with those recognized in any other part of Portuguese territory. It went on to say that this was one of the reasons why the Portuguese Government considered that the statement that the popular sentiment in the Portuguese possessions in India was in favour of merger with India was due to misapprehension. A totally different picture emerges from the record of events, which are known to have occurred in the Portuguese possessions in India during the past few years. There has been a progressive curtailment of political liberties, many persons professing sympathy with the idea of merger with India having been punished summarily and severely and, in some cases deported to far-away Portuguese prisons. Censorship of the press has been imposed, with consequent denial of freedom of speech and writing. Public meetings have been banned; arrests have been made without warrant; and resort has been had to trial by court martial.

"In addition to these repressive measures, many decrees have been issued which have had the effect of depriving Indian citizens in Goa of freedom of residence, commerce, trade and occupation, as well as the right to acquire property. This action is not only contrary to the traditional friendship professed by the Government of Portugal towards India, but has also imposed serious disabilities on a group of people who are undistinguishable from the other inhabitants of Goa, Daman and Diu, in race, culture and creed. The many representations made by the Government of India to the Portuguese authorities on this subject have led to no result.

"The hope has so far been entertained that, with time, a fuller understanding of the problem may incline the Portuguese Government to a more realistic approach. This hope has been disappointed, and the accumulating evidence of a policy directed to the suppression of all manifestation of sympathy with the cause of merger with India has hardened public opinion; and the demand is now widespread that the present unsatisfactory position should be brought to a speedy termination. Political barriers artificially created by accident of history can no longer stop the rising tide of national urge for unity. No longer, again, is it compatible with the status of India as an independent republic that the pockets of foreign territory, however small in area and however friendly the Powers occupying them, should continue to exist in Indian soil.

"The Government of India has accordingly come to the conclusion that no solution of this problem is now possible except on the basis of a direct transfer which will ensure the merger of these territories at an early date with the Indian Union. The Government of India would like, at the same time, to declare that it will be their desire to maintain the cultural and other rights, including language, laws and customs of the inhabitants of these territories, and to make no changes in such and like matters except with their consent.

"The Legation of India earnestly hopes that the Portuguese Government will agree to the opening of negotiations for the direct transfer of these territories to India. The Government of India has suggested that the principle of direct transfer should be accepted first and that this should be followed by a ***de facto*** transfer of administration. If this is agreed to between the respective Governments, the other steps, including such constitutional formalities as might be necessary, will offer no difficulty. The legal sovereignty of Portugal would continue until the steps then considered appropriate had been taken to give effect to the decisions arrived at. The Government of India would be glad if the government of Portugal would accept these suggestions as a basis for the proposed negotiations."

Note dated 1st May, 1953 Given to the Portuguese Foreign Ministry

"On January 14, 1953, the legation of India presented a note to the Ministry of Foreign Affairs[20] about the future of the Portuguese possessions in India. The note recalled the earlier efforts of the Government of India to enter into negotiations with the Portuguese Government and stated that, in view of the failure of the efforts, the Government of India had come to the conclusion that no settlement is now possible except on the basis of a direct transfer which would ensure the merger of these territories with the Union of India. The Government of India also made it clear that it is their desire to maintain the cultural and other rights of the inhabitants of these territories and to make no changes in suchlike matters except with their consent.

"The Portuguese Government were invited to agree to the opening of negotiations between the two Governments, on the basis mentioned in the note, for the direct transfer of these territories. Although more than three months have elapsed, the Portuguese Government have sent no reply to the note and have even refused to discuss this question with the Indian Charge' d'Affairs in Lisbon. The Government of India has established a Legation in Lisbon in the expectation that this would assist in reaching a settlement on this question. The attitude of the Portuguese Government has, however, rendered impossible the achievement of this purpose.

"The Government of India have accordingly come to the conclusion that their Legation in Lisbon has ceased to be of practical utility. They can see no advantage of keeping the Legation, if the Portuguese Government is unwilling to discuss the future of their possessions in India with the Government of India's representative. They propose, therefore, to withdraw their Mission from Lisbon unless the Portuguese Government are prepared, on further consideration, to discuss the suggestions which have been made by the Government of India."

Note dated 21st May, 1953

I am directed by the Government of India to state[21] that in a note delivered on 1st May, 1953, the Legation of India informed the Ministry of Foreign Affairs that in view of the continued refusal of the Portuguese Government to discuss the future of the Portuguese Possessions in India with the Government of India's representative in Lisbon, the Government of India have come to the conclusion that their Legation in Lisbon has ceased to be of practical utility. The note also stated that the Government of India proposed to withdraw their Mission in Lisbon unless the Portuguese

Government is prepared, on further consideration, to discuss the proposals, which have been made by the Government of India.

The Government of India have received the reply of the Portuguese Government dated 15th May, 1953. This reply indicates that the attitude of the Portuguese Government in regard to the possessions in India has undergone NO change and they have NOT appreciated the points raised in the Government of India's Note of 1st May. It has been made clear that the Portuguese Government is NOT prepared to discuss this question, much less to accept the solution proposed by the Government of India. In view of this, the Government of India has come to the conclusion that their Mission in Lisbon can serve NO useful purpose and have decided to close it. "This Legation will address a further communication to the Government of Portugal intimating the exact date on which the Legation will be closed and requesting the Government of Portugal to provide such facilities as may be required for winding up the affairs of the Legation and for the transfer of the staff and the property of the Legation of India."

Kewal Singh
Chargé d'Affaires Ad
Interim of India in Portugal

Note dated 26th May, 1953 Closure of Legation in Lisbon

"In continuation of letter No. Pol (P) dated 21st May, I write to inform you[22] that the Government of India having decided to withdraw their Mission in Lisbon, this Legation will be closed from 11th June 1953. With your Excellency's permission, I shall be approaching the Protocol Department with a view to obtain necessary facilities for winding up the affairs of this Legation and for the transfer of the staff and the property of the Legation."

Kewal Singh
Chargé d'Affaires Ad
Interim of India in Portugal

The Portuguese Government, however, decided to maintain its Legation in New Delhi, as it continued to consider its usefulness in relations between the two countries.

References:

10—20 anos de Defesa do Estado –Min. dos Neg. Esrtr. -Vol Ip-3
11—Salazar's Greetings. Ibid—p—5
12—Nehru's thanks. Ibid—p 5
13- -Ibid—p 63 and p-91
14—Ibid-VolI-p119-
15—Ibid-Vol-II –128
16—Aide Memoire dtd 20-02-1950—Ibid- Vol-II-p184-187
17—Salazar's speech—Ibid Vol II-p157
18— Portuguese reply to Aide Memoire-Ibid-Vol II –p219-221
19—Indian Note to Portugal- Ibid-p281-285
20—Note informing the intention of closure- Ibid-p292-299
21—Note –Ibid—p307-308
22—Note informing the closure- Ibid-p309-310

CHAPTER IV

LIBERATION OF DADRA and NAGAR HAVELI and SATYAGRAHA of 1955

Liberation of Dadra And Nagar Haveli

A very significant and historic event occurred on 21st July, 1954. Dadra, a detached Portuguese pocket about 160 kilometres (one hundred miles) north of Bombay, was liberated by Goan volunteers[23]. Eleven days later, the population of Nagar Haveli, another Portuguese pocket to the east of Daman and separated from it by a narrow strip of Indian Territory was also liberated.

The liberation of these two places can be termed as the "Beginning of the end of Portuguese Colonial rule in India". It ended the 175 years of Portuguese rule in these pockets. The success of this event encouraged the freedom fighters so much that a mass Satyagraha was planned to take place next year. The Congress party that was in power at the Centre could not spearhead this movement, as it had to be in line with the Government's policy. The agitation naturally went into the hands of opposition parties, notably the Praja Socialist Party popularly known as the P S P.

Meanwhile, Portugal accused India of having sent armed Indians to liberate the enclaves of Dadra and Nagar Haveli, and demanded the right of passage for her armed forces through Indian Territory to re-establish her rule there. On India's refusal to accede to this request Portugal went to the International Court of Justice at The Hague in December 1955.

(The case was fought from December 1955 to 12th April, 1960. We will not go into the details of the case as it is a subject worthy of a separate book, outside the aim of the present one)

The final judgment on this complaint was delivered on 12th April, 1960.

It said: "*In view of the tension then prevailing in intervening Indian Territory, the Court is unable to hold that India's refusal of passage to the proposed delegation and its refusal of visas to Portuguese nationals of European origin and to native Indo-Portuguese in the employ of the Portuguese Government was action contrary to its obligation resulting from Portugal's right of passage. Portugal's claim of a right of passage is subject to full recognition and exercise of Indian sovereignty over the intervening territory and without any immunity in favour of Portugal. The Court is of the view that India's refusal of passage in those cases was, in the circumstances, covered by its power of regulation and control of passage*".[24]

The liberated enclaves remained autonomous territories for some time; the Varishta Panchayat made requests to the Government of India for their merger with India. In August 1961, the Government of India acceded to the requests and carried through the Parliament two bills making the enclaves a part of the Indian Union, to be governed directly by the Centre, and giving them the right to be represented in the Lok Sabha.[25]

Satyagraha - The Non Violent Approach And Portugal's Violent Reply

The Goa Vimochan Samiti announced that it would launch a peaceful Satyagraha from 15th August, 1955. Portugal sent the chief of its armed forces General Barros Rodrigues to meet these peaceful freedom fighters. The concept of Satyagraha was beyond their comprehension. They decided to meet it with guns and bullets.

On the morning of 15th August, 1955, the eighth anniversary of India's independence, about 4204 peaceful Satyagrahis, including women, drawn from all political parties entered Goa, Daman and Diu in small groups. They were unarmed and were headed there to demonstrate their sympathy and solidarity with the Goan people's liberation movement and offer Satyagraha.

Satyagrahis entered from all sides during the night of 14/15 August from the northern Aronda border and from Castle Rock in the east.

Some even waded through the river Terekhol. On all fronts the Portuguese police and army units were ready to repel the "invaders", who had nothing more than a few flags in their hands. In all sectors, the police opened fire on the Satyagrahis, generally without warning. A woman Shrimati Subhadrabai Sagar, who was carrying the national flag, was shot down at point blank range. Sardar Karnal Singh from Punjab was shot in similar fashion. John Hlavacek of the United Press of America and Arthur Bonnear of Columbia Broadcasting brought the dead Satyagrahis and the wounded Mrs. Sagar to Indian territory. Twentytwo Satyagrahis were brutally killed. Two hundred and twenty five were injured, many maimed for life. Some were pushed back to India and several arrested. In many places Goans themselves offered Satyagraha and flew Indian flags on buildings. They were rounded up and brutally assaulted before and after the arrests.[26]

The foreign correspondents covering the Satyagraha for their papers were of the opinion that firing on peaceful Satyagrahis was unnecessary. Prime Minister Nehru charecterised the firing as brutal and uncivilized in the extreme. A wave of anger and resentment swept throughout the country. Demonstrations and hartals were held at many places in India, and the people demanded that the Government should take police action in the enclaves to save the lives of Satyagrahis.

The Government of India, to avoid an unnecessary bloodbath, sealed the borders of the Portuguese possessions, thereby stopping the entry of Satyagrahis into these enclaves, hoping that the Portuguese would respond by agreeing to negotiate and settle the question peacefully. The Portuguese Government did not react in the expected way.

The stalemate continued...

References:

23—Prabhakar Vaidya—Nagar Havelicha Mukti Sangram Ani Mee

24—Judgement of Int. Court of Justice dtd 12-04-1960

25—Resolution of Varishta Panchayat—dtd 12-06-1961.

26—Pt. Nehru's Statement in Lok Sabha
P.D.Gaitonde-Liberation of Goa-p 108

Martyr Sardar Karnal Singh

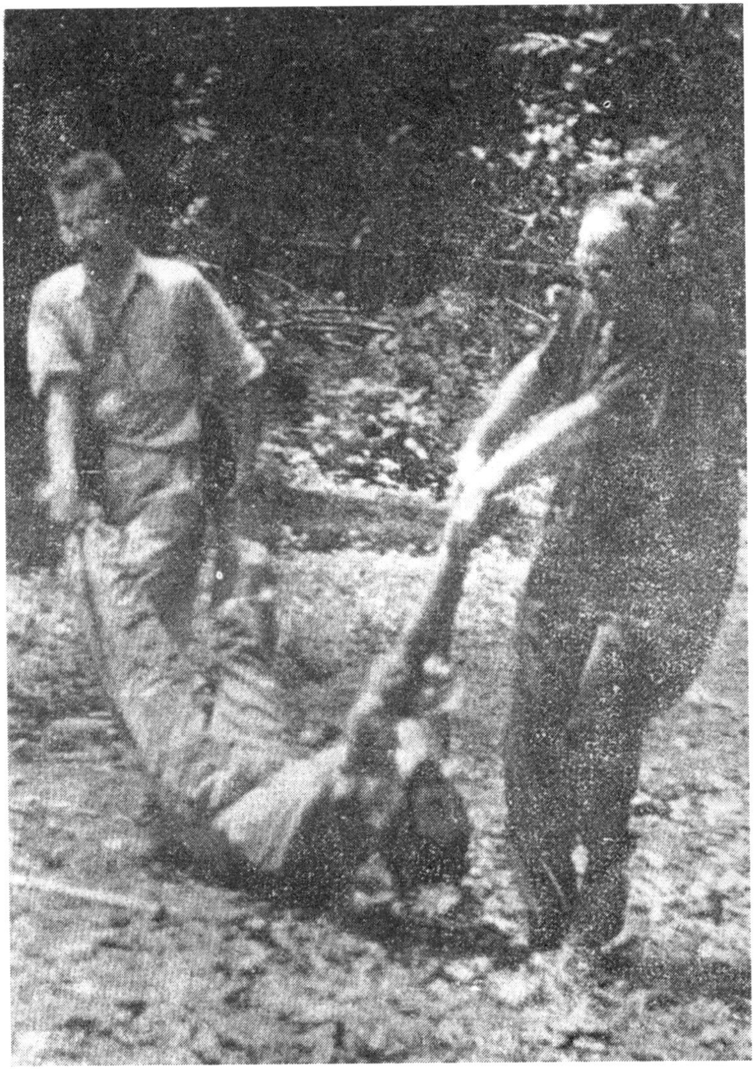

American journalists carrying the dead and wounded

CHAPTER V

WHAT WAS INDIA TO DO?

The Seminar On Portuguese Colonies

A four-day seminar[27] on Portuguese colonialism sponsored by the Indian Council for Africa was held in New Delhi beginning October 20th, 1961.

Delegates from different Liberation Movements in the Portuguese colonies, namely Angola, Mozambique, Cabo-Verde, S.Tome', Goa, Daman and Diu attended this seminar.

The delegates were Mario Andrade, Viriato da Cruz, Pascoal Luvualu (all from Angola), Adelino Guambe, Marcelino dos Santos, Dr Edward Mondland and J.F.Sigawke (all from Mozambique), Miguel Treveada (from S. Tome' and Principe) Alfred Bangoura and Malan N. Diaye (from Guinea) and Adriano Araujo (Cabo Verde). Among the delegates from abroad there were also two Goans –Joao Cabral and Aquino Braganza. Mr. Aquino Braganza later on became the right hand man of President Samora Mashel and died in the plane crash together with President Mashel.

Other foreign dignitaries were Mr. Julius Nyereri, of Tanzania Mr. Hastings Banda of Malawi, Mr. Tom Mboya of Kenya, Mr. Ronald Ngaya, Mr. Kenneth Kaunda of Zambia, Mr. Abdel Karim el- Khatib of Morocco and Mr. Wedgehood Benn of Britain.

In this seminar, Mr. Nehru assured his listeners that *"We are not in any sense tied down absolutely to pursuing the policy which we have thus far pursued in the interest of removal of colonialism. If we have to take some other action, we shall take it. We shall keep an open mind."*

As the seminar progressed it became apparent that what had begun as a condemnation of Portuguese colonialism had become an attack upon India's Goa policy. The Africans expressed their desire for a joint military venture against Portugal.

All the speakers were unanimous in considering that non-violence was unlikely to be effective in bringing freedom to the Portuguese colonies in view of the outmoded thinking of the Portuguese authorities. Marcelino Santos from Mozambique said that the greatest contribution India could make towards the liberation of Portuguese colonies was to liberate Goa. Winding up the discussion, the chairman Kenneth Kaunda described Portugal's so called 'civilising mission' as utter barbarism. He reiterated his faith in non-violence "as method and experiment in the affairs of man", but it could not be used against Portugal, which had no democratic institutions and no public opinion to exert pressure.[28]

The African representatives made it plain that they did not understand metaphysics. Nor were they interested in "pious resolutions", for they were involved in a bloody struggle with the Portuguese. What the Africans wanted from India was more positive action. They maintained the occupation of Goa by Indian Forces would not be a small step in aiding their revolution. Rather they regarded such an event as the key, for it was alleged that the Portuguese Empire in Africa would collapse once Goa fell. Moreover, the Africans acknowledged India was provided with the opportunity to give the anti-colonial movement direction and indicated their willingness to follow if only Nehru would reassert his leadership.

Speaking before a mass rally at Chowpatty, Prime Minister Nehru went even further towards the African position. He frankly admitted that the policy pursued by the Government of India toward Portugal had been a failure. He announced that since Goa was a part of India, "nothing" could prevent the completion of independence. He said further that the Government of India was compelled to do some fresh thinking and consider the problem anew. "When I say I think afresh, I mean that we have been forced into thinking afresh by the Portuguese to adopt other methods to solve the problem. When and how I cannot say now. But, I have no doubt that we will do it."[29]

Change In India's Stand

India's dilemma was great. On one hand, its stand that Goa was a colony of Portugal on the Indian sub-continent, and that geographically, linguistically and ethnically a part of India was admitted as valid on all sides. The U.N., the U.S., the U.S.S.R., and practically the whole civilized world was opposed to colonialism, and favoured the freedom of colonies from their foreign rulers. Countries friendly to Portugal and India saw no chance of persuading her to withdraw peacefully, and to negotiate on that basis. And yet everybody was requesting India not to take recourse to force in a cause with which they all seemed to sympathise with.

India herself was opposed to the use of force, and had refrained from using it for fourteen long years, in the hope that a peaceful solution to the problem might be found. A situation had now been reached when no other course seemed feasible, particularly in view of the intransigent attitude of Portugal and the failure of friendly powers to effect a change in that attitude.

During the debate in the Trusteeship Committee, the Portuguese contended that Nehru had renounced the use of force to end Portuguese rule in Goa. To this, the Indian representative Krishna Menon warned that "My country had at no time abjured the use of force in international affairs", and that "India would not hesitate to use force if provoked". This was in November, 1961.

There was persistent demand from the Parliament and the public to take military action against the Portuguese ruled enclaves in India. The Government, however, was reluctant to take military action and trying its best to solve the problem by peaceful means. The Portuguese Government was in no mood to come to the negotiating table with the argument that these were parts of Portugal–Overseas Portugal

In October 1961, speaking at the concluding meeting of a seminar on Portuguese colonialism, Prime Minister Nehru had confessed that the Government of India's policy of solving the Goa Question by peaceful means had failed and that *"we have been forced into thinking afresh by the Portuguese—to adopt other methods to solve this problem. When and how we will do it cannot be forecast now. But I have no doubt that Goa will soon be free."* The conflict in the mind of the Government to use or not to use force for a cause with which it had full sympathy was at last resolved.[30]

The Final Course Of Action

India had finally to fall back upon the course of action, so beautifully epitomized by Guru Gobind Singh more than 250 years ago in one of his Persian verses—a course of action which applies so aptly to just such situations:

Chu Kar az Hama Heelti Darguzasht
Halal ast burden b-Shamsheer Dast

(When a problem defies all other means of solution,
It is just and proper to take the sword in hand).[31]

References:

27—Hindu21September1961
28—Rubinoff-India's Use of Force-p 81
29—Ibid- p 83
30—Nehru's Speeches (1957-1963) p367-368
31—Guru Gobind Singh's verses quoted in Operation Vijay—p 54

CHAPTER VI

PROVOCATION FROM ANGEDIV

In November 1961, the Portuguese in Angediv resorted to provocative action[32] against Indian ships and fishing boats in the vicinity of the island. The decision to retaliate could not be postponed any longer. Initially it was decided to take action only against Angediv Island. However, a detailed consideration of this course of action from 27th to 30th November showed that there would not be any advantage if the action was restricted to only Angediv Island. Then it was favoured to take action for the takeover of Goa. The warning order dated 29th November to the Armed Forces said: ***"As a result of Portuguese hostile action against our nationals, the Government proposes taking certain steps in the area of Angediv Island."***

On further consideration, to eliminate the possibility of the Portuguese retaliating from the enclaves of Daman and Diu, it was found necessary to include these two territories also in the proposed action. Thus these provocative incidents created by the Portuguese authority of Angediv were the immediate cause, which forced the hands of the Government of India

On 17th November, the Portuguese garrison in Angediv Island fired upon the Indian steamship ***SABARMATI*** which was passing through the 1.6 kilometres wide expanse of water between the island and the mainland. The Chief Engineer of the vessel, Mr. Penha was injured in this action. A week later, during the night of 24th – 25th November, the Angediv garrison near about the same area between the island and the mainland fired on a group of Indian fishermen in about 20 boats. One of the fishermen, Atmaram Kochrekar died the next day as a result of the injuries received in this incident. This made the local fishermen nervous and hesitant to venture into the sea to carry on their normal fishing activities. In order to infuse confidence in them a frigate and a destroyer *KIRPAN* and *RAJPUT* were sent from Bombay to Karwar, on 27th November. The ships were directed to exercise off Karwar keeping clear of Portuguese territorial waters, which was to be considered as ten kilometres. Both these ships arrived at Karwar during the afternoon of 28th November. A day after that, Naval Headquarters instituted what was known as "Operation Chutney", which involved the maintenance of a linear patrol by two ships at a distance of not less than thirteen kilometres off the Goa coast. The ships on patrol were required to report shipping, air and personnel movements in and out of Portuguese territory, and retaliate with necessary force if engaged by any surface or air units. Other ships of the Indian Navy were alerted and ordered to be operational at the earliest possible date.

Meanwhile, it was learnt that from 18th to 25th November, the SEATO powers were holding naval exercises in the Arabian Sea about 240 kilometres off the Goa coast.

The Portuguese knew of the dispatch of the Indian warships from their informants in India. (Ref: Telegrams No 98 from Portuguese Ambassador in Karachi and No 573 from Ambassador in London).[33]

The Indian Government sent a strong protest to the Portuguese regarding the firing on *S.S.Sabarmati* by their garrison at Angediv on 17th November. The Portuguese Military Command asked their garrison commander to clarify the matter. His immediate reply was negative. However, later on he informed on 24th that indeed there was shooting on an Indian ship. This matter was worsened after the incident of 24th – 25th November. The Ministry of National defense in Lisbon demanded an in depth report of the incident from authorities in Goa as the matter had taken a serious turn. They feared that India might take military action taking advantage of these incidents.

Prime Minister. Nehru declared in the Rajya Sabha that a fresh situation had arisen in Goa, which might need a new approach from the one followed so far by India. He said: *"There had been strong resentment in the country against the policy of the Indian Government regarding the Goa problem. It had been suggested that the Government should take drastic steps to end this colonialism in our country and free the people from Portuguese rule over small pockets like Goa, Daman and Diu... It was important to remember that the Indian Government could not in haste abandon certain basic principles, which it had been pursuing in respect of such problems".* One thing was certain, he added, that the Portuguese hold on some pockets in Indian Territory was bound to end.

Angediv

Angediv is a small island off the western coast of India. It is situated in 14° 75' N and 74° 10' E, 8 kilometres South-West of Karwar. Its dimensions are quite small, the extreme length from north to south being

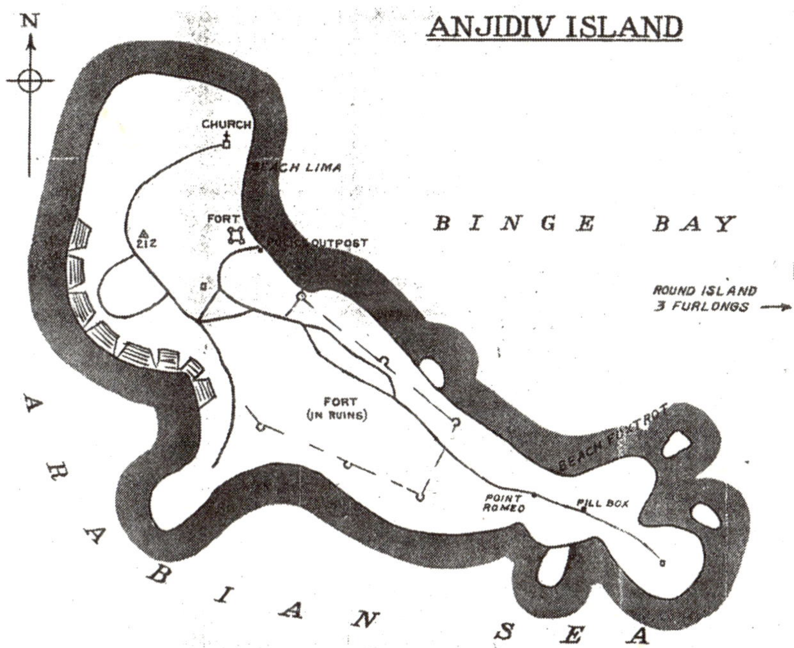

Angediv Island

only about 1.6 kilometres and the breadth from east to west about 0.3 kilometres. In the past it had been a flourishing outpost of the kingdom of Vijaynagar, but its fortune declined from the times the Muslims started navigation between India and the Red Sea. The Hindus were forced to leave the place and settle on the mainland. The Muslims destroyed the temple of Goddess AryaDurga.

Angediv is mentioned in ancient books like the one by Periplus. The famous Moroccan traveler Ibn Batuta, who landed here in 1342 A.D., also referred to it in his travelogue. The island was lost by the Vijaynagar garrison to the Arab traders in the 15th century. The Portuguese captured it from the Arabs and retained it till it was liberated in 1961.

The Portuguese connection with the island dates back to 1498 when Vasco de Gama visited it during his return journey to Portugal. He visited it once again in 1502-03, during his second visit to India. He made it as a base of operations against the Zamorin of Calicut. A fortress was built during the period of Vice-Rei D. Francisco de Almeida. It was the first fort built by the Portuguese in India. It was here that Afonso de Albuquerque took shelter after having been driven away from Goa by forces of Kamal Khan, the Adil Shahi general, after the monsoon of 1510.

Sir Abraham Shipman took shelter in this island during the monsoon of 1662. He had come with a body of 500 soldiers to take possession of the island of Bombay given to King Charles II of Britain as dowry during his marriage with Princess Katherine de Braganca of Portugal. Sir Shipman who died on 5th April, 1664 and many of his officers and men lie buried in this island.

The fort was renovated by D.Francisco de Ta'vora-Conde de Alvor in 1668, when he saw that the Marathas under Sambhaji were intending to build a fort in the island, which was lying unoccupied. (The island remained with the Portuguese till it was liberated in December 1961 by the Indian Navy.)

By 1856, the decline had set in due to epidemic caused by nearness of the cemetery to the water spring that supplied water to the inhabitants.

In 1961, the local population consisted of two old ladies, a retired Goan soldier and a teenager. There was a military detachment of thirty soldiers stationed in this island.

The Portuguese had set up six posts in the island: *Posto de Diligencia, Posto da Capela, Posto de Altinho, Posto de Fonte, Posto de Miradouro and the Posto de Alto da Bandeira.*[34]

Enquiry Ordered by Portuguese Government

The Portuguese Government asked Captain Carlos Alexandre Morais of ***Agrupamento Afonso de Albuquerque*** with its headquarters at Navelim to proceed to Angediv and conduct an on the spot enquiry[35] and submit his report on the incidents mentioned above. (The Angediv garrison was in the area under the command of Agrupamento Afonso de Albuquerque.). He was briefed about his mission by the Governor General Vassalo e Silva and by Lt. Colonel Ma'rio Marques de Andrade, *Chefe do Estado Maior* (Chief of the General Staff), and left for the island by the warship *Afonso de Albuquerque* on 27th November, 1961. The ship remained alongside during the time he remained in Angediv.

He reported: The incident that occurred with passenger ship Sabarmati, took place on 17th November.

> *The sentry, who was on duty at the post ALTO da BANDEIRA situated at the highest point on the island and where the National Flag (Portuguese) is displayed on the mast, temporarily handed over his charge to 1º Cabo (corporal) Fernando Carvalho Ferreira and another soldier as he had to take his meals. Around mid-day this relief party saw a passenger ship, which was, navigating in the direction North-South between Angediv and Indian coast, was in our territorial waters.*
>
> *Corporal Ferreira raised the national flag and waited so that the Indian ship would do the same, as per the norm followed for the identification of the ships moving in that zone. When he observed that Sabarmati did not reply and continued navigating in our territorial waters, Corporal Ferreira supporting the gun on steel structure around our post fired a warning shot on the ship. Noticing this fire, the ship speeded up in the direction of the coast and continued in the direction it was moving.*
>
> *Meanwhile the sentry on duty had returned and taken his position. He was informed about the incident. However none of these three informed their superiors. The incident remained*

unnoticed, as the sound of the fire was also not heard in the command post.

Later on, when the Quartel General (Headquarters) sent the first message inquiring about the matter, the post commander 2nd Lt Luis Manuel das Neves after due enquiries, which did not yield any result, informed the Military Command negatively.

Only after insistent queries from the Quartel General and other checks did the Corporal Ferreira explain the incident on that day. The commander checked the reason as to why all the three soldiers had covered up the incident and was satisfied with their explanations. Meanwhile, the enquiry conducted took into consideration the angle of the trajectory of the shooting and other details and concluded that the ship could not have been hit.

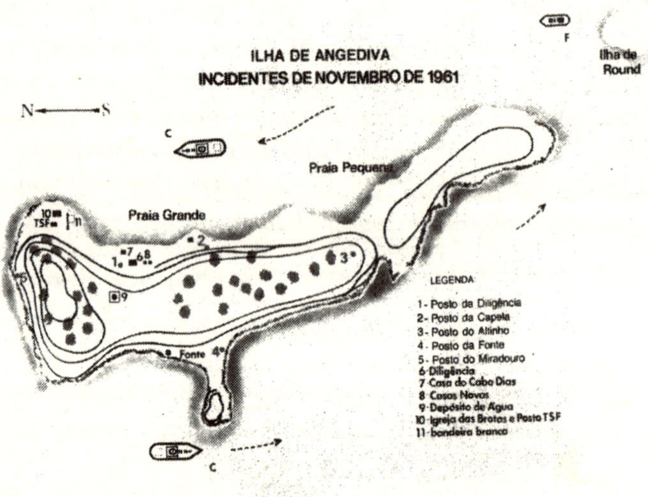

Incidents during November 1961

Incident During the Intervening Night of 24th–25th November, 1961

Captain Carlos A. Morais reported:

The Indian population around Angediv lived generally off fishing. Thus many fishing crafts–tonas- moved daily around the island for their normal activity. They never entered our waters without permission. There were other areas around where there were strong currents and were unsuitable for their activities.

After the receipt of messages on 23rd and 24th November the post commander mounted a system of vigilance and gave strict instructions in order to avoid any landing of the enemy which was expected any moment as the result of firing on the passenger ship Sabarmati.

On 24th, around 10 o'clock at night the "Posto of Miradouro" observed that a country craft (tona) a few metres from the land was moving slowly and without lights towards the island[36]. In order to force it to go away as it was very near to our land our defense personnel fired on it forcing it to move away.

The same post observed after some time another craft in similar circumstances, trying to approach the land rapidly. It was fired upon but it approached the land instead of turning away. It was again Corporal Fernando Carvalho Ferreira, who was part of this post, who gave a burst of his automatic weapon on this craft forcing it to go away hurriedly. Loud cries of injury were heard, presuming that the fire had hit someone.[36]

Around the middle of the night at the end of the small peninsula to the west of the island two crafts approached it and stationed there about. One of them remained at that place and the other silently followed the contour of the peninsula and stopped at a distance of a water spring at that place. The soldiers who were manning the "Posto da Fonte" followed the movements of the craft attentively and understood that someone wanted to come ashore. The post commander, 2nd Lt. Neves e Silva who happened to be present at this place observed that the craft had fled when the dogs started barking at the strangers.

To the west of the island at a place rarely used by fishing boats half a dozen crafts which had stopped there slowly started going away. Later on at around 2 o' clock another craft approached the land from the East but was forced to go away when warning shots were fired by the post near Igreja de Brotas.

Captain C.A. Morais completed the enquiry and having informed H.Q. by radio prepared to return to Goa. On 2nd December he started his return journey on the warship ***Afonso de Albuquerque***. "*Hardly had we left Angediv we saw in our front two frigates of the Indian Navy with their guns raised in our direction. We sailed in the direction of Mormugao. The two warships changed direction rapidly and started following us. Through our binoculars we could notice that they were ready to open fire. It was only near Mormugao that they stopped following us, which they had been doing throughout our journey. We did not understand the aim of this pursuit. On our return to Goa, we came to know that there was already the news that* ***'Afonso de Albuquerque'*** *was intercepted by Indian* warships".

INS KIRPAN

INS RAJPUT

These warships were Destroyer ***INS RAJPUT*** and Frigate ***INS KIRPAN.*** Obviously this pursuit was due to the operation of plan "***Operation Chutney***" unknown to the Portuguese. The Portuguese Governor General Vassalo e Silva said later that the Portuguese warship remained quiet as it did not want to fall prey to the provocation.

Meanwhile, the Portuguese Ambassador in London informed their Foreign Office (telegram No 573)[37] that they had come to know from reliable sources that the military action against Goa was to take place on 10th December. There were already two frigates in Karwar and three more had been ordered to start immediately for the same destination. All these ships were armed with four inch Guns. The cruiser '***Mysore***' which was in Bombay would also participate in this operation." In the same telegram, the killing of fisherman Atmaram Kochrekar was attributed to the Indian police themselves, as he was a smuggler!

References:

32— P. N. Khera-Operation Vijay-p 112
33—Min. Neg. Estr. -20 anos de Defesa—p 53,54
34—C.A. Morais –Queda da India Portuguesa—p63
35—Ibid—p 66
36—Ibid—p 67
37—Min. Neg. Estr. -20 Anos da Defesa, Vol IV p 54

CHAPTER VII

INDIA DECIDES TO USE OTHER METHODS

LT.-GEN. J. N. Chaudhuri,the Army Commander controlling OPERATION VIJAY

Towards the end of October 1961, the four-day seminar on Portuguese Colonialism was held in New Delhi. It was clear to the people from the speeches of Prime Minister Nehru that the Government of India, had at last, started thinking of using "other methods"[38] for liberating the colonies.

The military was given to understand verbally at the end of August that military action against the Portuguese-held territories was a "distinct probability". In view of this verbal view, Lt. Gen. J. N. Chaudhuri, G.O.C.-in C., Southern Command made a reconnaissance of the Goa border and prepared an Appreciation of the Situation and a Plan. This plan was ready by early November and submitted to Army Headquarters on the 11th of that month.

APPRECIATION OF SITUATION

by Lt.Gen. J.N.Chaudhury,

G.O.C- in C. Southern Command at Poona on 10 Nov. 1961.

Terms of Reference[39]

1. Army Headquarters TOP SECRET letter No 46715/GS/MO of 7 Oct 61 addressed to Lt. Gen. J. N. Chaudhury, G.O.C.-in-c Southern Command.

AIM

2. To occupy militarily the territories of **GOA, DAMAN and DIU** when so ordered.

FACTORS

GROUND

GOA

Objectives

3. The three Portuguese territories within the sub-continent of INDIA comprise Goa, Daman and Diu. Of these Goa is by far the largest and the most important. With its occupation, any serious resistance in Daman and Diu is unlikely; indeed operations in these two places may well turn out to be

unopposed, especially if they start after initial military success is achieved in GOA[40].

4. Within Goa, PONDA UX 9677, a military base and centre of communications, PANJIM UX 7589, the capital, VELHA GOA UX 8589 and MARGAO UX 9062, are politically and militarily the main objectives. With their occupation Portuguese resistance must cease. The occupation of subsidiary objectives is a matter of time. The subsidiary objectives are in the North: PERNEM Us 7317, MAPUCA US 7401, SANQUELIM UX 9797and VALPOY UY 1291; in the SOUTH: MARMAGAO UX 7178 (the main port), QUEPEM UY 0353, SANGUEM UY 1355 and CANACONA UX 9929. It is important to remember that in order to prevent any deterioration of law and order after military entry, these subsidiary objectives should be quickly occupied.

Terrain

5. Along the Indo-Portuguese border, the country consists of very heavily wooded hills with steep slopes in the East. Visibility is restricted to between 50 and 100 yards. The roads on the Indian sides are poorly maintained with an indifferent narrow surface and are only one-way fair weather roads. MT (motor transport) movement off them is confined to the occasional limited harbour area. Cross-country movement even for infantry is difficult. Because of the present political relations road sections in the immediate vicinity of the border are NOT maintained. On the Portuguese side the roads were originally better constructed and maintained, but intelligence reports state that all of these roads up to within 5 to 8 miles of the border, have either been put out of commission by demolished bridges and culverts or are prepared for demolition. Away from the border in Portuguese territory, the country is easier for movement, being typical of the undulating country around BELGAUM though more wooded.

6. The country can broadly be divided into the valleys of the three main rivers and their tributaries; from NORTH to SOUTH-
   (a) The CHAPORA or TILARI R. (river)
   (b) The MANDOVI / NAROA / MADEI R.
   (c) The RACHOL R.

As all these rivers run from EAST to WEST, an approach from the EAST follows the grain of the country and leads comparatively easily to the main objectives. The approaches from the NORTH and SOUTH run counter to the grain of the country and end at two serious river obstacles that cover the direct approaches to PANJIM and VELHA GOA.

The important bridges on these rivers are:

1.	ASSONORA	US 8505	A stone bridge on road MAPUCA-BICHOLIM.
2.	BICHOLIM	UX 9099	A large single girder bridge 8 miles from BICHOLIM on the way to SANQUELIM. Besides there is one more brick bridge 1 mile from BICHOLIM that is fit for light vehicles only.
3.	SANQUELIM	UX 9696	Steel structure bridge on road SANQUELIM –VALPOY.
4.	USGAO	UY 0182	Brick bridge fit for light vehicles only on SANQUELIM-MOLLEM road.
5.	CANDEAPAR	UY 0179	Large narrow stone bridge with cement concrete to take heavy traffic on road PONDA-MOLLEM.
6.	BANASTARIM	UX 9088	Bridge on CANDEAPAR River on PANJIM—PONDA road. Steel bridge with stone piers. Length 90 feet. NO diversion possible.

7. BORIM	UX 9570	A high 8 span heavy girder bridge over ZUARI River on PONDA-MARGAO road.
8. SANVORDEM	UY 0960	Steel structure bridge on road BORIM—SANVORDEM.
9. POINGINIM	PJ 0466	Cement concrete bridge on road CANACONA—POLLEM.
10. ARDINFOND	055696	Steel Structure Bridge on road CANACONA—POLEM.
11. QUEPEM	UY 0353	Steel structure bridge on road QUEPEM—SANVORDEM.
12. SANGUEM	UY 1254	Steel structure bridge on road SANVORDEM—SANGUEM.
13. SIRIDAO	UX 8082	Masonry bridge on road PANJIM-AGACAIM
14.LINHARES		Near PANJIM (not on map) Masonry bridge just outside PANJIM town.

7. While the roads are metalled all-weathered roads capable of taking heavy traffic, they frequently cross nalas and rivers. The bridges and culverts may be demolished in the event of military action. The metre gauge railway from MARMAGAO to COLLEM UY 2367 is functioning but has NO military value.

Approaches to the main Objectives

8. There are the following four main approaches to **PANJIM:**

ROUTE A

(a) PERNEM-MAPUCA-BETIM UX 7491-PANJIM and the linked approach to MAPUCA from DODAMARG 927104 via ASSONORA US 8503 and from BANDA Us 8127 TORXEM Us 7923.

ROUTE B

(b) BANDA-DODAMARG-ASSONORA-BICHOLIM-US 9000-SANQUELIM –USGAO UY 0382-PONDA-VELHA GOA and the linked possibility BICHOLIM-PILIGAO UX 9066 – VELHA GOA.

ROUTE C

(c) ANMOD UY 3179-MOLEM UY 2273 –PONDA-VELHA GOA.

ROUTE D

(d) KARWAR PJ 0847-CANACONA-MARGAO and then on to PANJIM either via:

(i) CORTALIM UX 8577 ferry; or

(ii) BORIM bridge UX 9570 –PONDA-VELHA GOA.

9. (a) **ROUTE A**

(i) This route though the shortest in distance to **PANJIM** would be the longest in time as two wide rivers have to be crossed, the last affording considerable protection to the built up waterfront of **NORTH PANJIM**. An opposed crossing, however lightly opposed and even an un-opposed crossing would be very difficult both from the tactical and administrative angles.

(ii)This approach is capable of taking a brigade group.

(b) **ROUTE B**

(i) This is a longer route but comparatively an easier one. Though two rivers have to be crossed, whether via **PILIGAO** or **PONDA**, these crossings are **NOT** as formidable as those on **Route A**. Of the two sub-approaches, the one via **PONDA** is easier though the one via **PILIGAO** would be strategically more profitable provided the crossing there was a tactical possibility. **NO** reliable information is available of the ferry site. The section from **SANQUELIM** to **PONDA** and beyond appears suitable for tanks.

(ii)This approach is capable of taking a brigade group.

(c) **ROUTE C**

(i) From the point of view of movement, though the initial few miles may be difficult, this route is the best. Again two water obstacles have to be negotiated; one across the **CANDEPAR R** and the other at **BANASTARIM UX 9188,** but these are easier than the ones on the other routes. The road is a metalled, all weather one and runs through reasonable country particularly suitable for armour. From the point of view of time also, this route seems the best.

(ii) This approach is capable of taking a brigade group.

(d) **ROUTE D**

(i) This is the present main approach from **INDIA** to the interior of **GOA**. It is metalled all weather road and is believed to be two way. However, the formidable **ZUARI** estuary 815786 obstructs the direct route to **PANJIM**, which is subject to tides. The offshoot to **PONDA** via the **BORIM** Bridge also has to cross the same river at a point about 800 yards wide. The bridge is likely to be blown.

(ii) The ferry crossing of the wide **KALINADI CREEK PJ 1151** presents a serious time and equipment problem.

(iii) This approach is capable of taking a brigade group.

10. **SEA APPROACH:** An approach by sea would have been a possibility, but is ruled out for the following reasons:-

(a) The availability of assault craft is to the best of our knowledge **NIL**;

(b) Troops will have to be taken off their present duties and trained in amphibious operations;

(c) It does **NOT** seem to give any particular tactical advantages.

11. **DEDUCTIONS FROM APPROACHES**

(a) All approaches are capable of taking a brigade group and from the point of view of road space **Routes D** and **C** are best in that order. On the other hand from the point of view of speed **Route C** is best.

(b) If the river crossing with their attendant difficulties are to be kept to a minimum **Routes C** and **B** are best and in that order,

(c) **PONDA** is an important focal point for both Portuguese and us and must be one of the initial objectives.

(d) On all approaches Armour can be used in limited quantities and in view of the road and bridge conditions in the vicinity of the frontier, a light tank is the better equipment.

(e) The start points for all the routes are widely separated and if all four routes are used, co-ordination of movement, inter-communication and administration will present serious problems. Also this tends towards initial dispersal of our already limited forces and this dispersal will **NOT**, in my opinion, be compensated for by the dispersal of Portuguese troops to meet us.

(f) The need for adequate light bridging and assault craft to support any military action is very apparent and will be provided for in excess of normal allotments.

(g) In view of the close country at the border, the initial advance along **Routes A**, **B**, and **C** will be difficult, especially if opposition is met at the border. Because of this correct grouping and determined infantry action will be essential in the opening phases.

CONCENTRATION and ASSEMBLY AREAS, START POINTS/ FUPs

12. As the troops allotted by Army Headquarters and those available in Southern Command will arrive from various formations they will have to be knit together under a divisional headquarters.

For this purpose a common concentration area is essential and BELGAUM is the obvious choice.

13. Suitable assembly areas for NOT more than a brigade group are as under: -

(a) Route A—Area north of PERNEM
(b) Route B—Area BANDA
(c) Route C—Area ANMOD
(d) Route D—Area MAJALI PJ 0757.

14. Suitable start points are available along the roads just short of the border. Should opposition be anticipated at the border suitable FUPs are also available.

DAMAN

Objectives

15. The town of DAMAN [41] is the main and the only objective. Its occupation will ensure the easy occupation of the remainder of the territory. The town lies astride the DAMANGANGA R and the important sector is the Northern one.

Terrain

16. Ground here is no serious problem. Two rivers, the DAMANGANGA and the KOLAK R divide the territory and flow from SE to the coast. A convenient approach runs through easy, slightly undulating country and between the two rivers, direct to the town of DAMAN. There is NO natural obstacle protecting the town.

Approaches

17. There are three possible approaches. In order of priority they are: -

ROUTE P

(a) **VAPI PR 9181—KUNTA PR 8688—DAMAN (NORTH).** This is the best, shortest and most direct route with **NO** natural obstacles.

ROUTE Q

(b) This approach enters from the NORTH through **MOTIWARA PR 9293** and entails the crossing of the **KOLAK R**. Thereafter the going is good.

ROUTE R

(c) This is the Southern approach from **DHANWA PR 8681**.It leads to **DAMAN (SOUTH)** before which lies the **KALU R.** obstacle. Thereafter the **DAMANGANGA R**. has to be crossed before **DAMAN (NORTH)** is reached.

18. **ROUTE P** is the best approach for the reasons given above.

CONCENTRATION AND ASSEMBLY AREAS

19. For Route P the following concentration and assembly areas are suitable:-

(a) Concentration area – DEOLALI

(b) Assembly area –VAPI

20. **MAIN DEDUCTIONS**

(a) The best approach is along ROUTE P.

(b) Tanks can operate along this approach.

(c) No assault equipment for a water obstacle is required.

(d) As culverts may be destroyed some bridging material is required.

DIU

Objective

21. The town of **DIU** [42]

Terrain and approaches

22. **DIU** is an island 14000 yards by 4000 yards. The map reveals three possible approaches mostly across wasteland: -

 (a) From the NE via **DELWADA VG 6371**,
 (b) From the NORTH via the causeway **VG 4967**.
 (c) From the EAST via **VELAN VG 3764.**

23. All approaches entail crossing a water obstacle, but it would appear that the Northern route is the best as the creek there is crossed furthest from the open sea.

Concentration and Assembly Areas

24. (a) Suitable concentration areas—**BARODA** and **JAMNAGAR**
 (b) Suitable assembly areas on each route exist.

25. **Main deductions**

(a) Assault equipment for water obstacle may be required.
(b) Irrespective of the approach finally accepted either **BARODA** or **JAMNAGAR** are suitable concentration areas.

RELATIVE STRENGTHS

The relative strengths[43] of both the sides will be:

26. PORTUGUESE FORCES

Intelligence reports state that there are in **GOA,** a total of three Infantry battalions of European Portuguese troops, consisting of about 2200 all ranks. In **DAMAN**, there are three companies (360 all ranks) and the same number is in **DIU**. The location of these troops and details of other arms (as known) are given below:-

(a) **Infantry**

Headquarters one Battalion—VELHA GOA

Headquarters one Battalion—VASCO DA GAMA UX 7377.
Headquarters one Battalion—NAVELIM (near MARGAO) UX 9062.

The above battalions have detachments, varying between a company and a platoon each at the following places:-

PERNEM
MAPUCA
BICHOLIM
VALPOY
PONDA
CANACONA
BALLY UX 9747

Army detachments are reported to be located on important bridges.
In addition there are police and customs outposts all along the border. The strength of these outposts varies from one section to one platoon. The area round some of these outposts is believed to be mined with anti-tank and anti-personnel mines.

(b) ARMOUR
One squadron each is reported at:
MAPUCA
BICHOLIM
PONDA
BALLY

These are possibly reconnaissance squadrons equipped with armoured or scout cars. They may include tracked 'A' vehicles but these cannot be either of heavy or modern designs.

(c) ARTILLERY
One company each at:

MARGAO
VASCO DA GAMA
BICHOLIM

These units are equipped with 6 x 105 mm howitzers each. Anti-aircraft artillery is located at DABOLIM for the protection of the airfield and at Mormugao for the protection of the harbour. In addition there are some coastal guns at Mormugao.

(d) **Equipment**

The Portuguese Army in Goa, Daman and Diu is equipped with the following small arms and infantry weapons:

(i) Semi automatic rifle 7.9 mm
(ii) Sten 9 mm
(iii) Bren gun 7.9mm
(iv) MMGs
(v) .32 pistol
(vi) Mortars
(vii) 6 pdr Anti-tk gun

In addition, there are approximately **3000 armed Goan police personnel** and **Customs Guards** in **Goa**, backed by some Europeans. These indigenous forces are equipped with mortars and light automatics. They are deployed mainly along the border. The strength of the **police in DAMAN is about 350 with 100 customs guards** to assist and in **DIU** there is apparently a small force of **70 men.**

27. It is stated that the Portuguese forces generally are immature and inadequately trained, the better-trained troops having been drafted to AFRICA. It is also stated that the Portuguese military officers are disinclined to fight over GOA while the Goan officers have no influence in military councils.

NAVY

28. The Naval Command of Portuguese India is responsible for the operational area of Goa and the maritime defence of Portuguese India. In an emergency it is believed that the Naval Command is placed under the C-in-C of the Armed Forces. At present there are **three small ships**, presumably armed with 3 X 120 mm cannons and four multiple Pom Poms each. These move between **GOA, DAMAN and DIU.**

AIR FORCE

29. The Portuguese have NO air force[44] in GOA worth consideration. There are perhaps a few military transport planes and there may be some fighter-bombers all located at **DABOLIM UX 7876** airfield which is equipped to international standards. Both **DAMAN** and **DIU** have an airstrip, each capable of taking Skymasters.

Reinforcements

30. It should be noted however that naval and air force units are more flexible than ground forces. If **Portugal** is given too long a notice of our intention to take action in **Goa,** both naval and air force units deployed for the defence of Portuguese India can be fairly quickly reinforced except over a long period.

OWN TROOPS

Troops available within this Command[45]

31. The following troops (major units only) fit for war and, in my opinion, available for military operations against the Portuguese territories in India, are available within this Command. In selecting these, the fact that the INDO-PAK border cannot be left unguarded during the period of operations

against the Portuguese has been kept in view as also the fact that some troops have to be held in reserve for possible IS (insurgency) commitments.

(a) **INFANTRY**

One infantry battalion –JAMNAGAR
One infantry battalion –POONA
One infantry battalion –MADRAS
One infantry battalion – MHOW

(b) **ARTILLERY**

One field battery—DEOLALI
One field battery—MHOW
(Subject to the approval of Army Headquarters)

(c) **ARMOUR**

One squadron 18 CAV –MHOW. (Subject to the approval of Army Headquarters)

Troops allotted by the Army Headquarters

32. The following troops have been allotted by Army Headquarters for planning purposes:

(a) **HEADQUARTERS**

One infantry division headquarters.

(b) **ARMOUR**

(i) One squadron(light Armour) (Stuarts)
(ii) One divisional regiment armoured corps (AMX).

(c) **ARTILLERY**

(i) One field regiment (towed)
(ii) One mountain battery/ heavy mortar battery.

(d) **ENGINEERS**

Two field companies.

(e) **INFANTRY**
One infantry brigade
50 independent Para Brigade group.

INDIAN NAVY

33. As NO naval units[46] have been specifically allotted detailed tasks cannot be suggested. However the following tasks would assist the ground forces:
(a) Blockade of the ports of **MARMAGOA**, **PANJIM** and **DAMAN**,
(b) Prevention of the removal of important stores and equipment.
(c) Close support by naval aircraft if required.
(d) Close support by naval guns in any emergency.

INDIAN AIR FORCE

34. Air force[47] formations have also NOT been allotted. Possible tasks are:
(a) Close support of ground forces.
(b) Air maintenance (airdrops) when necessary and possible limited air maintenance when Portuguese airfields have been occupied.
(c) Provision of intercommunication flights, also in the preparatory stage.
(d) Interdiction
(e) Immobilisation of Portuguese aircraft in GOA.

35. I consider that there is NO requirement for taking on any strategic targets in GOA. In fact, politically, this may do more harm than good. I do consider, however, that close support and the engagement of tactical targets in support of the ground forces will be essential and feel that two squadrons of FBs

(Fighters and Bombers) should work directly under the command of the Force Commander. POONA and BELGAUM airfields are both suitable for the operation of FBs.

MORALE

36. Linked with the factor of relative strengths is the factor of morale. Traditionally and with their backs to the sea, the morale of the Portuguese troops cannot be of high order. Once our decision to enter their territory is apparent to them as also our probable strength, the inevitable conclusion that they cannot win is bound to cause a further drop in morale. This is satisfying situation which, in the event of military operations must be exploited by forceful leadership at all levels and by initially driving into GOA in a most determined manner without being unduly casualty conscious. Should the Portuguese resist, as it will be India's first war with European nation, an initial tactical reverse or lack of momentum must, at all cost be prevented. This can only be avoided by the careful selection of formation and unit commanders.

37.This morale factor, as operations are ordered, must also be exploited by all forms of propaganda. Broadcasts into GOA exhorting the military forces to surrender and assurances that they will be well treated if they do, will, in my opinion, have considerable effect. Broadcasts to the people of GOA outlining our aims and asking them to continue their normal life calmly will also have good effect. Leaflets from the air may also be used.

38. **DEDUCTIONS**

(a) Considering the overall superiority there can be NO question of NOT fulfilling my aim with the troops allotted to me. However, speed is essential as also good leadership qualities at all levels.

(b) From the overall force at my disposal relative to the Portuguese forces, and bearing in mind my conclusions from the ground factor, it is apparent that I should form two brigade groups and three infantry battalion groups.

(c) Because of the bridging problem in the initial stages and possibly later, an extra complement of engineers will be necessary.

(d) An important weapon missing, which is essential for infantry support, is the MMG. Some are required.

(e) For troop transport and maintenance there is a need for GT (General Transport) companies. Only civilian GT companies exist in my command and the required number of those manned by combatants is essential.

(f) There are for the Indian Navy and the Indian Air Force but the details can only be worked out when the allotment is known.

(g) PAKISTAN may attempt harassment on the KUTCH border during the preparatory stages and during operations. Vigilance in that area must, therefore, NOT be relaxed; if anything it must be increased.

TIME AND SPACE

PREPARATORY STAGE

39. In view of the ad hoc nature of forces that will be placed at my disposal, it is essential that the formations and units concentrate early enough to get some form of cohesion and to carry out the necessary reconnaissance. Time will also be required for the suitable locating of stores, equipment, ammunition, and administrative units and for the move forward to assembly area. Against this must be taken the factor of giving too much information regarding our concentrations to the Portuguese. Taking both factors into

consideration I consider that all troops should be concentrated in the BELGAUM, DEOLALI and JAMNAGAR/ BARODA areas 14 days before D-day.[48]

OPERATIONS

40. Once operations commence it is imperative that they are conducted with utmost speed. This speed will eliminate any UN interference unfavourable to us and will also have a salutary shock effect. Further it will ensure the least disruption to law and order in Portuguese territory by so called nationalist elements or goondas. The least disruption of and quickest return to settled conditions will be politically most advantageous.

41. My estimate is that with determined troops and subordinate commanders, it will take 72 to 96 hours for the completion of my main task, i. e. the occupation of PANJIM and VELHA GOA. This time factor is calculated both on possible Portuguese military resistance as well as delays caused by demolished bridges and culverts. Should NO resistance be offered these objectives could possibly be reached in a matter of 24 hours. Thereafter it should be only a matter of another 48 hours to bring the rest of GOA under military control.

DEDUCTIONS

42. My main deduction is the need for speed, which can be attained by correct initial grouping along each approach used and by the initiative and determination of all ranks, particularly of officers.

SURPRISE AND DECEPTION

43. Strategic surprise[49] is NOT possible. As troops for the operation are NOT stationed in the close vicinity of GOA, DAMAN and DIU; any movement forward to concentration areas cannot be hidden from the Portuguese. Moreover as the entries into Portuguese territory are limited, varying routes of approach will also afford little strategical surprise. Thereafter, I consider a cover plan is NOT possible and will be of NO value. Tactical surprise and deception are possible to a limited extent in respect of our actual strength along approaches, the equipment employed and our speed of operations. This will be incorporated in the final plan. As our possible intentions will be known early to the Portuguese, the matters of explaining any of our movements and concentration or admitting to them will primararily be the responsibility of the Government of India.

44. In this context, I put forward the suggestion that it may be worthwhile to disclose at an appropriate time, something of our intentions to the Portuguese, even to the extent of giving them an approximate dateline. Realising that we are firm in our decision to occupy their Indian enclaves and its eventual outcome, they may well decide to save lives and surrender without a fight. However, for reasons given earlier, this date line should NOT be extended as to permit the Portuguese to improve considerably their defences. I would suggest that after troops have reached their assembly areas, 48 hours might be allowed.

WEATHER

45. In view of the terrain, fair weather is essential for successful operations. The best period of these operations is during the months of February to April. Previous to this aftermath of the winter rains make the going difficult and after this, early rains may set in.

ADMINISTRATION

46. Distances still demand an extended logistical organisation. The administrative policy will include *siting* of maintenance areas for the GOA, DAMAN and DIU forces and refilling points close to the border along each route.

47. The setting up of this organisation will take time, which is another reason for ensuring that units, stores and equipment must be in position 14 days before D-day.

48. Deductions

The ground indicates the following deductions:

(a) Maintenance areas.
For GOA—BELGAUM
For DAMAN—DEOLALI
For DIU—JAMNAGAR or BARODA
In all these places the nucleus exists.

(b) Refilling points
(i) GOA operations
Route A –area BANDA
Route B –area DODAMARG
Route C—area Customs House 287787 near ANMOD
Route D—MAJALI
(ii) DAMAN operations—VAPI
(iii) DIU operations possibly the area of DELVADA or SOKHRA VG 4574
to be decided later.

(c) The following military Hospitals can cater for the needs of GOA, DAMAN and Diu respectively: -

BELGAUM
DEOLALI
JAMNAGAR or BARODA

It will also be possible to use the civil hospitals at SAWANTWADI Us 7638 and LONDA UY 5380 in the chain of evacuation as far as GOA is concerned, while so few casualties are expected for DAMAN and DIU that local arrangements will suffice.

(d) Advance surgical teams are required on each approach.

CIVIL AFFAIRS

LOCAL POPULATION

49. The most we can depend on from the majority of the local population[50] is their being generally pro-Indian, more so after a successful entry. On the other hand it would be incorrect to assume that they could usefully assist us as a guerrilla force or with arms in any way. I consider that all nationalist and subversive movements should be discouraged from independent action of any nature and, in fact should be prevented from entering GOA while military operations are on. Any action by these groups however well meant, can only hinder military operations and possibly leave a serious aftermath. Some use could possibly be made of own police contacts as guides and informers but this should be the limit of civilian assistance.

50. The setting up of a Civil Affairs organisation in good time and its subsequent induction into GOA are such apparent points, that they are NOT overstressed here. Once general approval to the military plan is obtained, a civil affairs set up can be suggested.[50]

OWN COURSES

GOA

51. In view of my deductions from the factors of ground and relative strength I consider I can employ two brigade groups and a battalion group in GOA, one battalion group each for DAMAN and DIU and keep a minimum of one battalion group in reserve.[51]

The courses therefore are limited and reduce themselves to a choice of approaches and the strength of troops on each.

52 The courses open to me in GOA are:

COURSE A

(a) One brigade group along route B, one along Route C and a battalion group along Route D.

(b) This course has the following advantages:-

(i) The shortest routes to the main objectives in time and space are used.

(ii) It allows for the quicker concentration of the two brigade groups.

(iii) It permits flexibility as the two brigade groups can easily concentrate on the PONDA/ BANASTARIM areas, or advance independently on VELHA GOA via PONDA and PILIGAO.

(iv) By approaching along three routes, it compels the dispersion of the already weak Portuguese forces.

(c) The disadvantage is that it lacks surprise

COURSE B

(d) One brigade group along Route A, one along Route B and a battalion group along Route C.

COURSE C

53. The advantage of Courses B and C are very limited. As in case of Course A they compel Portuguese forces to disperse while Course C enables one brigade group to use the best highway in Goa i.e. through MARGAO. The disadvantages on the other hand, far outweigh the advantages. Approaches end at the two wide rivers: the ZUARI and the MANDAVI. To reach the main objectives recourse must eventually be made through PONDA.
54. For the reasons stated, Course A is the only acceptable one.

PORTUGUESE COURSES

55. Broadly there are two courses open to the Portuguese[52]. Both must be defensive.

(a) COURSE X

To put in their main holding effort along the border at the entries into GOA. Here the country is difficult and will assist a weak defender. The hopes for advantage of this course would be to hold us at the border for as long as possible and thus get sufficient time for possible UN intervention and a policy of destruction if so decided upon. The disadvantages of this course are an extended L of C for which they cannot be prepared, some difficulties of terrain and dispersion of their limited forces.

(b) COURSE Y

To hold, as strongly as possible, an inner perimeter roughly along the line MANDAVI—VELHA GOA—PONDA—MARGAO, with light covering troops located near the border and then falling back under pressure.

56. Of the two courses open, Course Y seems more likely as it shortens the perimeter of defence and it allows for greater concentration along water obstacles.

57. Irrespective of the course adopted by the Portuguese my Course A should succeed.

DAMAN

58. There is only one course open to me and one open to the Portuguese. I consider I must advance directly on DAMAN (NORTH) by route P with a battalion group.[53]

DIU

59. Here there are three courses open to me[54]. Each caters advancing along one of the three routes mentioned in paragraph 22 above. A detailed reconnaissance is required.

60. The Portuguese have NO option but to concentrate their small route of advance. They have the advantage of the fairly good water obstacle.

PLAN

The plan[55] consists of:

AIM

61. To occupy militarily the territories of GOA, DAMAN and DIU when so ordered.

INTENTION

62. A division will advance and occupy VELHA GOA and PANJIM as soon as possible with a view to subsequently occupying the remainder of GOA. X Infantry battalion group will occupy DAMAN and Y Infantry battalion DIU.

METHOD

GOA[56]

TROOPS and AXES

63. (a) One infantry brigade group—Route B
    (b) 50 Para brigade group –Route C
    (c) One infantry battalion group—Route D

GENERAL OUTLINE

64. The operation will be carried out in three phases:-

(a) **Phase 1**
Concentration area –BELGAUM.

(b) **Phase 2**
Move to assembly area as under: —
(i) Infantry brigade group –BANDA area
(ii) 50 Para brigade group –ANMOD area
(iii) Battalion Group –MAJALI

(c) **Phase 3**
The advance into GOA.

TASKS

65. **Infantry Brigade Group**
(a) To clear opposition on Route B and occupy VELHA GOA by forcing the PILIGAO crossing; or alternatively,
(b) To advance to PONDA and become reserve to 50 Para Brigade operating on Route C.
(c) To occupy MAPUCA.

66. **50th Para Brigade Group**
To clear opposition on Route C and occupy PONDA as soon as possible with a view to the further advance on to PANJIM.

67. **Infantry Battalion Group**
(a) To clear opposition on Route D and occupy MARGAO and MORMUGAO.
(b) Alternative task: to cross in the area of BORIM bridge and assist in the occupation of PONDA.

ADMINISTRATION

68. (a) Maintenance area –BELGAUM with forward dump at MAJALI for Route D.
(b) Two second lines ammunition (all natures) each at Maintenance area and at refilling points.
(c) Medical –MH BELGAUM.

INTERCOMMUNICATION

69. Division Headquarters will advance along Route C and co-ordinate the action of the three combat groups.

DAMAN[57]

TROOPS

70. One Infantry Battalion Group.

GENERAL OUTLINE

71. The operations will be carried out in three phases:
(a) Phase 1
Concentration area—**DEOLALI**
(b) Phase 2
Move to assembly area at **VAPI**
(c) Phase 3
Advance into **DAMAN**

TASK

72. To occupy DAMAN (NORTH) and subsequently the remainder of the territory of DAMAN

ADMINISTRATION

73. (a) Maintenance area—DEOLALI: Refilling Point at VAPI.
 (b) Two second line ammunition (all natures) at VAPI.
 (c) Medical—MH DEOLALI.

DIU[58]

TROOPS

74. One infantry battalion group

GENERAL OUTLINE

75. The operation will be carried out in three phases:-
 (a) Phase 1
 Concentration area –**JAMNAGAR or BARODA.**
 (b) Phase 2
 Move to assembly area (to be decided later).
 (c) Phase 3
 Advance into **DIU**

GENERAL-ALL OPERATIONS

COMMAND and CONTROL

76. (a) For the command of the three operations a Tactical HQ Southern Command will be set up in BELGAUM with Command representatives located with HQ of the three forces.

(b) An ASSU set up is required to cover the three areas of operation.

COMMAND RESERVES

77. (a) One infantry battalion group.
(b) Location—**BELGAUM.**

INDIAN NAVY[59]

78. (a) Blockade of the ports of **MARMAGOA, PANJIM and DAMAN**.
(b) Prevention of the removal of important stores and equipment.
(c) Close support by naval aircraft if required.
(d) Close support by naval guns in an emergency.

INDIAN AIR FORCE [60]

79. (a) Close support of ground forces.
(b) Air maintenance (airdrops) when necessary and possible limited air maintenance when Portuguese airfields have been occupied.
(c) Provision of intercommunication flights, also in the preparatory stage.
(d) Interdiction.
(e) Immobilisation of Portuguese airfields in **GOA.**

The appreciation of situation is an important exercise for the execution of attack or defence. It is prepared by studying all the inputs shown in acronym **KITBM**.

KHABAR or Intelligence describes enemy's strength, his weapons and formations gathered with meticulous care.

IRADA or Aim tells in clear-cut terms the aim of operation. As seen in this case it is to capture Panaji and Velha Goa in 24 hours and complete the operation in four days.

TARIKA or Method tells about the routes to be followed, the short targets to be achieved before attaining the ultimate aim.

BANDOBAST or Administration tells about refueling, replenishment of ammunitions, medical points, and casualty evacuation.

MELMILAF or Inter Communication is explained.

The thoroughness of the APPRECIATION OF SITUATION is as important as training and fighting qualities of the men participating in the operation.

Although **Lt Gen. Chaudhuri (G.O.C.-in -C Southern Command**) had prepared his appreciation on 10th November, no actual preparations were made, since the Government had not conveyed to the Army authorities any decision to take military action against Portuguese enclaves.

References

38—Khera-Op. Vijay-p40
39—Khera-Op.Vijay Appendix I-p145
40—Ibid, Appendix I—p145
41— Ibid, Appendix I-p149
42— Ibid, Appendix I-p150
43— Ibid, Appendix I-p151
44— Ibid, Appendix I-p153
45— Ibid, Appendix I-p153
46— Ibid, Appendix I-p154
47— Ibid, Appendix I-p154
48— Ibid, Appendix I-p156
49— Ibid, Appendix I-p156
50— Ibid, Appendix I-p158
51— Ibid, Appendix I-p158
52— Ibid, Appendix I-p159
53— Ibid, Appendix I-p160
54— Ibid, Appendix I-p160

55— Ibid, Appendix I-p160
56— Ibid, Appendix I-p161
57— Ibid, Appendix I-p162
58— Ibid, Appendix I-p162
59— Ibid, Appendix I-p163
60— Ibid, Appendix I-p163

CHAPTER VIII

PORTUGUESE PLAN OF DEFENCE OF ESTADO PORTUGUES DA INDIA

After the independence of India on 15th August, 1947, the Portuguese knew that the problem of their enclaves in India would arise sooner or later and had formulated a plan for the defense of Estado Portugues da India. The Indian Government wedded to the principles of non-violence tried its best to bring the Portuguese Government to the negotiating table. To start with the diplomatic relations were established. The Portuguese Government did not want to discuss the time table of transfer of these enclaves with the argument that they were an unalienable part of Portugal. On 1st July, 1955 by a legal magic the Colonies were transformed into Overseas Provinces, "Provincias Ultramarinas-and the Empire-"Imperio" into ULTRAMAR PORTUGUES. With this magic, a pluricontinental nation was born.[62]

Due to the intransigence of Portugal India was forced to close its Legation in Lisbon and later on it asked Portugal to close down theirs in New Delhi[63].

In 1954 and 1955 there was peaceful Satyagraha offered by volunteers, coming from all parts of the country. Portugal answered by firing on these peaceful Satyagrahis, killing, wounding and maiming several of them.

During the Governorship of General Paulo Benard Guedes a plan was prepared to defend Goa militarily[61]. The document dated 26th January, 1955 shows the intention of the Commander-in-Chief and Governor –General Paulo Benard Guedes in case armed action took place against Goa, Daman and Diu.[64]

1 - He wanted to guarantee the defence of Diu till the last.

2 - To begin in Goa a decisive battle with prolonged resistance.

3 - To maintain at whatever cost the link by sea with Daman and Diu.

Directives for the Defence of India

CCEI
COMANDANTE
PANGIM
261200 JAN 55
No 256/54/OC

GENERAL DIRECTIVE

(For the Defense of India)

I-ENEMY

1-It is my impression that the enemy will try:

a)- To attain a victory, as Daman and Diu are small in size. Above all, it will be a political victory of great projection, both in the international as well as national arena. The conquest will have great historical significance for the presence of Portugal in India. A lightning action against those two territories, by surprise action from 'civilian' elements supported by the Police Force will be carried out;

b)- To carry out a violent action against Goa, essentially by Armed Forces, aided if possible by internal uprisings, with a view to rapidly achieve the politico-economical objectives, fundamental to the actual position of Portugal in India–Panjim and Mormugao;

c)- To facilitate such actions by a previous intensification of economic blockade of all the territories and make use of the isolation caused by the monsoon season for carrying out these objectives.

II-OPERATIONS

2 – My intention is to safeguard the presence of the National Flag in India;

a) Defend, in Daman and Diu, to the last, the national honour and sovereignty, on the walls of their historical forts;

b) Engage, in the territory of Goa, with all available means in a decisive battle, making the resistance as long as possible, and prolong it beyond the organised phase;

c) Maintain at any cost the sea link with defensive fortifications of Daman and Diu and the defensive positions of Goa.

3—MISSIONS

a) Land Forces

-To face all the attacks on land, irrespective of its nature and its span, fighting to the last at the allotted positions and with the organised resistance, prolong the fight wherever possible, by means of an intense guerrilla action;

b) Naval Forces

-To guarantee the exercise of national sovereignty in the territorial waters and cooperate with Land Forces, either supporting them directly, or by safeguarding the sea link between the territories of Goa, Daman and Diu.

Paulo Benard Guedes
General

DIRECTIVE FOR DEFENCE OF DAMAN
Directive No. 2

1-ENEMY

1-It is my impression that the enemy, in case of conflict, will try to occupy Daman, carrying out a swift and surprise action, initially based by civilian elements, and later on by using armed forces, possibly with a ground of re establishing order.

II- OPERATIONS

2-It is my intention:

a)-To wear down the enemy as much as possible, within the existing availability of means, during the advance along the territory and concentrate in the forts of DAMAO-GRANDE and DAMAO-PEQUENO the defence of national sovereignty, by organizing the same right from now;

b)-To guarantee by sea all the operational and logistic support to the Forces in operation and to the population.

III-MISSIONS

a) LAND FORCES

-To defend, upto the last, the honour and the national sovereignty, in the forts of Damao-Grande and Damao-Pequeno

b) NAVAL FORCES

-To cooperate with the garrisons of forts in the defense and honour of national sovereignty, by supplying and supporting by means of fire and if necessary and possible, by landings;

c) PARA MILITARY FORCES

-To start operating directly, on receipt of order from the Governor of Daman, integrating with the Land Forces, at the positions to be allotted at the opportune time by the Military Command.

Paulo Benard Guedes
General

DIRECTIVE FOR DEFENCE OF DIU
DIRECTIVE NO. 3

I-ENEMY

1-It is my impression that the enemy, will try to occupy Diu in case of conflict, carrying out a swift and surprise action, backed by civilian elements supported by Armed Forces.

II-OPERATIONS

2-It is my intention:

a)To concentrate in the fort of Diu, the defence of national sovereignty, organising the same right from now;

b)To guarantee all the logistical and operational support by sea, to the Forces in operation and to the population.

III-MISSIONS

a) LAND FORCES

-To defend, to the last, the honour and the national sovereignty in the Fort of Diu;

b) NAVAL FORCES

-To cooperate with the garrison in the Fort in the defence of honour and national sovereignty, by supplying and supporting the same by fire and if necessary by landings;

c) PARA MILITARY FORCES

-To start operating directly, on receipt of order from the Governor of Diu, integrating with the Land Forces, at the positions to be allotted at the opportune time by the Military Command.

Paulo Benard Guedes
General

There were several other directives given from time to time, such as:

Directive No. 5 dated 9th February, 1957,for the defence of Goa against the subversive and terrorist actions;

Directive No. 17 dated 10th August, 1957, for acting against possible events on 15th August, 1957;

Directive No. 21 dated 22nd October, 1957, for acting against possible events during the month of November 1957;

Directive No. 23 dated 26th December, 1957, for the defence of Goa against the subversive and terrorist actions. (Replacement for directive No. 5);

Directive No. 24 dated 19th January, 1958, for the defence against the possible events on 26th January, 1958;

Directive No. 25 dated 15th May, 1958, for the defence against the possible events expected from 14th to 16th May, 1958;

Directive No. 26 dated 19th July, 1958, for the defence against possible events expected from 20th to 24th July, 1958;

Directive No. 27 dated 25th July, 1958, for the defence against the possible events expected during the months of July and August.

In November 1955 the Military Commandant, 'Coronel Tirocinado' Antonio Miguel Monteiro Liborio had prepared various secret plans for counter-attacks against the possible attacks in various sectors of Goa.[65]

There were 8 plans of counter-attack. These were:

1- Plan 'PI': Counter-attack in the direction of **Salem** (3090) and **Carpal** (3780).
2- Plan 'TETA'. Counter-attack in the direction of **Tudou** (6040) and **Paitem** (6040.
3- Plan 'ALPHA'. Counter-attack in the direction **Amonem** (5010) and **Pedem** (5000).
4- Plan 'DELTA'. Counter-attack in the direction **Dongurli** (5080) and **Codal** (6080)
5- Plan 'GAMA'. Counter-attack in the direction **Linguem** 94080 and **Podocem** (4070).
6- Plan 'OMEGA'. Counter-attack in the direction of **Borial** (6060) and **Matconda** (7060).
7- Plan 'BETA'. Counter-attack in the direction of **Edda** (6010 and elevation of **Enadquem** (6010).
8- Plan 'RO'. Counter-attack in the direction of **Yarconda** (2090) and **Naibaga** (2090).

PLANO SENTINELA

The plan for defence of Goa was named as "PLANO SENTINELA"[66].

Many plans were conceived. However they kept on changing depending on many factors. The last one was prepared when an armed military action from India was foreseen to be imminent. The previous plan prepared to face unarmed Satyagrahis was discarded.

As usual these plans were submitted for approval to the Military Command of the territory and then to the competent military authorities in Portugal (Metropole).

In 1960 the military strength was considerably reduced after the inspection done by Under Secretary of Army, Tenente Coronel Francisco da Costa Gomes. Major Joaquim Ramos de Freitas, Sub-Chefe do Estado Maior, prepared a new plan.

As per this plan three "Agrupamentos" or Groups were created. These groups had units of Infantry, Cavalry (Armoured) and Artillery.

Agrupamento **D. Joao de Castro** covered the Northern part of the territory; the Centre and the South were to be the part of Agrupamento **Afonso de Albuquerque** and the Agrupamento **Vasco da Gama** covered the Mormugao peninsula.

The new plan also envisaged the creation of an additional fourth Group. This Agrupamento **CENTRO** was to be created once there was an attack from Indian Forces.

It covered the northern part of the territory and the **Island of Goa**[67]. Its headquarters was located at the old city of **Velha Goa**. It had under command Esquadrao doReconhecimento Nº1 (E. Rec. 1) stationed in Mapuca, Companhia de Cacadores 9 (C.Cac. 9) stationed at Ucaçaim, and also the Companhia de Cacadores (C.Cac.1) stationed in Ilha de Goa and consisting of indigenous troops.

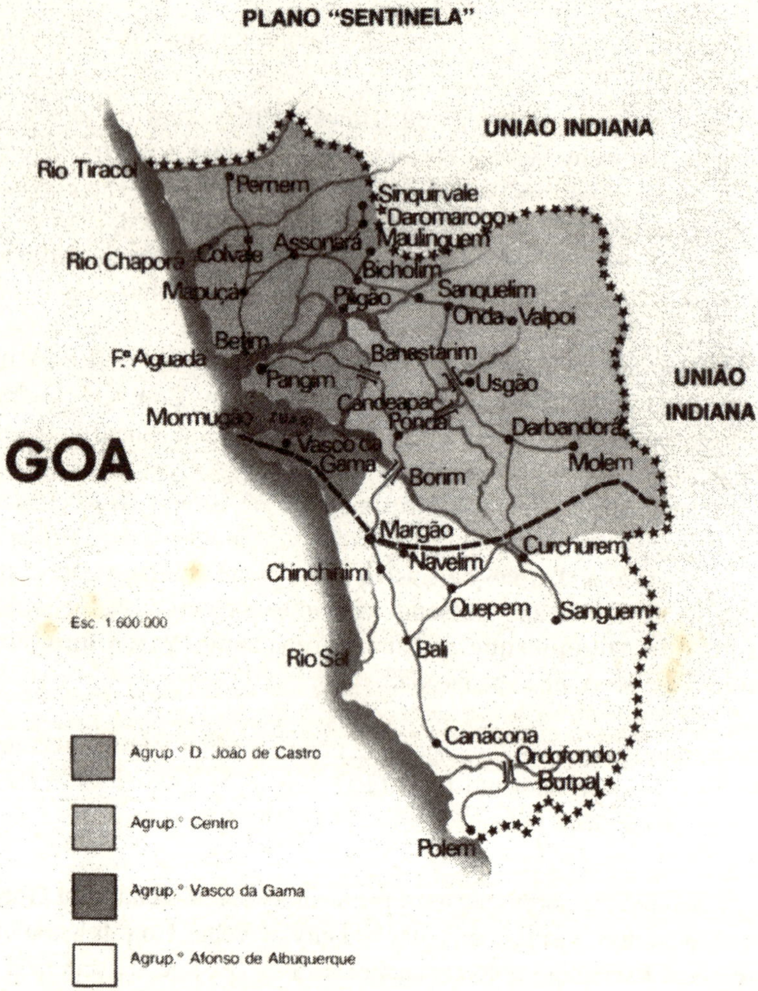

PLANO "SENTINELA"

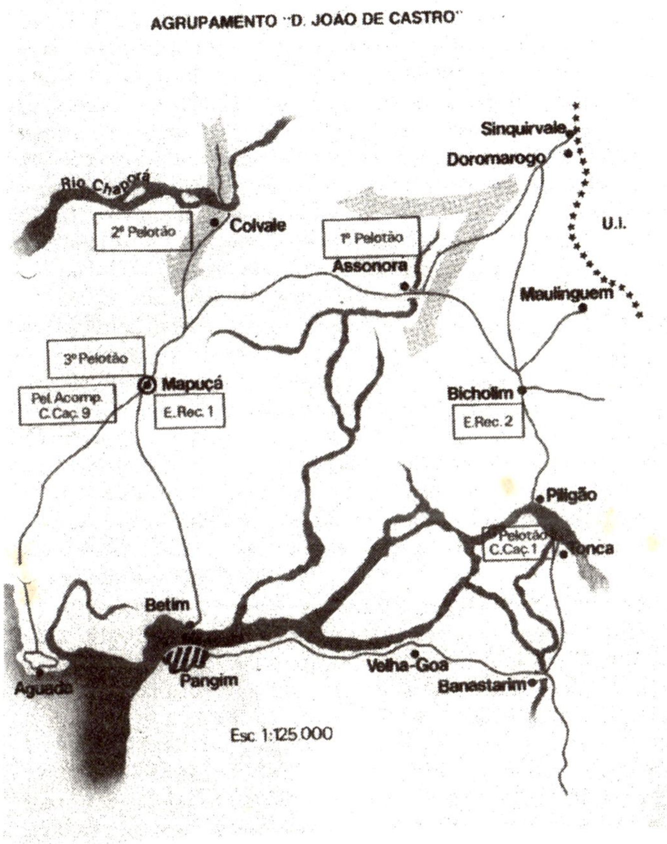

Agrupamento D. Joao de Castro

The Companhia de Cacadores 6 stationed in Velha Goa, and belonging to this group was put under direct command of Q.G. (Quartel General) and treated as Command reserve force. Similarly the Companhia de Cacadores 8, (C. Cac. 8) stationed in the **Aguada Fort** was included in the Agrupamento **Vasco da Gama** just a few days before the Indian action. However one of its platoons remained in the Fort and the other at Radio Station at **Bambolim**.

AGRUPAMENTO CENTRO

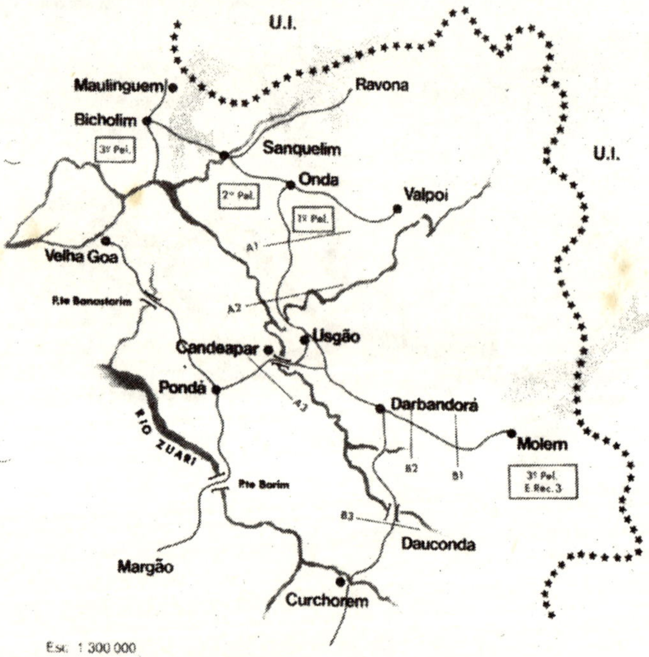

Agrupamento Centro

AGRUPAMENTO CENTRO

It covered the **Northeast and Central parts of Goa**[68] and would have its **Posto do Comando (P. C.) at Ponda** once the action started. It had at its disposal Esquadrao de Reconhecimento No 2 (**E. Rec. 2**) stationed at **Bicholim** given by Agrupamento D. Joao de Castro, Esquadrao do Reconhecimento No 3 (E.Rec.3) minus a platoon stationed in **Ponda**, a platoon of Companhia de Cacadores No 3 (C.Cac 3) also stationed in **Ponda**. (Agrupamento Afonso de Albuquerque ceded both of them.)

AGRUPAMENTO "AFONSO DE ALBUQUERQUE"

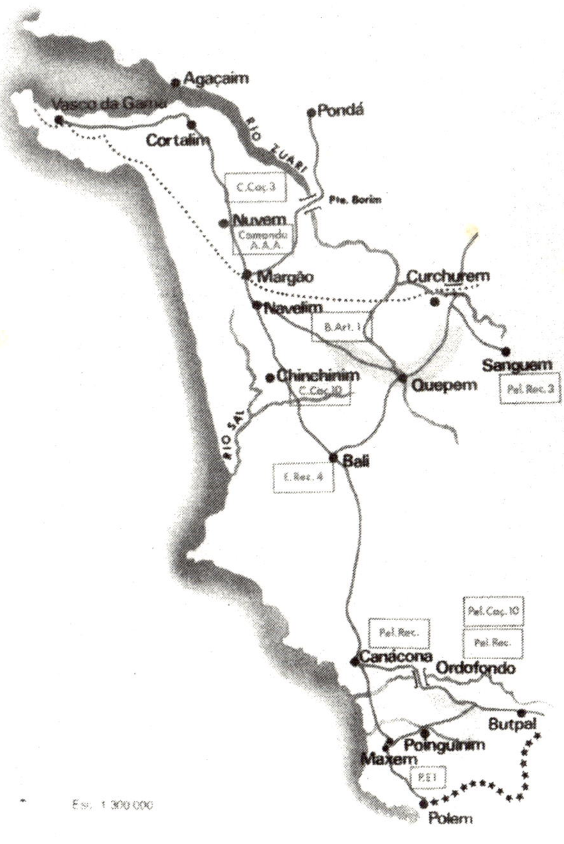

Agrupamento Afonso de Albuquerque

Agrupamento Afonso de Albuquerque covered a part of the centre and the south of the territory and had its headquarters located at **Navelim.**[69]

It had an Esquadrao de Reconhecimento No 4 (E.Rec.4) stationed at **Bali,** a platoon of E. Rec. 3 of Bateria de Artilharia No

1 (B. Art.1), with its headquarters at **Alto Margao** and consisting of indigenous troops. Besides, it had Companhia de Cacadores No10 (C. Cac. 10) stationed in **Navelim**, and Companhia de Cacadores 3 (**C. Cac. 3**) minus a platoon stationed at **Ponda** also consisting of indigenous troops.

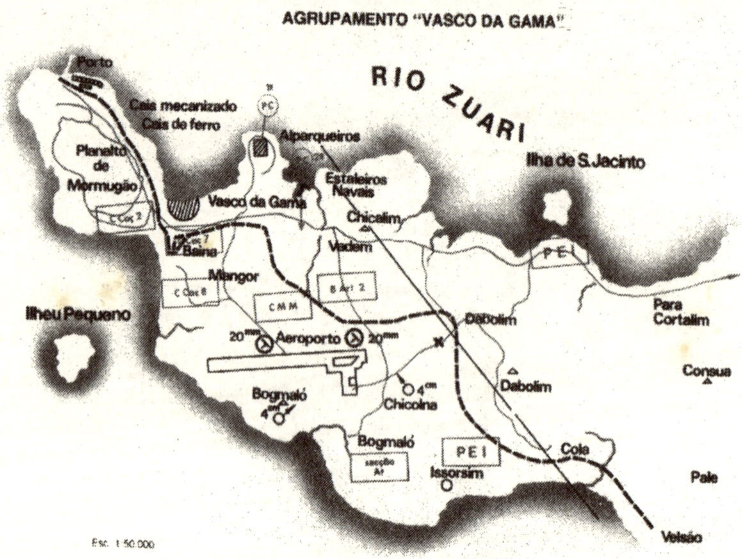

Agrupamento Vasco da Gama

Agrupamento Vasco da Gama covered the Mormugao Peninsula and had its headquarters at **Alparqueiros.**[70]

It had Companhias de Cacadores Nos 2 and (C.Cac 2) and (C. Cac 7) both **at Vasco da Gama** the first having indigenous troops. It had also a Companhia de Bateria de Artilharia No 2 (B Art.2) located at **Alto Mangor** and also consisting of Goan troops. It also had a Companhia de Manutencao de Material (C. M. M,) and a Companhia de Cacadores no. 8 (C.Cac 8) minus two platoons.

There was also a Destacamento de Engenharia da India **(D.E.I.)** (Engineering Detachment) which from operational point of view would be divided in sections and would belong to respective Agrupamentos. These had the main function of execution of **Plano de Barragem** (Demolition of Bridges and Roads). The left over personnel would be stationed in **Marmagoa** peninsula.

The Aim of Plano Sentinela

The aim of this plan[71] was to

- Concentrate in the Mormugao Peninsula and Island of Goa around 2/3 and 1/3 of forces in Goa,
- Resist at any cost in the Mormugao Peninsula,
- Delay the control of Island of Goa by the enemy, especially CIDADE de GOA (PANJIM), for maximum period of time,
- Provide fire and delay the enemy advance along the principal destinations in the direction of island of Goa and to the Mormugao peninsula.
- Exercise the delay effort in the south to make it difficult for the enemy to have access to the bridges at Sanvordem and Borim and to the Mormugao peninsula. The following lines will be crossed only after order from the Commander–in-Chief:

  Sanguem—Quepem—Bali
  Maina—Navelim—Adsuli
- Exercise a temporary defensive action along the rivers Mandovi, Candeapar and from there to Sanvordem, especially based in the regions of the crossing of these rivers. These lines could only be abandoned with the order of the Commander –in- Chief.
- Try to permanently guarantee the safety of Mormugao peninsula and Island of Goa especially of the former from the action of parachutists and the landings coming from the sea.

Thus in case of invasion the **Plano Sentinela** would immediately come into action and **Agrupamento Centro** would come into existence. Simultaneously it will be the responsibility of other two Agrupamentos in the frontier zone to face the enemy.

During the first phase it will be the duty of **Reconnaissance platoons**, located at the frontier to collect all the personnel of **Police** posts as well as of **Customs**. These personnel would immediately go to Mormugao peninsula to occupy the pre-determined locations.

During the second phase, the reconnaissance platoons and squadrons would take steps to delay the enemy advance, along the predetermined axis and follow the Plano de Barragem (**Demolition Plan**) for blowing up bridges and viaducts (roads) so as to hinder or at least make it difficult for the enemy to advance.

ALSO...

The Esquadrao do Reconhecimento No1 (**E.Rec.1**) stationed at **Mapuca** and two of its platoons at **Assonora** and **Colvale** would start its delaying action along the axis **Mapuca-Betim** before retreating to island of Goa. It will occupy the predetermined positions in defence of this island. It will be supported in this action by Companhia de Cacadores No.9 (**C.Cac. 9**) (**Ucassaim**).

The Esquadrao de Reconhecimento No 2 (**E. Rec.2**) stationed at **Bicholim** with its two platoons in **Sanquelim** and **Valpoi** (later on in **Onda**) would execute its delaying action along the axis **Bicholim-Sanquelim-Onda-Usgao-Ponda**, and retreat to the Island of Goa. It will occupy the positions for the defence of that island. From this moment onwards it would be under the command of **Agrupamento D. Joao de Castro.**

The Esquadrao de Reconhecimento No 3 (**E.Rec.3**) stationed at **Ponda** would execute together with its two platoons at **Molem** and **Sanguem** the following missions:

(a) The platoon at **Molem**, which belonged to Agrupamento Centro, will start the retreating action along the axis **Molem-Darbandora-Curchorem**. It will now pass to be under the command of **Agrupamento Afonso de Albuquerque**. It will now continue its retreating action along the axis **Curchorem-Quepem-Margao**. It will then retreat to Mormugao peninsula where it will occupy its predetermined position.

(b) The platoon at **Sanguem**, which belonged to Agrupamento Afonso de Albuquerque, would conduct a retreating action along axis **Sanguem-Quepem-Margao**. It would then gather at Mormugao peninsula, where it will occupy a position near the platoon from **Molem** and the **squadron command** to which it belonged. In this way they would be reunited.

The Esquadrao de Reconhecimento No 4 (**E. Re 4**), stationed at **Bali**, together with its platoons at **Canacona and Ordonfondo,** would execute a retreating action along the axis **Ordonfondo-Bali-Margao** gathering thereafter at Mormugao peninsula where it will occupy the predetermined positions. Its **3rd platoon** would remain in the region of **Quepem** in order to support if necessary the platoon from **Sanguem** in its delaying action. Later on it would gather in the Mormugao peninsula.

The delaying actions were as per **Plano Sentinela**. These corresponded to number of days required to guarantee the successive positions. In this way all the units, except the ones that would gather in the **Island of Goa** for its defence, would concentrate in the Mormugao peninsula. The personnel belonging to **Police** and **Customs** together with other forces gathered at the Mormugao Peninsula would constitute the final force in defence of territory of Goa.

Meanwhile, on 15th November, 1961 **Instrucoes Pessoal e Secretas** No. 5 from Chefe do Estado –Maior General das Forcas Armadas were received. These were:-

"The mission of the Armed Forces of Estado da India consists in:

(a) Avoiding uprising,

(b) Opposing the invasion of the territory.

*"The fulfilment of the second part of the mission implies that there would be delaying actions at the important penetration points and the final resistance in the positions which would cover the **Mormugao peninsula** and the **island of Goa.** Simultaneously it covers the defence of the peninsula against the actions from air and sea."*

"The delaying actions naturally would consist of temporary resistance and mobile actions. The aim of the final resistance would be to defeat the invader showing him its incapacity to win or die in fulfilment of its mission."

"In Daman and Diu the defence of respective territories is entrusted to their garrisons. In extreme cases they should hold the possession of the respective forts. (One may note the language used in these instructions, especially referring to the final resistance. It uses the same words as used by Presidente do Concelho in his message sent to Goa on the eve of invasion).

There were many objections to the **Plano Sentinela** but the military participated in the execution of the plan. The concentration of forces at one place, as a final defensive position was unimaginative. When the pressure exerted along the frontiers by the enemy forces could not be faced it was ridiculous to assume that it would face it at a minuscule perimeter of the peninsula. It was a real "**beco sem saida**" (cul-de-Sac) –a narrow street without outlet.

General Vassalo e Silva said later in an interview:

*"As per this plan the first Portuguese troops positioned behind the frontier police posts were to retreat in a staggered manner till they reached their final location in **Panaji** and **Vasco da Gama**".*

"It was not possible to run away from these locations. We were not in Dunkirk. There was no British channel nor were there any ships to evacuate the soldiers. There was however an order to resist till... death!"

DR. SALAZAR'S FINAL ORDER

On 14th December, 1961 *Presidente do Conselho* **Dr. Oliveira Salazar** sent the following message[73] to the Governor General and the Commander-in-Chief of the Portuguese State of India:

"Your excellency will understand the bitterness I feel while writing this message. It is impossible to imagine whether the Indian Union would attack or no, a few territories of this State... We all are aware of the smallness of our forces, but even if the neighboring state decides to multiply its attacking forces by an arbitrary number it will always show a great disproportion"

"The politics of the Government has always been, due to the impossibility of having an efficient defence, to maintain in Goa such forces that would compel the Indian Union a huge military operation, as it is seen now, which would create a scandal in the world and thus dissuade her from taking simple police action".

"This means that the first mission of our forces has been fulfilled. The second mission consists in not dispersing against the terrorist agents, so called freedom fighters, but organize the defence in a way it would put the valour of Portuguese in a very high pedestal in tune with our old traditions in GOA."

"It is horrible to think that this may mean the total sacrifice, but I recommend and await that this sacrifice as the only form for us to maintain the height of our traditions and render greater service for the future of the nation".

"I do not foresee any truce or Portuguese prisoners, as also there will be no ships surrendered, as I feel that there would be only victorious or dead soldiers and sailors. The severity of the attack that is expected against Goa would reduce the fight to the minimum duration. Politically it would be convenient that it would continue for minimum eight days, a period necessary for the Government to mobilize international forums as a last recourse."

"These words by virtue of their gravity could not have been addressed but to a military man conscious of his high duty and entirely ready to fulfill them. May God forbid that this man be the last Governor General of Estado da India—Oliveira Salazar."[74]

We do not know the exact words used by Governor General in his answers to the messages sent by Professor Oliveira Salazar. We know however that General Vassalo e Silva had thanked him for reposing faith in him and had guaranteed that he would honour the traditions adding further that it would be possible to resist for a period of eight days only if the Presidente do Conselho "expected a miracle"[75].

References:

61—C.A.Morais—Queda da India Portuguesa—p47
62—Fernando Rosas—Preface "Goa ou o principio do fim—p12
63—Min.Neg.Estr. —20 anos da Defesa—Vol I p311-312
64—HAG-Purabhilekh Dec. 86 IV/2, Military records file No 118
65—HAG-Purabhilekh Dec 86 IV/2 Military Records File No 627.
66—C.A.Morais—Queda—p47
67—Ibid—p49
68—Ibid—p49
69—Ibid—p49
70—Ibid—p50
71—ibid—p50
72—Botelho da Silva—Dossier Goa-Vassalo e Silva—p98
73—Queda—p116
74—Ibid—p117
75—Ibid—p118

Dr. Salazar

V. K.Krishna Menon
Defence Minister of India in 1961

CHAPTER IX

INDIA TAKES FINAL DECISION

The Government of India finally took the decision[76] to liberate these territories by Military Action on or about 29th November. This was the date on which Headquarters Southern Command was informed of this decision. It was told that it (H Q Southern Command) would be in charge of the operations for the liberation of the foreign colonies in India. The same day Maj. Gen. K. P. Candeth was also told that he had been selected to command the Task Force to be assembled for the operation against Goa. It is from this date, therefore that the active steps in furtherance of the plans already prepared, began to be taken.

Orders were issued for certain troop movements. Some train services were cancelled for this purpose from 4th December. "It was obvious that the large-scale troop movements had been ordered by the Government. Civilian traffic from North India to Bombay and Madras came to a stop. Military specials and goods trains carrying military vehicles and equipment had started moving from Delhi to Bombay."

The Plan of Attack

The operations in Goa[77] were to be conducted by troops under Maj. Gen. K. P. Candeth, G.O.C. 17th Infantry Division. There were four main approaches to Panjim. The advantages and disadvantages of each of these were discussed in the appreciation of Gen. Chaudhury dated 10 November, and the final choice had fallen upon two routes—one affording entry into Goan territory from the east and the other from the north. A 'decoy' entry or feint from the south was also envisaged.

The eastern thrust was to be made along the route Anmod—Molem—Ponda by 17th Division troops, and the northern from Dodamarg—Assonora—Bicholim by troops of the 50th Independent Para Brigade, with the possibility of the latter moving a part of its force westwards towards Mapuca, and from there southwards to Betim.

From the studies already done the main thrust was to be from the east, referred as Route C. This was considered to be the best route, as on this the river crossings were easier and it also had an all-weather metalled road running through the country suitable for Armour. The employment of a division on this route and only a brigade on the northern route strengthen this impression.

For the purpose of deception a small force simulating brigade strength was to enter Goa from the south along the route Karwar—Majali—Canacona. This was intended to draw away, and contain, some Portuguese troops towards the south so as to weaken the opposition to the main thrusts from the east and north. This force, though only of company strength, was nicknamed 20th Infantry Brigade and was to operate directly under HQ Southern Command.

No strategic surprise was possible, as the Portuguese expected the Indian forces to attack and made all possible preparations to meet it or hinder the advance by mining the approaches or setting up bridges for demolition. Therefore once the movement of troops began, the operation would have to be concluded speedily. It was feared that any delay in finishing the task quickly might lead to the destruction of public utilities, the massacre of Indian and Goan nationals. It could also lead to bringing up of the question in the U. N., leading to a premature cease-fire agreement.

Both the routes were capable of taking a brigade group each. The northern route was comparatively longer but it was easier on account of the fact that, although two rivers had to be crossed the crossings were not likely to be formidable. The section from Sanquelim to Ponda and beyond was considered suitable for tanks. The eastern route (Anmod-Ponda) initially ran through hilly country for a few kilometres but it was considered the best. On this route also there were two water obstacles to be crossed, but these were easier than on the other routes. The road was an all-weather metalled one running through country particularly suitable for armour.

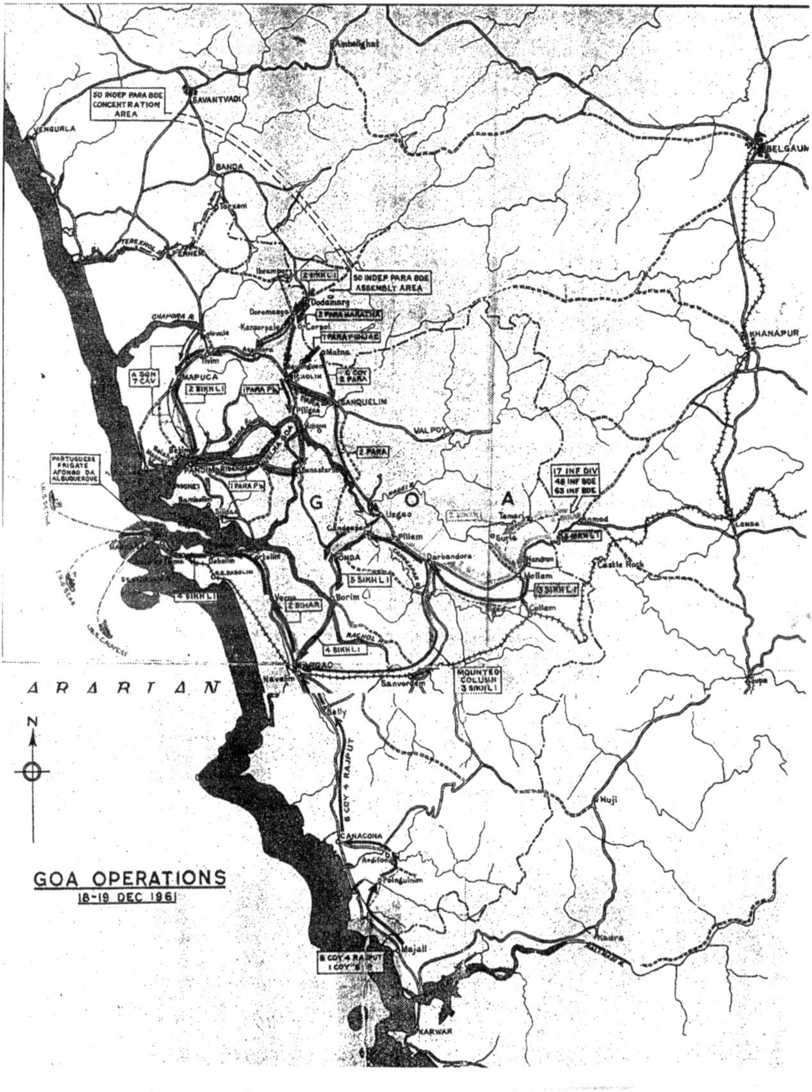

Map of Goa Operations

Goa Operations

General Chaudhury later commented that that his tactics were that the northern thrust being easier it was to be the hammer with the 17th Infantry Division as an anvil on which any pocket of resistance could be driven.

The initial objective of the forces entering Goa was to be the line Mapuca—Bicholim—Sanquelim—Ponda—Margao and the final objectives were to be Velha Goa—Panjim and Mormugao.

The Air Force was to give tactical support to the ground operations from the airfields at Poona and Belgaum. At the start of the operations, it was to neutralise the Portuguese Air Force by destroying the runway of the airfield at Dabolim and the wireless station at Bambolim in Goa, thereby gaining air supremacy over that territory. The wireless station was the only Portuguese link with Lisbon[78]

The Navy's role was to support ground operations by neutralising coast batteries and blockading the ports of Mormugao, Panjim and Daman. It was to ensure that no Portuguese ships, either naval or merchant, entered or escaped from these ports.[79]

Earlier, it was thought to approach Goan territory by landing; however this option was ruled out as it was found that it did not offer any tactical advantage. In any case, sufficient assault craft would have to be made available or assembled. Also the troops would be required to be trained for an amphibious operation for which there was no time.

The plan for Daman was that the 1 Maratha Group would enter it via Vapi, occupy the airfield north of Daman in the first instance, and then move to the town and capture it. Air support, limited to two aircraft every two hours, was to be provided to the ground operations. The airfield was not be bombed, but kept under observation to prevent its use.

The original intention was that the operations in Daman should begin after the completion of operations in Goa, so that the morale effect of the Portuguese defeat or surrender in Goa might be utilized to induce the Daman authorities to surrender without fighting. However this plan was changed and the final decision was to start operations in all the three enclaves simultaneously.[80]

Diu Island is separated from the mainland by a narrow tidal creek. As there was no time to move sufficient assault crafts to the site of operations, it was decided that 20 Rajput should cross the creek at night on improvised rafts at some point north of the island. Then it was to turn southeast towards the airfield and capture it. Thereafter it was to move east to the town and fort of Diu. Meanwhile a company of 4 Madras was to capture Gogla (north-east of the citadel of Diu) one hour before the assault crossing by the 20 Rajput, so as to be in a position to provide covering fire to the troops attacking the fort from the west.

Air support for this operation too was very limited, being restricted to one aircraft at a time, available at call from Jamnagar.

Close naval support was to be given by the cruiser *I.N.S. Delhi* moving along the coast, but only during the hours of daylight.

As in Daman, the Diu operations were also planned originally to begin some time after the commencement of the Goa operations, but the final decision was that all the three operations should have the same H hour, namely the first light on 18 December.[81]

These Indian army units ignored requests from Wg Cdr MPO (Micky) Blake, planning-in-charge of the Indian Air Force operations in Diu, to attack only on first light when close air support would be available.[51]

(Non-provision of adequate assault crafts resulted in the deaths of quite a number of Jawans. This situation could have been averted and valuable lives saved.)

PREPARATIONS FOR OPERATION VIJAY

G.O. C. in C. Southern Command, Lt. General J.N.Chaudhuri having received definite instructions from the government on 29th November began his preparations[82] to assemble a strong force near the Goan border.

Troops for the operation, which was to be called **"OP VIJAY"**, were to be stationed by 11th December at the following areas:

BELGAUM for GOA
VAPI for DAMAN and
UNA for DIU.

Troops for *DIU* and *DAMAN* were to be found from the Southern Command itself, but the bulk of the task force for GOA was to come from *AMBALA* and *AGRA*. The following troops were earmarked for these operations:

(a) **GOA**:

(i) 17th Division less one brigade.

(ii) 50th Independent Para Brigade less one battalion, under command of 17th Division.

(iii) 2 Sikh Light Infantry to join 50th Para Brigade.

(iv) Two light armoured regiments, One Medium Artillery Regiment and a number of engineer units under its command.

(b) **DAMAN**

1 Maratha, with under command an ad hoc 25 pounder battery from Artillery School *DEOLALI*.

(c) **DIU**

20 Rajput and one company of 4 Madras, under command of a brigadier.

When the move order was received by the 17th Infantry Division on 30th November, it was under the command of Maj. Gen. M.M. Khanna MVC, who was due to proceed to the U.K on a course as nominated earlier. Before he handed over the charge of the Division to Maj. Gen.

Candeth, Director of Artillery at Army Headquarters, three days later, he issued certain administrative orders for the issue of stores and ammunition to the units and the movement of the troops to six different railway stations from which they were to entrain. The first steamed out of *AMBALA CANTT*, Railway station on the morning of 2nd December carrying the Divisional Advance Party for *POONA*. Soon after taking over the divisional Command next day (3rd December), Maj. Gen. Candeth too left for POONA, where he was briefed by the Army Commander on the 4th before flying to *BELGAUM* which had been selected as railhead, airhead and the site of the Tactical Headquarters of the Southern Command.

On 29th November, the Commander of 50th Para brigade, Brigadier Sagat Singh, was called from Agra Cantonment to Army Headquarters, New Delhi. He was told of the impending operations in *GOA* by the special task force and that his Brigade had been placed under the command of the Force Commander. In a conference held the same evening at Army Headquarters, it was decided that a battalion group from this Brigade would be employed in an airborne role either in the north of *GOA* near *MAPUCA* or near the important road communication centre of *PONDA*. When Brigadier Sagat Singh returned to Agra Cantt with the news, there was great jubilation in the entire Brigade at the prospect of air- borne operations for which 2 Para (Maratha) was chosen. The jubilation was, however, short lived, as the idea of dropping parachutists in *GOA* was soon given up, to the disappointment of all concerned.

An expensive air-borne attack against *GOA* was not really necessary, and it is claimed, represented merely an exuberance of spirit on the part of Army H Q. The proposal was given up when Gen. Chaudhuri assured all concerned that the whole operation would be over within a maximum of three days.

Three days before D-Day, COAS, General P.N.Thapar, accompanied by Lt. General P.P.Kumaramangalam the adjutant General, and Lt. General J.N.Chaudhury, the Army Commander, visited the brigade, and Brig.Sagat Singh went through his plan for operation with them. At the end of the presentation, the Army Commander expressed some reservation. He felt that Sagat's

timings were too optimistic and it may not be possible to keep to them. But Sagat Singh insisted that the timings were feasible, and the visitors left after wishing the brigade good luck. On his return to tactical HQ, the Army Commander conveyed his doubts to his staff. However Air Vice Marshal Pinto and the Chief of Staff, Major General P.O.Dunn, as well as G.N.Handoo of theIB, who knew Sagat well, supported him and he was allowed to proceed with his plan. As it happened Sagat had already kept four hours in reserve, and was able to remain well ahead of the estimated timings when the operations took place.

The move of the Para Brigade troops from *AGRA* to *BELGAUM* began in the early hours of 2nd December. By 1000 hours on 6 December the entire Brigade less vehicles, heavy equipment and certain personnel belonging to administrative units, gathered in an area between kilometres 9 and 14 at BELGAUM-SAWANTWADI. From *BELGAUM* the Brigade moved to *SAWANTWADI* by the 13th and was concentrated in the assembly area east of *DODAMARG* by the evening of the16th.

The Portuguese representative at the UN complained, "*Indian Paratroopers, from 50th Unit, comprising about 2000 in strength, have concentrated at Poona.*" They presumed that they would be Para dropped into GOA.[83]

Brigadier Jaswant Singh of 112th Brigade and Lt. Col. S.J.S.Bhonsale of 1 Maratha, who were to conduct the *DIU* and *DAMAN* operations respectively, were sent off immediately to do their own reconnaissance. They were to operate directly under HQ Southern Command.[84]

It was estimated that the forces earmarked for the operation in *GOA* would be concentrated in *BELGAUM* by the 11th. However, the troop movements, which began on the 2nd from *AMBALA CANTT*, and other railway stations, were mostly completed by 6th December. In the words of the G.O.C-in-C. Southern Command this was a remarkable achievement, as it involved long rail journeys, a change of railway gauge in the *POONA* area, and in the case of mechanical transport, detraining near *POONA* followed by a road move to *BELGAUM*, a distance of over 200 miles.

All large stock of supplies, ammunition, oil and bridging equipment had arrived from various depots located in different parts of the country.

Although the bulk of the administrative concentration was completed by 12th December, some stores were still coming in, when operations started on the night of 17th /18th December.

Conferences were held almost daily at *POONA* from 30th November, sometimes by the Army Commander, sometimes by his Chief of Staff with the heads of branches, arms and services. The operational plans were explained, the administrative problems arising from them discussed and orders and instructions to various officers and services decided upon and issued.

Everything moved according to plan and the Tactical Headquarters, Southern Command, started functioning at *BELGAUM* on 13th December when the Army Commander, Chief of Staff and other staff officers and Heads of Branches/Arms and Services arrived there in the morning. Earlier, on the 12th, the troops had moved to their forward concentration areas along the borders of *GOA, DAMAN* and *DIU.*

INSTRUCTIONS N° 2 to MAJ. GEN. K.P.CANDETH, G.O.C. 17 INFANTRY DIVISION

Instructions [85]

Information and Appreciation

1. As a result of provocative action by the Portuguese in *ANJEDIV* Island and recently along the Indian border, it is anticipated that we will have to take retaliatory steps against them in the very near future. With this in view suitable forces are now being concentrated in the *BELGAUM* area.

Portuguese forces in Goa

2. All available information in respect of Portuguese forces in *GOA* has already been sent to you under this Headquarters, TOP SECRET letter No 391505/GST (I) of 6th Dec 61. Further information when received will be forwarded to you. There are unlikely to be large reinforcements to the Portuguese ground forces either in manpower or equipment.

3. The Portuguese Army may initially offer coordinated resistance to our advance. In any case, they are likely to be adequately equipped and to have prepared for demolition of certain portions of the main axes of advance into *GOA* plus the bridges and culverts along them. You may encounter some modern jet aircraft in close support of their forces. Their Navy may also operate against our own in the immediate vicinity of their territories in India. Once orders for our entry into *GOA* issue, any delay by us may lead to:
   (a) The Portuguese raising this matter in the UN, which may result in a premature ceasefire agreement,
   (b) Massacres of Indian and Goan nationals, and
   (c) The destruction of public utilities.

   Your operations therefore will be conducted with the utmost speed and determination.

Appreciation of enemy action

4. My appreciation of two possible military courses open to the Portuguese are given in my Appreciation of 10th Nov 61, paragraph 55 and 56, a copy of which is with you.

Forces available

5. See Appendix "A" attached.

Navy

6. The Indian Navy will be supporting ground operations by neutralizing coast batteries and controlling shipping movements in and out of ports of *GOA*. Co-ordination with them will be maintained through my Headquarters.

Air Force

7. The Air Force will support ground operations from airfields at *POONA* and *BELGAUM*. Its primary task will be the neutralisation of the Portuguese Air Force in *GOA* on the first day of operations thus gaining air superiority over that territory. Thereafter it will provide close air support to the ground forces.

8. The Air Forces that will be deployed by 9th Dec 61 in support of your operations are given in Appendix "B" attached.

9. As far as so-called nationalist groups are concerned the instructions previously issued apply.

Operations in *GOA* conducted directly by Headquarters Southern Command[86]

10. In furtherance of your plans I intend operating a small mixed army and Police Force along the route ***KARWAR-CANACONA***. The purpose of this force is to draw away and contain as many Portuguese troops towards the South. This force will come under your command when you have gained your main objectives but till then I will control and maintain them. I will also move the SRP

behind you all along the border and will see that they will not interfere with your operations.

Intention

11. My intention is to occupy the Portuguese territory of *GOA* with the utmost speed.

Method

Tasks

12. (a) in the first instance to advance to the general line *MAPUCA, BICHOLIM, SANQUELIM, PILLIEM*; and thereafter
(b) To the general line *PANJIM, VELHA GOA, PONDA* and
(c) Occupy the rest of the territory of *GOA*.

13. In the event of the Portuguese surrendering before you have completed tasks (b), you will immediately dispatch a brigade group to *PANJIM* and then undertake task (c) with speed. You must be prepared for this contingency.

14. The terms and conditions of any surrender if given to you will be referred back to me immediately before acceptance or discussion.

Troops available to you

15.For details see Appendix "A". Your plans will be made on the assumption that in addition to your own command 17 Infantry Division less one infantry brigade group, you will have under command 50 (independent) Para Brigade group whose ORBAT is shown in appendix "A"

7 Cavalry less1 squadron
24 Medium Artillery Regiment
74 Mountain Battery
3 Air observation posts (OP) Flight (FLT)
1 Svy Tp (troop) except 20 Loc Regiment

16. In making your appreciation, you may consider the employment of additional engineer and signal troops as shown in Appendix" A".

Administration

17.The Army Maintenance Area is located in *BELGAUM* where also will be located in the first instance your adm area. You will be responsible for drawing all your administrative needs in your own transport.

18. As your advance progresses you may establish administrative areas forward, along the routes of your advance. These new administrative areas will not be established without permission from my Headquarters.

19. Treatment of all Portuguese forces captured or surrendering will be under the normal usages of war. P.W. or civilians taken into custody will be segregated into 3 groups: Portuguese, African and Goan.

20.Women and children must be protected and the behaviour of troops must be according to our highest standards. You will also ensure as far as you can that looting by lawless and mischievous elements is prevented.

Intercommunications

21. Being issued separately.

Wireless silence

22. Wireless silence will be observed till further orders.

Sitreps (Situation reports)

23.Sitreps as at 0600 and 1800 hours will be submitted to this Headquarters daily.

Other Reports and Returns

24. Being issued separately.

25. **Code words**

(a) Code name for operation—VIJAY

(b) Entry into *GOA*—VARAHA

(c) Break wireless Silence—MEENAKSHI.

"D" Day

26. You will be informed of "D" Day personally by me.

27. Acknowledge

Lt. Gen. J. N. Chaudhuri
General Officer
Commanding-in-Chief

FORCES AVAILABLE

The following forces[87] will be available:

1. **17 Infantry Division** less 64 Infantry brigade Group

2. **50 (Independent) Para Brigade Group**
   - (a) **H Q**
     H Q 50 Independent Para Brigade
   - (b) **ARTILLERY**
     17 Para Field Regiment
   - (c) **ENGINEERS**
     411 Para Field Company
   - (d) **SIGNALS**
     - (i) 50 Independent Para Brigade Signal Company
     - (ii) 17 Para Field Regiment Signal Section
   - (e) **INFANTRY**
     - (i) 1 PARA
     - (ii) 2 PARA
     - (iii) 2 SIKH Light Infantry ex MM and K area
     - (iv) Independent Para Company MAHAR MG (Borders)
   - (f) **A S C** (Army Supply Corps)
     - (i) 272 Para Company P1
     - (ii) 622 Company ASC (GT) Para less one P1
   - (g) **MEDICAL**
     60 Para Field Ambulance.
   - (h) **ORDNANCE**
     50 Independent Para Brigade OFP
   - (j) **E M E** (Electrical Mechanical Engineers)
     - (i) 50 Independent Para brigade LAD Type II
     - (ii) 17 Para Field regiment LAD
     - (iii) 2 Para infantry Workshop Company
     - (iv) 1110 Para Transport Company Workshop Section Type "C"
   - (k) **LIASION** Sections
     - (i) 50 Para GL section Type 'B'
     - (ii) 51Para GL section Type 'C'

(iii) 52 Para GL section Type 'C'

(l) **PROVOST**
50 Independent Brigade Provost Section

3. **7 CAVALRY** less one squadron including signal section and LAD

ARMY TROOPS

4. **ARTILLERY**
   - (a) 24 Medium Regiment including signal section and LAD
   - (b) 74 Mountain battery
   - (c) 3 Air Observation Flight
   - (d) One Svy troop ex 20 Loc Regiment.

5. **ENGINEERS**
   - (a) HQ 20 Infantry Division Engineers including signal section
   - (b) 21 Field Company
   - (c) 380 Field Company
   - (d) 44 Field Pk Company including LAD
   - (e) 86 Bridge Company Engineers Maintenance P1
   - (f) 87 Bridge Company Engineers MaintenanceP1
   - (g) One Jp1 ex 651 Engineers Plant Company (ex CME)

6. **SIGNALS**
   - (a) Detachment 1 Air Sp Signal Company comprising:-
     - (i) Tcls 5
     - (ii) Control dets 2
     - (iii) Air field dets 3
     - (iv) Tac R det 1
     - (b) 1 Medium Radio Relay Section
     - (c) Det 1 line Carrier Section consisting of: -
       - (i) Terminal stations 2
       - (ii) Repeater station 1
     - (d) 2 line section

(e) 5 Wing Signal section ex 2 Air formation Signal Regiment

(f) 6 Terminal Equipment Section 2 Air Formation Signal
regiment.

(g) 2 tcls ex 2 Air Special Signal Company.

7. **ASC** (Army supply Corps)

(a) HQ 602 Company ASC (AD) with 1 platoon ex CHANDIGARH

(b) 688 Company ASC (GT) (3 Ton) including transport workshop Section

(c) 704 Company ASC (civilian GT) (3 Ton)

(d) 706 company ASC (civilian GT) (3 Ton)

(e) 656 Company ASC (Br Normal) including transport Coy Workshop Section

(f) 657 Company ASC (Br Heavy) including transport Coy Workshop Section

(g) 651 Company ASC (Amph) including transport Coy workshop Section

(h) 666 Amb Platoon ASC.

8. **ORDNANCE**

(a) 55 Ordnance Maint Platoon

(b) One man Platoon ex Amn Company

9. **LIAISON** section Type 'B'

(a) 18 GL section Type 'B'

(b) 21 GL Section type 'C'

(c) 24 GL section Type 'C'

(d) 41 Air Transport liaison section Type 'D'.

10. **1 APIS**

Maj-Gen. K. P. Candeth,
in command of the Goa Operations

HQ 17 DIVISION Operation Order No 1/61 dated 11 Dec, 61

Operation Vijay —17 INF DIV OO No 1/61, 11 Dec 61[88]
(No change from verbal orders except Paras 12 (a). 15, 16 and 17)
Maps: Bombay Deccan States and GOA I into4 miles sheets 48/J and 1into1 mile sheets 48E/14, 15 and 481/2, 3, 7.

INFO

General

1. As a result of provocative action by the Portuguese in Angediv Island and recently along the Indian border, it is anticipated that we have to take retaliatory steps against them in *GOA*.

Portuguese Forces

2. For strengths and dispositions see 17 Infantry Division PERINTREP No 1of 9 December 61.

Own Troops

3. Under instructions HQ Southern Command, elements of 4 Rajput with civilian police are to advance simultaneously with us from *KARWAR* (PJ 04) along coastal road to *CANACONA* (UX 93) *QUEPEM* (UY 05) with a view to distracting Portuguese forces opposing us.

Air

4. (a) ***For close support***
8 Vampires – approximately 12 FB (fighting/ bombing) Missions of 2 actions per day.

(b) ***For tactical Reconnaissance and air photo recce (oblique)***
Two Vampires. Air photo can be airdropped after 2 hours if required.

(c) ***For target identification and spotting***
Two Harvard.

(d) ***For communication, casualty evacuation and limited logistics***
Two Otters. Two Helicopters directly under TAC (tical) HQ.

(e) ***Location JOC***
Main division HQ

(f) ***Tac Radio Broadcasts***
At 0800hrs and 1600 hrs daily.

5. **Additional Troops**
Coming under command in present concentration area:-
50 Independent Para Brigade
7 Cavalry less one squadron
24 Medium Regiment
74 Mountain Battery
3 OP Flight
One Svy troop ex 20 Lac Regiment

Engineers
HQ 20 infantry Division Engineers including Signal Section
21 Field Company
380 Field Company
Detachment 86 Br Company Engineers Maint Platoon
Detachment 87 Br Company Engineers Maint Platoon
One platoon ex 651 Engineers Plant Company

Signals
Detachment 1 Air Sp Signal Company comprising –tels 3.

ASC
HQ 602 Company ASC (AD)

688 Company ASC (GT)
704 Company ASC (Civ) GT–In concentration area after completion of Army dumping.
656 Company ASC (Br)
657 Company ASC (Br)
651 Company ASC (Amph)
666 Amb platoon ASC

Liaison Sections
Two GL Sections type C

Intention

6. 17 Infantry division and attached troops will advance with utmost speed into GOA to capture *PANJIM* (UX 78) *MARMAGAO* (UX 77)

Method
General Outline
7. Operation will be carried out in two phases as under:-
(a) Phase I – Advance and capture of *PONDA* (UX 97).
(b) Phase 2—Capture of *PANJIM* and *MARMAGAO* (order for phase 2 later)

Phase 1
8. **General**
Advance will be two up on three axes as under:-
(a)Axis RED *DODAMARG* (US 9210)—*ASSONORA* (US 80)—*SANQUELIM* (UX 99)—*USAGAO* Br (UY 0182)—*PILLIEM* (UY 07).
(b) Axis YELLOW ANMOD (UY 3179)—*POLEM* (UY 27) *PILLIEM* (UY07)—PONDA
(c) Axis GREEN *MOLEM* (UY 27)—*COLLEM* (UY 26)—Tr junc UY 1270—Nala crossing UY 0671—*PONDA*

9. Order of march

(a) Axis RED
50 Para Brigade Group

(b) Axis YELLOW
63 Infantry Brigade Group
Divisional R Group
Engineers Group with Br (bridge)/raft equipment (divisional troops)
Artillery Group
Main Divisional HQ
48 Infantry brigade group
B Ech(echelon)
Rear Divisional HQ
Divisional Adm Group

10. Grouping—Axis RED

50 Para brigade Group (as already composed) with under command-
7 Cavalry less one squadron
B squadron 8 Cavalry
135 Heavy Mortar battery
P battery 24 Med Regiment
Battery less one troop 45 LAA regiment
Br (bridge) equipment
Section 85 Field health Section
Forward repair team (AFV) 4 Special workshop Company
Detachment 17 infantry Division Recce Company
One ACT
663 FPO

11. Grouping Axis YELLOW

(a) 63 Infantry brigade leading with—

(i) <u>Under Command</u>
8 Cavalry less one squadron
377 Field Company (with Bridge Equipment)
Section plant Engineers

C Company 7 MAHAR MG
One ACT with tel
ADS 152 Field Ambulance (TA)
AWD 210 Field workshop Company
Forward repair team 4 Special workshop Company
Detachment 17 Infantry Division Recce Company
One section 17 infantry division Provost Unit

(ii) <u>In direct support</u>
74 Mountain Battery
10 Field Regiment
137 Heavy Mortar battery
Q battery 24 Medium Regiment

(iii) <u>Under command for move</u>
Artillery brigade Recce party (restricted scale)
Engineer's Recce party
One platoon 637 Company GT ASC
One Section-17 Infantry Division Provost Unit.

(b) Engineer Group
376 field group
Bridge equipment

(c) Artillery Group
17Artillery brigade less those allotted
RHQ 24 Medium regiment
3 AOP Flt.
Svy Troop 20 Loc Regiment

(d) Main Division HQ with
JOC
ACT with one tel

(e) 48 Infantry Brigade with

(i) Under command
A company 7 MAHAR MG
ADS 152 Field ambulance (TA)
Half section 17 Infantry division Provost Unit
AWD 209 Field Workshop Company
Detachment 17 Infantry division Rec Company
One ACT with tel

(ii) Under command for move
69 TCVs (641 Company ASC (GT) and other elements.

(f) B Echelon Group
B Echelons of all formations/units moving on the axis

Tasks

12. (a) Para Brigade Group
(i) Will secure *ASSONORA* and *BICHOLIM* (US 80) and *USAGAO* Bridge (UY 0182) with a view to advance on PONDA.
(ii) Secure *MAPUCA* (US 70). Force at *MAPUCA* will come under command this HQ on issue of nickname SUGAR LOAF.

(b) 63 Infantry Brigade Group
Will capture *MOLEM* with a view to securing *PONDA*.

(c) 48 infantry Brigade Group
Will be Division reserve and be prepared to take over advance from 63 Infantry Brigade if necessary.

13. Time of Start

(a) 50 Para brigade Group
Head of Advance Guard crosses frontier at 0515 hrs D Day

(b) 63 Infantry Brigade

To cross frontier at 05 15 hrs D Day.

14. Axes of Advance

(a) 50 Para brigade Group
Route RED

(b) 63 Infantry Brigade
(i) Route YELLOW
(ii) From MOLEM onwards, YELLOW and GREEN routes

15. CL

YELLOW Route

16. **Bounds**

(a) Axis RED	Nickname
ASSONORA	TIR KAMAN
BICHOLI M	AMAR RAHO
SANQUELIM	RAM RAJ
USAGAO Bridge	JAL DIN
(b) Axis YELLOW	Nickname
MOLEM	HEER SYAL
PILLIEM	RAJA FAKIR
CANDEAPAR R (0079)	JACK SPAN
PONDA	DAHI BADA

17. **Report Lines**

(a) Axis RED	Nickname
Road Tri Junction (TISK) (UX 9888)	CHALTAADMI
(b) Axis YELLOW	Nickname
Road Junction	GUL JANI

18. **Harbour Parties**

(a) Standard Composition

(b) Divisional Harbour master's party to move behind Div R Group.

19. **Supporting Arms**

(a) Armour

Tasks—(i) Axis RED

(aa) Destroy any enemy AFVs

(bb) Protection of 50 Para brigade from hostile AFVs

(cc) Recce of *PILIGAO* (UX 9196)

(ii) Axis YELLOW

(aa) One squadron 8 Cavalry with one bn to advance along GREEN route with all possible speed to secure *PONDA*

(bb) To provide protection to 63 infantry Brigade advance on *PONDA*.

(b) Artillery

(i) All artillery resources on both the axes will be deployed before first light D Day to support advance initially on respective axes.

(ii) Ammunition expenditure

3.7 HowitzerTypes	150 rpg	All
25 pr	150 rpg	do
75 mm	300 rpg	do
5.5 in	120 rpg	do
4.2 in Mor	100 rpg	do
LAA	100 rpg per day less	
P Battery.		

(iii) **Recce parties**

Allowed with leading brigade on restricted scale.

(iv) **Likey gun areas**

(v) **Allotment of LAQ**

One battery –SAMBRE Air field

One Battery less one troop for tank concentrations and gun areas on axis YELLOW.

(c) **ENGINEERS**

Tasks

(i) Clearing mines;

(ii) Making detours;

(iii) Making of class 9and class 18 bridges and rafts;

(iv) One Field Company ex 20 Infantry Division Engineers to be in support of 50 Para Brigade in 50 Para Brigade Area.

(v) HQ 20 Infantry Division Engineers with one Field Company to be in reserve in Divisional Adm Area;

(vi) Build airstrip for AOP.

(d) **M G**

(i) Normal affiliations

(ii) Provide Divisional HQ Defence Company.

(e) **AIR**

(i) Be prepared for air strike at *ASSONORA* at first light D Day.

(ii) Be prepared for air strike at *MOLEM* soon after first light D Day, if necessary.

(iii) Interdiction along two main axes.

(iv) Destruction of enemy AFVs.

20. Patrolling by leading Brigades

May commence after last light D-1 across the border.

21. **D Day**

Later on nickname "BULL DOZER" followed by date.

22. **Movement Table**

(a) At Appendix B attached for route YELLOW. HQ Para brigade will issue for route RED.

(b) SP for RED route–later.

A D M

23. **Maintenance**

(a) A M A

Remains present location

(b) Division / Brigade maintenance areas

(i) To be established separately for routes RED and YELLOW

Route RED—*SAWANTWADI* (US 73)

Route YELLOW and GREEN—LONDA (UY 58)

(ii) When link up is affected at *PILLIEM* maintenance for whole Division less force at *MAPUCA* will be along route YELLOW.

24. For further details, refer 17 Infantry division Administrative order No 1/ 61

25. **Location HQ**

(a) Tactical HQ Southern Command *BELGAUM*

(b) Main Divisional HQ

Area *TERNAIGHAT* railway station (UY 48)

26. **Signal Comns**

(a) For details see 17 Inf. Div. Sig. Regt. 00 No 1 of 11 December 61.

(b) Wireless silence until H Hours; to be broken on code word MENAKSHI from this HQ. All wireless stations to be on listening watch 30 minutes before H Hour.

27. **Summary of important nicknames** Given

Diplomatic activity and Postponement of D –Day

All was now set for the operation to begin on 16th December. This was the date given by the G.O.C-in-C. Southern Command to the Defence Minister and the Chiefs of Staff on 2nd December as that on which the operation could start. Although the feasibility of starting the operation a day earlier, i.e. on the 15th had been considered and accepted a few days before, the Army Commander was informed in writing on the 14th that the D-Day had been fixed for 18 December[89]. It is highly probable that the postponement of the D-Day to the 18th was dictated by political considerations and the diplomatic activity going on at the U.N[89] and among other interested Governments to avert a showdown. It also proves the desire of the Government of India till the last moment to arrive at a peaceful solution of the problem if possible.

D-Day had been postponed to the 18th in the hope that diplomacy might achieve something, resulting in the cancellation of operation or a further postponement. This hope having been frustrated, the die was cast and the Indian forces started their move on the night of 17th /18th December.

Brig. Sagat Singh,
Commander, 50th Para Brigade

Brig. Gurbux Singh,
Commander, 48th Infantry Brigade

Brig. K. S. Dhillon,
Commander, 63rd Infanry Brigade

Brig. Mohinder Singh
The Artillery Commander of 17th Division

17 INFANTRY DIVISION TASK FORCE FOR OPERATION VIJAY[90]

ORBAT

Formation/Unit	Commander
HQ 17 INF DIV	Maj. Gen M M KHANNA MVC. Upto4 Dec 61
	Maj. Gen K P CANDETH
HQ 48 INF BDE	Brig. GURBUX SINGH
5 GUARDS	Lt. Col. JAI SINGH
13 KUMAON	Lt. Col. B S CHAND Vr. C.
1 SIKH LI	Lt. Col. MUNSHI SINGH BRAR
HQ 63 INF. BDE	Brig. G. BHARAT SINGH Upto 30 Nov 61
	Brig. KS DHILLON
3 SIKH LI	Lt. Col. JD BOBB
2 BIHAR	Lt. Col. KULDIP SINGH CHADHA
4 SIKH LI	Lt. Col. RAGHBIR B. NANDA
HQ 17 ARTY BDE	Brig. MOHINDER SINGH MC
3 Fd Regt	Lt.Col. LACHHMAN SINGH LEHL Vr. C.
10 Fd Regt	Lt. Col. DC NORONHA
30 Hy Mor Regt	Lt. Col. CKR SESHADRI
45 LAA Regt	Lt. Col. VK NAIR
8 CAV	Lt. Col. FONSECA
HQ 17 INF DIV ENG.	Lt. Col. TD BADHANI
376 Fd Coy	Maj. DD KADAM
377 Fd Coy	Maj. VM WARTY
47 Fd Pk Coy	Maj. RR MALIK
17 Inf Div Sig Rgt	Lt. Col. SVS JUNEJA

7 MAHAR MG	Lt. Col. BM BALI
17 Inf Div ASC Rgt	Lt. Col. BAWA SUNDER SINGH Upto 12 Dec 61
	Lt. Col. DR SURI
256 Comp Pl ASC	Maj. RAMACHANDRAN
306 Comp Pl ASC	Maj. SS KALRA
308 Comp Pl ASC	Capt. HARBANS SINGH
641 Coy ASC (GT)	Maj. SS GYANI
637 Coy ASC (GT)	Maj. AMAR SINGH RAI
680 Coy ASC (GT)	Maj. JASWANT SINGH
ADMS 17 Inf Div	Col. HL KAPOOR
152 Fd Amb (TA)	Lt. Col. TM SEETHAPATHY
85 Fd Health Sec	Maj. BL GUPTA
MSU (TA)	Maj. NS BAWESA
40 MSU (TA)	Maj. DN GANGULI
120 DU	Capt. BK HAZRA
HQ CAOC 17 INF DIV	Lt. Col. KC CHOPRA Upto 10 Dec 61
	Lt. Col. SLN REDDI
17 Div OFP	Maj. AS CHAHAL
HQ CEME 17 INF DIV	Lt Col. VISHWAMITTER
209 Fd Wksp Coy	Capt CHARANJIT SINGH Offg
210 Fd Wksp Coy	Maj. PL CHADEV
4 Specialists Wksp Coy	Maj. JAGDISH CHANDRA
701 Tpt Wksp Coy	Maj. RG VERMA
17 Inf Div Rec Coy	Maj. JS GREWAL
17 Inf Div Pro Unit	Capt. PUSHPINDER KUMAR

646 FS Sec	——
17 Div Postal Unit	Lt. RATTAN SINGH
HQ 50 PARA BDE	Brig. SAGAT SINGH
17 Para Fd Regt	Lt. Col. ARJINDER SINGH
P Bty 24 Med Regt	
64/45 LAA Bty	
135 Hy Mor Regt	
7 CAV	Lt. Col. BHUPINDER SINGH
B Sqn 8 Cav	
411 Para Fd Coy	Maj. RASTOGI
380 Fd Coy Engrs	
50 Para Bde Sig Coy	Maj. RR CHATERJEE
1 Para (Punjab)	Lt. Col. SUCHA SINGH Vr. C. MC
2 Para (Maratha)	Lt. Col. UK GUPTA
2 Sikh LI	Lt. Col. T CHERIAN
Indep Para Coy	Maj. HARIPAL SINGH
MAHAR MG	
272 Para Comp ASC (Para) less one Pl	Maj. HARBANS SINGH
602 Coy ASC (AD)	
50 Indep Para Bde	Capt. BS SOMAN
2 Para Inf Wksp EME	Maj. SUSHIL KUMAR
50 Indep Para Bde PRO	Jam. CHAGGAN LAL
50 Para GL Sec	Maj. MY KHAN
51 Para GL Sec	
52 Para GL Sec	
41 Air TPT Liaisons Sec	Cap. DARUWALA
60 Para Fd Amb	
50 Indep Para Bde LAD	
663 F P O	

References:

76—Khera—Op. Vijay—p 44
77—Ibid-p55
78—Ibid-p57
79—Ibid-p57
80—Ibid-p57
81—Ibid-p58
82—Ibid-p45
83—Min.Neg.Estr. -20 anos da Defesa-Vol IV –p122
84—Khera—Op Vijay—p47
85—Khera—Op. Vijay—App.II-p166
86—Ibid- App.II-p167
87—Ibid-App. III-p170
88—Ibid-App IV-p173
89—Ibid-p49
90—Ibid-App.VI p183-185

CHAPTER X

OPERATION IN FORCE

Gen. P. N. Thapar,
Chief of Army Staff in 1961

Special Order of the Day from Chief of the Army Staff, Gen. P. N. Thapar before Operation Vijay 16-17 December 1961

My Special Order of the day[91] to all forces taking part in OP VIJAY.

This will be read out to troops before they go into action.

Firstly the people of GOA have caused the collapse of colonial rule. The colonialists can NO longer maintain themselves law and order in GOA.

Secondly the people of GOA are Indians and have suffered colonial rule longer than we in the rest of our motherland.

Thirdly you will now enter GOA NOT as conquerors of a foreign land but as part of the Indian defence forces who has always served the motherland to defend the honour and security of people

Fourthly GOA never belonged to the colonial rulers. It belonged to our people from whom it could NOT be kept away forever. The colonial occupation has ended. The colonialists have now been unseated and the land and people there join in the greater freedom of our country.

Fifthly let our courage as well as the high purpose of your mission and your high sense of duty and discipline be evident to all GOA whatever you stand by doing..

Sixthly in GOA you are in India and with your compatriots. Your duty is as at home. GO DEFEND and PROTECT the people. Let no one suffer violence.

Seventhly this is for your guidance. Whilst you are engaged in the task of assisting in the establishment of stable conditions which the colonialists have destroyed leaving behind them chaos and destruction.

Eighthly I have no doubt you will take special care to respect sanctity of places of worship and see that no damage is done to them.

The Operations in Goa

On 15th or 16th December all the troop movements were completed, and the units had been briefed about the objectives to be achieved and their respective roles. D-Day was 18th December, and the moves were to begin almost simultaneously on all sectors at 'first light' on that day.

The atmosphere in the camps, on the evening of 17th was tense. However there was complete confidence among all ranks about the outcome of the coming operations.

At the Tactical Headquarters of Southern Command in Belgaum Lt. Gen.Chaudhuri and Air Vice Marshal Pinto were busy giving the finishing touches to all the arrangements. Already the Civil Affairs Officer designate Shri Noronha and DIG Nagoo of the Indian Police had arrived.

The 17th Infantry Division was to carry out the operations in Goa. Its plan was already explained verbally to the three Brigade Commanders and written down as operation order after finalization. (OO No 1) of 11 December. The intention mentioned in the order was as follows:

"17 Inf Div and attached troops will advance with utmost speed into Goa to capture Panjim (UX 78) and Marmagoa (UX 77)"

The general outline of the method was "an eastern and a northern thrust and a decoy entry from the south." Duties and responsibilities were assigned to the various units for the northern and eastern thrusts and details of phase I of the operation were given (to be conducted on D Day). Detailed instructions such as wireless silence to be observed until H Hour and patrolling before that time were also given. In addition to this Operation Order, the Division also issued seven perintreps (intelligence reports) from 9th to 17th December, informing its brigades and other units under it of the day-to-day developments and news received about the morale of the Portuguese troops, and the Goans in service. It further gave information about the topography of the country to be traversed, condition of roads and buildings, enemy gun positions, ammunition dumps, strength and disposition of enemy troops, and other matters likely to be of tactical use.

Although the H Hour had been fixed for first light on 18 December, some patrols were allowed to cross the border earlier at different times during the night of 17th /18th December. The object of the patrols was to liquidate the enemy posts near the border on the contemplated routes of the main forces in order to facilitate advance and to gain information especially of road communications and state of defences. As the wireless silence had been imposed, all information had to be brought back by runners.

Maj. Gen. K. P. Candeth, G.O.C 17th Infantry Div, directed the operations against Goa. He had under command also 50 Para brigade, 48 Infantry Brigade and 63 Infantry Brigade.

Patrol Activity On Northern Or The Red Axis

The main advance here was to be made by three columns under the 50th Para Brigade Group from the Dodamarg side. Patrols from all the three columns were sent out after nightfall on 17th December, from 2 Para Maratha, 1 Para Punjab and 2 Sikh Light infantry[93].

A patrol from 2 Para Maratha was ordered to move from Matna, along the smuggler's route to Sanquelim, and secure the concrete bridge there by 05:15 hours on the morning of 18th December. This bridge, if captured intact, would facilitate the advance of the rest of that Battalion on the route to Usgao and from there to Ponda. An iron bridge was also reported to be in existence in the same area.

C Company of 2 Para Maratha, therefore, left Matna with two local guides at 21:00 hours on 17th December and crossed the border an hour and a half later. By 04:00 hours on 18th December it was well inside Goan territory and stopped in a lone house at a place not far from the concrete bridge, preparatory to capturing it.

However, at about 04:20 hours it noticed intense vehicular traffic moving on the Bicholim-Sanquelim road in the vicinity of the bridge. A few minutes later a loud bang was heard and a bright flash seen in the direction of Sanquelim. The Portuguese had demolished the bridge in the nick of time. At 05:00 hours two more bangs were heard and the iron bridge was also gone. (*The Portuguese came to know about the Indian troops crossing the border from the All India Radio broadcast.*

But for this broadcast it was reasonably certain that these bridges would have been captured intact.) The Portuguese had not blown the bridges earlier on this axis, due to misleading intelligence reports.

The 50th Independent Para Brigade group moved from Belgaum to the forward concentration area southwest of Sawantwadi from 11th to 13th December, and had reached the assembly area east of Dodamarg only on the evening of 17th December. The Portuguese authorities in Goa were not aware of this movement and believed to the last minute that the Parachute Brigade was concentrated in Poona for an airborne landing in Goa. They were thinking to counter the "vertical approach" of the brigade and therefore the bridges were not demolished earlier but only on the 18th after the advance had begun.[94]

As bridges were found blown up the Company Commander made a quick change of plan. He decided to capture Sanquelim itself to remove the possibility of any interference by the Portuguese troops or Police in the work of putting up a Bailey bridge on the river when the main column should come up to cross it. Defensive positions were taken on the road junction to prevent any further enemy movement. A move towards the town was made; the military and police barracks of the place were occupied. By first light the company group was firmly established. The riverbank at the bridge site was also secured. The main column of the battalion, which had started its move at the scheduled time, could now come up and cross the river by throwing a Bailey bridge over it.

A little to the west of where the 2 Para (Maratha) patrol had crossed the frontier, patrols from 1 Para (Punjab) also entered between 20:00 and 21:00 hours on 17th December. Their objective was to secure three villages across the border before H hour. One of the villages (Ibrampur) was occupied without opposition. The second (Maulinguem) was also occupied, after overcoming slight opposition in which some casualties were inflicted at a cost of one Indian soldier wounded. (*The Portuguese casualties were: six killed and three wounded.*) The third place (Dodamarg) was however held by a platoon of infantry and a troop of Portuguese armoured cars. The Portuguese were inside a building surrounded by trenches and fortified by barbed wire. When C Company less one platoon of 1 Para attacked the position; they came under heavy fire from the Portuguese inside the building. Company Commander, Major Sushil Kumar, realized that he had to create gaps in the barbed wire in order to carry home the attack, and also deal with the armoured cars quickly. Men were detailed to cut the wire and to deal with the cars. Lance Havaldar Gulzar Sigh lost his life while on this mission. The attack was driven home with skill and determination and met with success. An armoured car and some trucks were knocked out, a few Portuguese killed and wounded in the process and twenty-four taken prisoners. (*The Portuguese casualties were: 3 killed, 2 wounded and 24 captured*). With the establishment of the patrols in these three villages well before H Hour the entry into Goa from the northern approaches could now be safely undertaken by the troops of the main columns.

This battalion which had to advance from Dodamarg to Assonora and from there to Mapuca and Panjim in the most westerly route also sent a patrol to Kansarpale to see if the culvert there, reported to be mined, had been blown up or not. The patrol returned at 02:00 hours with the required information.

Patrol on Eastern Axis

The advance of the 63rd Infantry brigade from the eastern side of Goa was to be on two routes named the **Yellow axis** and the **Green axis**. The yellow axis was from Mollem to Collem track junction UY 1270, Nala crossing UY 0671 and then to Ponda.

On these two routes also, patrols were sent between 1900 hours to 20:00 hours on the night of 17th December[95]. One of these arrived at a place called Tamari at 23:00 hours, only to find that the Portuguese had vacated it earlier that day. Another patrol starting from Anmod and going by a by-pass route to secure the bridges at Nandron and Mollem found that its vanguard using the shorter main route had already secured the bridges. Yet another patrol went on the Anmod- Mollem road and by 20:30 hours brought back data on the state of culverts, craters and mines *en route*. It had gone about 1.6 kilometres inside Goan territory and, apart from other useful information, had brought a mine also, which its commander had de-fused to carry back.

Thus all the patrols had achieved their objectives both on the northern and eastern routes successfully. Thus the entry into Goa by the main forces had become an easier task.

Advance of Main Columns

On the northern route 2 Sikh Light Infantry and 1 Para (Punjab) were both ordered to reach Panjim, by different routes. Each was keen to have the honour of entering that place first, and therefore both tried, once the march began at first light on 18th December, to overcome all obstacles on the way and reach the objective before the other could do so[96].

1 PARA PUNJAB

The battalion[97] started from its forward assembly area at 05:00 hours and arrived at the border police post at Matna at 06:00 hours. After a stop of one hour, it arrived at Maulinguem, which had been cleared earlier by a patrol. The battalion halted for about an hour awaiting the success signal indicating the occupation of Bicholim. The vanguard of 2 Para (Maratha) was known to be moving to that place.

The battalion was moving on foot so it reached Bicholim at 10:30 hours and Piligao at 12:45 hours. It had to cross the river at this place. No local boats were found at the ferry site. Four storm boats were brought up by engineer vehicles and after a short while a fairly large boat and a small boat also appeared. The local civilians revealed that the ferry site on the bank opposite Piligao was mined. There was also another ferry site opposite Amona which was not mined and the crossing there would put the battalion nearer Banastarim. The first company got ready to cross over and the guns were placed in position to provide firing support.

A company was sent across to investigate the ferry site opposite Amona. After the reconnaissance, it was found that the site was all right for infantry but the jeeps carrying recoilless guns could not be landed. Even the track inland was very difficult and unsuitable for vehicles. The Commanding Officer, however, ordered that the infantry would land at that site and get ready to march forward. Consequently the infantry started crossing over. It was decided that the jeeps would land opposite Piligao, as intended originally, and that the engineers would prepare a diversion. As there was no full engineer element the work was done with help of local civilians. A diversion was quickly made and the jeeps could start crossing the river. As soon as two jeeps carrying guns landed, the battalion began using the diversion and moved towards Banastarim without waiting for the jeeps to cross over. The second in command remained behind at the ferry site to organize the crossing of the remaining vehicles and join the battalion later. This crossing took place at about 16:30 hours.

When they reached Banastarim bridge around 17:45 hours, they found that the bridge had been blown up. As there were no boats available, the battalion took up positions on the eastern side of it and waited for the remainder of the vehicles and troops to come up from Piligao. There was a message from Brigade HQ that the Army Commander would visit the battalion at 09:30 hours the next day. This meant that they would be able to move towards Panjim only some time after that hour on the 19th and their hopes of being the first to reach that place were not destined to be realised.

2 Sikh Light Infantry Group

This battalion[98] was to advance on the Maroon axis, by road Dodamarg-Assonora-Tivim-Mapuca–Betim and then to Panjim. Its advance was to be led by Armour, namely "A" squadron of the 7th Cavalry and a troop of "B" squadron 8th Cavalry. The force assembled three kilometres north-east of Dodamarg on the 15th and carried out reconnaissance of the route it was to follow. (Another squadron of the 7th Cavalry was to move on the Red axis under command of HQ 50th Independent Para Brigade from Dodamarg to Bicholim, Sanquelim, Usgao and Pilliem).

7th & 8th CAVALRY SQUADRONS

On 17th December the commandant addressed all ranks of the Cavalry Squadrons and emphasized the importance of speed, discipline, maintaining the good name of the regiment and treating the Goans **"as our brethren"**

At 05:15 hours on the morning of the 18th, A squadron moved out of night harbour and crossed the starting point at 06:30 hour. The Commandant, who had reached there earlier, saw them off and wished Major Sidhu, the column Commander, the best of luck. After a delay at village Dodamarg (three kilometres inside the border) caused by the necessity to search the village for mines and booby traps, the squadron pushed forward with speed and was soon at village Assonora. The bridge over the creek was found demolished. The Pioneer Section, with the willing assistance of the locals, prepared a temporary causeway by 08:40 hours, over which the squadron crossed the creek and resumed the advance to Tivim. Some Portuguese barracks on the way were found deserted. The Portuguese had left one fully stowed armoured car and also two jeeps in the compound before withdrawing. The squadron reached Tivim at 10:15 hours and again found the bridge destroyed. There was no suitable crossing place near the bridge; however the bridge at Colvale, 6 kilometres north of Tivim was reported to be intact. The whole squadron was ordered to proceed to that place. This was at about 11:30 hours.

The advance was slowed down as the route to Colvale was bad. It was reached at 14:00 hours. There were no Portuguese there too, and the place was secured and the advance to Mapuca continued. The road from Colvale to Mapuca was found covered with hastily laid anti-tank mines. The Pioneer troops moved along clearing the mines as they went, and the squadron reached Mapuca. A roadblock consisting of two big trees felled across the road was encountered at the outskirts of the place. The only possible diversion was cleverly mined. After completing the clearing work the advance to Mapuca was resumed. There were no Portuguese to cover the roadblock with fire. Mapuca was reached at 15:30 hours.

The squadron was informed by the locals that on the road from Mapuca to Betim all culverts, bridges, etc., had been destroyed, so it could be desirable to advance along a track west of the road, which joined the main road 1.6 kilometres short of Betim. After moving on the track the squadron hit the main road again. Near Betim, an enemy LMG opened fire on the leading troops. After firing only two bursts all was quiet again. The leading troops reached Betim at 17:02 hours. Panjim the capital was only 549 metres across the river Mandavi. It was thrilling to feel that they were the first among the Indian troops to reach within sight of the Portuguese capital of Goa in such a short time.

As it was considered that all the boats at the ferry would be required for crossing over to the capital, the squadron fired a few bursts of 30 Browning to warn the boats in the area not to move. One boat on the far side however, succeeded in getting away, while another in making a similar attempt was fired upon and sunk.

2 SIKH LIGHT INFANTRY

This unit[99] was in command of the operations on this axis and was following on the heels of the Armour. It had begun the move at the scheduled time on the morning of 18th December, but after getting inside the border it had begun to encounter light opposition from Portuguese infantry outposts, supported by armoured cars and mortars. The first sizeable opposition was met in the Kansarpale area. This was easily overcome in about half an hour's time; three Portuguese officers being captured and an armoured car destroyed. After that the advance continued fairly rapidly till Assonora was reached. This place on the Mandavi River (tributary) was easily secured, but the bridge was found demolished, and the advance beyond the river to Tivim was held up for a while. Eight enemy Armoured Fighting Vehicles were reported on the other side of the river, which held out the prospect of some real fight.

The battalion's engineers with the help of local labour prepared a diversion and by 11:15 hours the force began crossing the river. By 12:00 hours the bulk of the force (including the guns) was across the river and moving on to Tivim. The Portuguese Armoured Fighting Vehicles earlier reported to be in the area were, however, nowhere to be seen. The bridge at Tivim was also found demolished, making further advance along the axis difficult. A diversion was then taken to proceed on the Pernem-Mapuca road. At 14:00 hours the head of the column hit the road, where numerous anti-tank mines were encountered. Some delay occurred as these had to be removed and disarmed. By 16:00 hours the head of the column was on the Pernem-Mapuca road. This road too was a fairly well mined, and blocked with felled trees at several places. The whole column reached Mapuca at 17:00 hours.

One company group was detached from the main group, and given the task of rounding up Portuguese stragglers, creating confidence among the public and affording protection to the town. The rest of the force continued its march towards Betim. This route too had obstacles, which were overcome or bypassed, and the entire column reached Betim by 18:00 hours, only an hour behind the armoured column. The battalion was keen to cross Mandavi River the same night and have the honour of being the first to reach Panjim –the capital of Goa and the seat of the Governor General. There were, however, no orders to do so. Efforts were made by various means of communication to contact the Brigade HQ from 18:30 hours to 21:15 hours to obtain permission, but no contact could be established. The troops were disappointed as they had overcome or bypassed many hindrances and obstacles on their march from Dodamarg to Betim. Now, that they were within easy reach of their objective they were not allowed to reach for their prize for want of orders. Thus they were forced to harbour for the night at Betim.

A squadron of the 7th Cavalry had reached Betim an hour earlier than the main force of the 2 Sikh Light Infantry. Major Sidhu warned the boats not to leave the ferry site, and had to sink one boat, which tried to ignore the warning. On hearing this firing, the Portuguese flag in front of the Governor-General's Secretariat across the river in Panjim was lowered and a white flag was hoisted in its place, which was considered as indicating surrender. The time was 18:00 hours on 18th December, 1961. Major Sidhu sent a civilian across the creek to the other side to order the ferries to come over to Betim side and to collect the Portuguese flag, which had just been hauled down.

The civilian succeeded in sending the boats across but he could not trace the person who was in possession of the flag. Soon the ferries started coming over to the Betim side, full of cheering crowds. At 19:30

hours, the 7th Cavalry moved into night harbour within a kilometre of the ferry towards Aguada fort side.

At about 20 00 hours, a priest *(**Padre Gregorio Magno de Sousa Antao**)* from Panjim came in a boat to the Squadron's harbour site with a communication written in Portuguese. This document[100] was understood to be a letter of surrender from the military Commander of Panjim to the Military Commander of the Indian Forces in Betim. It said:

"The military Commander of Panjim declares that he wishes to open talks with the commander of the Indian Forces of the Indian Union, to finalise surrender, so that peace could take effect immediately. This is to avoid massacre of the population and damage to the city".

The Commander
Acacio Tenreiro
Major

Major S.S.Sidhu took the letter to Lt. Col. Cherian, C.O. 2 Sikh Light Infantry, who, however, declined to order the crossing of the creek to accept surrender of Panjim, as he had not been able to contact the Brigade Commander to get his orders.

2 PARA MARATHA

The eastern- most column on the northern route was of 2 Para (Maratha)[101], which had to make a southerly advance via Sanquelim and Usgao to Ponda.

This battalion supported by Armour, made its move from the forward assembly area at 04:00 hours in order to be able to cross the Start Point at the exact H Hour, viz 05:15 hours. En route to the Start Point and immediately to the South of the abandoned Portuguese Customs post was a culvert in bad shape, and the vehicles could negotiate it with great difficulty. The tanks could not cross it at all. However, the culvert was quickly strengthened with steel decking and the move to the start point resumed.

(A company of this battalion group had already reached Sanquelim and secured the place, though both the bridges were demolished.)

The vanguard company crossed the Start Point at the given time and continued the advance, which was, however slow due to darkness and the difficult nature of the track, especially at the nullah crossings. By first light it had covered only about 3 kilometres to **Corpol** where it contacted the company of 1 Para Punjab which was escorting back Portuguese prisoners captured earlier.

As the going to Bicholim was slightly better, it was reached and cleared at about 08:30 hours. On the way to this place a Portuguese armoured car had been sighted, but on seeing the Indian column it had turned and sped away in the opposite direction. No engagement could take place as the tanks were very much in the rear.

At Bicholim also the bridge was found demolished, and so a ford had to be used to cross the river. Later, the advance was continued with

Destroyed Bridge at Bicholim

Destroyed Bridge at Usgao

great speed on a good tarmac road towards Sanquelim to which a company was sent earlier. This company was firmly established at that place, but as both the bridges had been blown up, it guided the column to a ford through which it crossed and moved on towards Usgao. Considerable time was lost as the tanks could ford the river only with great difficulty. Nevertheless, the mobile troops and the vanguard had moved on and reached Usgao at 11:40 hours, to find the bridge demolished.

The river Madei at this place is 183 metres wide. It is a formidable obstacle and unfordable, with the banks on either side reported to be mined. Two country boats were acquired for ferrying only the infantry troops, for whom a safe landing place was discovered south of the bridge. Some jeeps were also taken across for recoilless guns on improvised rafting. After the river was crossed the advance towards Ponda was resumed on foot. Only two detachments of 106 mm RCL, one-section of MMG and heavy mortars were in jeeps.

By 13:45 hours, they had reached and secured Ponda, while B and D companies were crossing the Candeapar River.

There was complete disorder in Ponda. The Portuguese had left after setting fire to their equipment and baggage, and some buildings were still burning. Hooligans were busy looting whatever they could lay their hands on. Parties of Indian troops were immediately posted at the three Army Barracks in the town, and the fire was brought under control.

As more troops arrived, guards were placed at places of public utility like petrol pumps, municipal offices, the post office, police station, etc. The bazaar area was also patrolled and the unruly crowd dispersed. By the evening the town was effectively occupied. Meanwhile, C Company, which had been left at Sanquelim, also joined the Battalion in Ponda at 1900 hours.

After occupying Ponda, the battalion commander along with a platoon went northwards to see the condition of the ferry at Undir and the bridges on the road to Banastarim. Both the bridges were found blown, but the ferry owner's agents were warned to stay with their ferries and be prepared to move at short notice during the night. This however proved unnecessary as, on returning to Ponda, the party learnt from the Brigade Commander that 1 Para Punjab had reached Banastarim. However, a party from 2 Para was sent next morning to establish contact with 1 Para at Banastarim. Contact was established with rear elements at 07:30 hours on 19th December –the forward elements having already moved towards Panjim.

It was found on all axes, by the afternoon of 18th December that the Portuguese troops had given up all intention of fighting. They were abandoning their positions hastily, in some cases after setting fire to them, and "breaking into wine shops on their retreat, and making as fast as they could for Marmagoa or Panjim, whichever was nearest."

Thrust from the East

Simultaneously with the movement of the three columns from the north sent in by the 50th Para Brigade, a thrust from the east [102] of Goa by units of the 63rd Indian Infantry Brigade of the 17th Infantry Division, was taking place. The 3 Battalion of the Sikh Regiment was to act as the advance guard. Starting from the Anmod side, the 63rd Brigade was to move in two columns: one along the existing road and the other on a track to its right, with one battalion on each. The first object was to capture Mollem, where both the columns were to link up, and then go again by separate routes to Ponda. As all the rivers in Goa, run roughly from east to west, the approach from the east followed the grain of the country and for that reason was considered easier. Also there were metalled, all- weather roads capable of taking heavy traffic. Against these advantages, the roads frequently crossed nullahs and rivers, on which bridges and culverts were sure to be destroyed or prepared for demolition, since the Portuguese expected the advance from this side. The advance, when it actually did take place, had therefore, to be on foot. It was naturally slower than the one from the north, though as it turned out, the Portuguese withdrawal was so hasty that quite a few bridges and culverts were left intact.

3 SIKH

3 Sikh Battalion[103] of the Sikh Regiment was to act as the advance guard of the 63rd Brigade. This battalion was to move on the Yellow route up to Mollem and from there go to Ponda via Collem on the Green route, while the other battalion (2 Bihar) was to reach Mollem by the Green route and then go to Ponda by the Yellow route.

Two patrols had been sent on the night of 17th /18th December for a few kilometres on the route to see if the culverts and bridges were mined, and to find out possible diversions. One of these patrols returned at 02:30 hours on the 18th and reported that the road was badly cratered and mined. It was therefore decided that the advance could not be led with Armour (tanks) as originally planned. Guns and other arms had also to be reduced to the minimum necessary.

The vanguard of 3 Sikh crossed the start line at 04:00 hours and the remainder of the battalion at 05:15 hours. Up to a distance of eight kilometres, the vanguard found many craters but the engineer element accompanying it went a little ahead and found places to cross these craters. All culverts and bridges were blown up. But the vanguard pushed through. By 06:45, when it came up to two bigger bridges, it found them intact and neither occupied nor prepared for demolition. So the vanguard pushed on and reached the outskirts of Mollem at 07:30 hours

The advance guard that was following the vanguard also reached Mollem half an hour later. There was no opposition on the route and there was none at Mollem, as the Portuguese soldiers had all left early that morning. The advance of 3 Sikh from Mollem onwards was to be on the Green axis. One company of the battalion, therefore moved towards Collem at 08:30 hours and that place was reached at 09:30 hours without opposition. The remainder of the battalion also reached Collem by 11:00 hours. Until then either side had not fired a single round on this sector.

It was learnt here that the Portuguese were fast withdrawing towards Ponda, and that if there was any delay in pursuing them, they might reorganize and give a determined fight at that place. So it was of paramount importance that the move to Ponda should be at full speed, so as to deny the Portuguese any breathing time.

After another brief reorganization, the advance guard (less one company) pushed along the road Collem—Sigao—Candeapar River crossing towards Ponda. In the interest of speed only medium machine guns were moved forward to cover the advance. After a march of about five kilometres during which only a few stray shots from the enemy were met, the column reached Sigao, where it found a number of civilian vehicles belonging to a mining company (E M C O mining Co). The owners were very helpful and placed the vehicles at the disposal of Indian troops.

A part of the battalion got into these vehicles. Even the medium machine guns were left behind and only 3-inch mortars accompanied the move forward. Thus the mounted troops reached Darbandora at 17:00 hours. As the bridge on the river Candeapar was found demolished, further advance was not possible. It was therefore decided to 'firm in' at Darbandora for the night and wait for the rest of the battalion, which was following on foot to catch up. This column on foot reached Darbandora at 22:00 hours, and the whole battalion was concentrated there. This battalion did not know it, but Ponda had already been captured by troops of the 50th Brigade (2 Para Maratha) in the afternoon.

2 BIHAR

2 Bihar[104] battalion which was concentrated in the Anmod area, had also to cross the border on foot. Every man had to carry his personal

Destroyed Bridge at Khandepar (Candeapar)

arms, three days rations and considerable amounts of ammunition. Considering the rough terrain through which they had to pass, particularly in the first portion of the route, which was a hilly area full of thick jungle and undergrowth, the load was heavy. But the men were in good spirits, physically fit and keen to be in action.

The battalion moved from the Start Point at 04:00 hours and soon approached Tamari (Tambadi Surla) village, where minor opposition was expected. The vanguard could clearly see the village in the moonlit night and hear the dogs barking away furiously. One platoon took up positions near the village and the medium machine guns were deployed to cover them. As another platoon got ready to enter and search the place a few shots were fired from a thicket to the left of the village. The MMGs immediately directed their fire towards the area from where the shots had come, but when the troops entered and searched the thicket they found nothing but a smoldering fire. It seems that the dogs had warned the Portuguese soldiers and they had run away after firing a few shots. This was later confirmed by the villagers, who were all up and waiting for the Indian troops outside their houses.

The vanguard moved on to Surla, where more action was expected. Here a bridge was to be crossed, but as the moonlight was waning, following the track was becoming difficult. However the location of the bridge was discovered from the sound of water flowing under it. When the leading platoon advanced towards it two shots were heard from the area beyond the bridge. The MMGs fired back and the troops charged, forgetting that the bridge could have been mined. Fortunately, it was not. The battalion continued its advance, cleared Surla and pushed on and reached within 914 metres of Mollem at 05:50 hours.

The battalion had orders to stop at Mollem till such time as the town was cleared by 3 Sikh coming along the main road from Anmod, a distance of about 18 kilometres, whereas 2 Bihar had to march 35 kilometres to reach that place. But 3 Sikh had not reached Mollem, so 2 Bihar was ordered to press forward and clear the town, which it did by 09:00 hours. By that time 3 Sikh and a little later 4 Sikh also, joined them there.

2 Bihar, after a little reorganization and planning, were now asked to continue the advance on the main axis to Ponda (the yellow route). Only four civilian trucks were available, in which a part of the battalion (The CO and B company) left, while others marched off on foot. The mounted company along with the CO found, after traveling about 16 kilometres, at Darbandora, that two culverts had been blown off, flooding the right side of the road. The left side was mined. While efforts were being made to clear and mark a diversion, the local people pointed to an alternative route to Ponda called the Miner's route. Proceeding by this route, the mounted column reached Candeapar river by 16:15 hours. The bridge here too was destroyed, but the company group waded across and established a firm base on the far bank, where they harboured for the night. As the water level of the river had increased, meanwhile, due to the tide, wading across was temporarily out of the question. So the foot column stopped on the near side of the river for the night.

4 Sikh Light Infantry, which was following behind the brigade 'R' and 'O' groups, reached Mollem at 11:30 hours on the 18th, and reached

Candeapar river crossing at 01:00 hours on the 19th, where it harboured till 06:00 hours the next morning. The men had marched 43 kilometres from the border with all their load. It led the brigade advance on the 19th.

HQ 17 Division Operations Order No. 2
18th December, 1961

Operation immediate
To: To units listed
Info: Tactical HQ Southcom

OP VIJAY-17 Inf Div 00 no 2/61 of 18 Dec for advance on 19 December- Ref 00 No 1/61 following changes ordered.[105]

Firstly

Info

-Alfa-Enemy has withdrawn on axis YELLOW behind BANASTARIM bridge having demolished the bridge at CANDEAPAR and BANASTARIM –VELHA GOA and PANJIM positions expected held with two battalions- MARMAGOA also expected to be held on axis RED –All enemy cleared except SOUTH of MAPUCA.

Bravo- Own troops- on axis YELLOW leading elements of 63infantry Brigade and 50 Para Brigade in area CANDEAPAR –on axis RED 50 Para Brigade holding line MAPUCA excluding –BICHOLIM-USGAO in area Mapuca 2 SIKH Light Infantry in area south of MAPUCA.

Secondly-

Method–grouping and task-

ALFA

ONE-48 infantry Brigade with- under command one squadron **8 CAV** field regiment 27 medium battery 376 field company section plant engineers –A company 7 MAHAR ADS 152 field ambulance- AWD

FRT detachment rec one section provost-ACT with tel-in sp remainder division artillery-under command for moving 75 TCVs and bridge equipment. **TASK**-advance along axis YELLOW-PONDA-VELHA GOA- PANJIM so as to secure PANJIM as soon as possible.

TWO-63 infantry Brigade with –under command **8 CAV** less two squadrons -10 field regiment- 137 heavy mortar battery-377 field company section plant engineers –C company 7 MAHAR-ADS 152 field ambulance (TA) –AWD FRT detachment rec –one section provost and one ACT with tcl.-in sp remainder division artillery-under command for moving 75 TCV and bridge equipment. **TASK:** capture MARGAO and MORMUGAO as soon as possible

THREE- 50 Para brigade group less one battalion to establish firm base at PONDA and be prepared to take over advance from 48 or 63 infantry brigade in their tasks.

BRAVO

Grouping will be completed by 190200.

CHARLIE

Order to march on axis YELLOW. 48 infantry brigade group-artillery group-main division HQ-rear Division HQ- division Adm group.

DELTA

Bounds: axis YELLOW- BANASTARIM bridge nickname BABY GIRL-VELHA GOA nickname MADHU BALA-PANJIM nickname FRENCH TOAST-axis BROWN (63 brigade axis)-BORIM bridge (9570) nickname DALL MOTH-DABOLIM (UX 77) nickname RAT DIN- Mormugao nickname PREM PUJARI.

ECHO

Report lines: axes YELLOW-road junction MARDOL (9281) nickname COCA COLA-MANGUEXIM (7989) nickname SABZI MANDI.

FOXTROT

Special arms: Armour-left over NORTH of SANQUELIM to mop up enemy there-artillery-ammunition expenditure same as for phase I.

GOLF

Movement table for route YELLOW: at apex Alfa-

THIRDLY

Intercommunications-location main Division HQ area sq 1671.

FOURTHLY

Acknowledge -all info.

Ground Situation On 18/19 Night

Thus the overall position on the fronts in Goa on the night of the 18th was that in the north, a general line- Betim and Piligao- and in the east-Banastarim and Ponda-had been secured.[106] Behind the advancing troops the engineers had repaired all the culverts, etc., with strenuous effort and sound organisation. Once the main road was open, units, brigade groups, vehicles of the artillery, reconnaissance parties, field regiments and brigade Headquarters had begun moving forward. The reserve brigade (48th Infantry Brigade) also moved up behind the brigade train during the night of 18/ 19 December.[106]

During the night of 18th / 19th December, Maj. General Candeth, the G.O.C 17th Division, had reached Mollem at 22:00 hours, and after taking stock of the situation, had issued orders to the different units to advance on the 19th. The 48th Brigade Group was to advance and capture Panjim, the 63rd Brigade was to turn towards Margao and Mormugao, and the 50th Para Brigade Group was ordered to "firm in" at Ponda and be prepared to take over from the 48th or the 63rd Infantry Brigade. However, as the 17th Division Headquarters was for the moment out of touch with the Tactical HQ Southern Command, the latter issued an order during the night to the 50th Para Brigade to capture Panjim as soon as possible on the 19th. This order was different from the orders of the HQ 17th Div. This was inevitable due to temporary interruption of wireless communication between different headquarters and units, and also due to the unexpectedly rapid advance of the various units. HQ 17th Div was not aware at that time that the units of Para Brigade had already reached points from where they could quickly move to Panjim and capture it. However, the information that such an order had been issued to Para Brigade Units was received by HQ 17th Div at 10:00 hours on the 19th.

The 48th Brigade, which according to the 17th Div orders was to pass through the 63rd Brigade positions at Ponda and capture Panjim, was stuck on the road. It was trudging behind the bridging fleet, which consisted mostly of old vehicles which experienced frequent breakdowns along the narrow one-way road, thereby blocking the move of the 48th brigade. The result was that this brigade could reach and pass Mollem by 09:00 hours on the 19th.

Capture of Panjim

The 17th Div Communication vehicles were stranded along a certain section of the Anmod-Mollem road, however they were able to resume control with a relay station vehicle in the Mollem area by 08:00 hours on the 19th. Still, it was not in touch with the 50th Para Brigade and did not know that Panjim was being ingressed[107]. As a result its orders of the previous night were repeated to 48th Infantry Brigade, to overtake 3 Sikh at Candeapar and dash down to Panjim[107].

When Maj. Gen. Candeth met Brig Sagat Singh he was informed that Lt. Gen. Chaudhury had ordered the Para Brigade to proceed directly to Panjim. The matter was discussed and Gen. Candeth agreed to it, as the 48th Brigade was not in a position at that time to move through the 63rd Brigade, which was advancing on to Marmagoa.

After this meeting, Candeth and Sagat Singh moved on to Ponda and went round the Engineer Barracks of the Portuguese who had fled. Sagat Singh then moved on to Panjim and was joined there by Candeth the same afternoon of the 19th

Two battalions from the 50 Para Brigade were engaged on the 18th in a race for Panjim. 2 Sikh Light Infantry had reached Betim in the evening, and was separated from Panjim only by the river Mandavi, which it could have crossed easily if it had orders to do so. 1Para Punjab had reached Banastarim Bridge, but it was told to stop and receive the Army commander next morning at 09:00 hours. It had no boats with which to cross over.

The O C of 1 Para Punjab, Lt. Colonel Sucha Singh, in order to be prepared for all eventualities, such as a change in orders, had during the night, sent his second in command to somehow procure some boats. It so happened that his premonition turned out to be correct. There was a change in orders. Early next morning he was contacted on wireless and the Brigade Major passed a personal message from the Army Commander that he (the Battalion Commander) should get into Panjim as quickly as possible. He was also told that the 2 Sikh Light Infantry which had arrived at Betim ferry crossing the previous evening had also been given similar orders.

"General Chaudhury has stated that he had kept open one of his signal sets for just such a contingency. Consequently, when he saw an opening, he took immediate advantage of it and passed direct orders." [112]

Could 1 Para Punjab reach Panjim before the other battalion? Here it was 16 kilometres from Panjim, but on the wrong side of a major water obstacle, and without any boats and without any transport after it got across. The other battalion was almost opposite Panjim, though across a bigger obstacle, but with all the boats in the world they needed. The odds were heavy against 1 Para winning the race, but an attempt would certainly be made. Meanwhile, the second in command turned up to say that a boat would arrive in 30 minutes at the bridge site.

"This raised a little hope, but I felt that waiting 20 minutes would be too late," said Lt. Col. Sucha Singh the OC of 1 Para. "At the same time, I saw a civilian truck arrive on the other side of the river and its passengers get out and cheer us. That was the real signal to enter Panjim. So without a second further I ordered two companies to swim across on two-man equipment rafts."

The troops eager to capture the prize of Panjim were on the other bank in about 25 minutes. In the excitement and haste, one raft sank. Casualties: one rifle and a Sten. Meanwhile some boats also had arrived. The OC with a few other officers hurriedly paddled across. Realising that there was very little time if the race for Panjim was to be won, they commandeered a civilian car and two trucks which had brought Goans to welcome the Indian troops, and collecting whatever men had put on uniforms after their swim, they started for Panjim in the car and the two trucks. Other troops were to follow them as soon as they could, in whatever civilian transport was available. "It is worth mentioning that civilians were so enthusiastic that they were begging to be given a chance to lift troops in their vehicles," reported Lt. Col Sucha Singh.

Meanwhile, the 2 Sikh Light Infantry at Betim had after all succeeded in contacting the Brigade Headquarters early in the morning and had been permitted to cross the creek. Arrangements for crossing were made immediately. The Armour, Artillery, Guns and Mortars were deployed to cover the crossing, and two rifle companies were sent across into Panjim at 07:35 hours. So the 2 Sikh Light Infantry won the race and were first in Panjim, Their objectives in town being Police Headquarters, Customs House, Governor General's House, Secretariat and Military Camp. Except for minor rifle and two automatic guns fire, which were soon neutralized, there was no opposition to the entry of the troops.

Although the Indian 50 Para Brigade - also called the Pegasus Brigade - led by Brigadier Sagat Singh was charged with merely assisting the main thrust conducted by the 17th Infantry, its units moved rapidly across minefields, roadblocks and four riverine obstacles to be the first to reach Panjim.

On Sagat Singh's orders, the troops entering the capital removed their steel helmets and wore the Parachute regiment's maroon berets. This was Sagat Singh's way of making a statement.

The people of Goa welcomed Sagat Singh and his Para Brigade as liberators. When the army started redeploying the Para Brigade to Agra, numerous telegrams and petitions were sent to the Prime Minister Nehru to reinstate what they called as the "Maroon

Beret Friends" back in Goa. Under popular pressure, Nehru ordered the Para Brigade back to Goa.

Sagat Singh's fame as liberator of Goa was carried all the way to Portugal. Soon after his brigade moved back to Agra, one day Sagat was visiting the Clarke's Shiraz Hotel in Agra. He was in civilian clothes when four American tourists approached him and enquired if he was " Brigadier Singh" When a surprised Sagat asked them how they recognised him, they told him that they had just come in from Portugal. Apparently they saw posters with his photograph in many café's and restaurants announcing an award of Ten Thousand US Dollars for anyone who captures and delivers Sagat Singh to government of Portugal! Sagat Singh made a good natured offer to surrender to the tourists and asked them to take him and hand over to the Portuguese. The offer was declined.

THE WELCOME BECOMES A NOVEL HINDRANCE

The civilian population had come out of their houses on foot and in vehicles in such large numbers to welcome the Indian troops, that the roads were jam packed making the movement of the troops to their objectives extremely slow.[108] This delaying factor was of an entirely different nature. It hampered the troops in getting to their objectives for an hour- and- a half.

Meanwhile, some troops of the 1 Para (Punjab) had crossed the water obstacle at Banastarim by swimming and were moving fast in civilian vehicles towards Panjim. They entered the town from another side and arrived at the Governor General's Secretariat (The Palace) at 08:30 hours and occupied it.

Thus **they lost the race for entry into the capital by just about an hour.** Then they found that the 2 Sikh Light Infantry was already in control of the police station. The OC 1 Para Punjab then went with his few troops towards the officer's mess area where the Portuguese troops were reported to have assembled. **They found a large number of Portuguese Officers and soldiers in their vests and underpants, cowering with fright. When asked why they were dressed so**

Lt. Col. Sucha Singh Vr. Ch, MC, accepting Portuguese surrender in Panjim

strangely, they confessed that they have been told that the Indian troops would kill all those found in uniform. Lt. Col. Sucha Singh VrC, MC, and his men had a good laugh at this absurdity. (Perhaps the Portuguese might have thought that the Indians would retaliate the cold-blooded murder of unarmed Satyagrahis by the Portuguese in 1955).

Their senior commander was sent for and asked if he wished to surrender. On his reply in affirmative, their surrender was taken by OC 1 Para Punjab, and orders for their custody were issued. Another company was put in charge of the camp. The surrender of some Portuguese naval personnel on shore was also taken.

Thus the 1 Para Punjab, though it had lost the race for Panjim by reaching there a little after the 2 Sikh Light infantry, had the honour of taking the surrender of the Portuguese soldiers and sailors there and occupying some of the important objectives, such as the G.G.'s residence, Government Godown, Civil and Military Hospital, Treasury, High Court, Power House, etc. The Army Commander also arrived soon, and the Portuguese soldiers in the Customs House surrendered to C Company of 1 Para Punjab in his presence.[113]

The Army Commander had flown in by helicopter from Belgaum, and had landed in a field about 8 kilometres outside Panjim, where a military jeep met him. Accompanied by Air Vice Marshal Pinto and B.N. Mullick of the Intelligence Bureau, the Army Commander drove into the town. A few shots were still being fired. As the Army Commander and Air Vice Marshal Pinto started moving into Panjim they too were (like the troops before them) surrounded by the local people cheering them on. In fact the crowd was delaying the movement. On the way,

Jubilant Reception by Rejoicing Crowd

the Army Commander stopped at the Hospital and he assured the Portuguese soldiers there that no harm would come to them and ordered that any medical supplies required should be given to them.

One factor contributing to the lack of co-ordination in the Portuguese defence was the fact that their communications had been disrupted at the start. Dabolim airport had been bombed by the IAF 'Canberras' at 07:00 hours on the 18th, and partially put out of action. The wireless station at Bambolim had also been subjected to a rocket attack at the same time, and was completely off the air till the engineers of All India Radio repaired it some weeks later. This had completely destroyed their link with the outside world and with the other districts of Daman and Diu.

Action of 63rd Infantry Brigade Group

As Ponda had been captured by 50th Para Brigade (2 Para Maratha) at last light on the 18th, the task of the 63rd Brigade for the 19th was to go south from Ponda and capture Margao with the 4 Sikh Light Infantry leading the advance.[109] This battalion, after a grueling march of 24 hours beginning at 01:00 hours on the 18th (passing through Molem and Darbandora) had reached Candeapar riverbank exactly at 01:00 hours on the 19th. During this long march, with only two brief halts for meals, they had to handle one recoilless gun and a section of mortars. When they reached the river they found, as was the experience everywhere that the bridge had been blown up. It was one hour past midnight and nothing could be done at that time but to harbour there for the night or whatever was left of it. For they had to be up and moving by 06:00 hours to lead the Brigade's advance to Margao via Borim. There were however no boats. A recce of places suitable for wading across was made, keeping in mind the tidal conditions affecting the depth. Finally at 06:00 hours, the battalion crossed the Candeapar by wading through chest-high waters. The leading company commandeered some civilian transport, and the whole battalion pushed on eagerly, some in vehicles and others on foot. The mounted company reached the Zuari River at Borim ferry crossing (about 10 kilometres from Margao) at 08:30 hours and the marching column a little later. Once again the bridge was found blown up. The river is 546 metres wide at this place and there was no question of wading through it. A barge was commandeered, and the whole battalion was on the other bank of the river by 09:00 hours. (The Company Chowgule provided transport for ferrying the troops)

On this bank, Goans from Margao and other places were waiting to receive them. Jubilant at the arrival of the Indian troops, they placed their trucks and cars at the disposal of the battalion, which gratefully got into them and rolled into Margao by mid-day without any incident. The throngs of people who came out to greet the troops in the town and rent the sky with national slogans and cries of joy were so overwhelming that, for a time, the battalion found itself moving at a snail's pace. Some people remarked that though they were being librated after 450 years of

Destroyed Bridge at Borim

foreign domination, it was never too late. However, Margao had a little earlier been occupied by advance elements of a company of the 4 Rajput coming up from the south.

Many invitations for a civic reception and food for the whole battalion were politely declined, and the troops managed somehow to pull out of the town and halted on its outskirts. The Officer Commanding, Lt. Col. R. B. Nanda, went to contact the Brigade Commander for further orders.

He was told that he should pass through 2 Bihar positions (some 8 kilometres north of Margao in the Verna area at that time) and resume the advance once again on a northerly and then westerly direction to Vasco and the port of Marmagoa via Dabolim.

The battalion resumed advance towards the new objective at 13:30 hours, passed through Verna at 14:45 hours, and moved on to Dabolim. On the way it found that several bridges and culverts, though prepared for demolition, had been left intact by the Portuguese forces. This was due to speedy advance of the Indian troops. This had forced the Portuguese to fall back on Vasco da Gama as hurriedly as possible and without risking any action. Perhaps all the culverts and bridges might have been blown up if the battalion had wasted time in Margao.

By 15:30 hours the battalion had reached the outskirts of Dabolim, where by a swift outflanking movement a number of Portuguese officers and men with large quantities of equipment, arms and ammunition were surprised and made to surrender. The Chief of Staff of the Portuguese Army along with an interpreter met the CO to express the desire of the Governor General of Goa for an unconditional surrender. Taking him along, the battalion continued its advance to Vasco da Gama, which was soon reached and encircled. Patrols were sent into the city to ensure that there was no looting. Then **CO took the initial, informal surrender of the forces in Goa from the Governor-General at Alparqueiros Camp, the main headquarters of the Portuguese forces.**

A small party of the enemy was however still holding out in the area of the Baina beach near Marmagoa. A platoon sent out to liquidate this position captured 40 of the enemy with a large booty of arms and ammunition. This completed the occupation of the western tip of the peninsula.

(Due to breakdown of communications between the 63rd Brigade headquarters and the main Division, the capture of Marmagoa was not known to the latter till about 23:00 hours.)

At 18:00 hours, the 63rd Brigade Commander K.S.Dhillon, also arrived at the Alparqueiros Camp in Vasco da Gama and arrangements were made for receiving the formal surrender of the Portuguese authority. The ex-Governor-general of Goa,

General Vassalo e Silva, in his capacity as the Commander-in-Chief of the Portuguese armed forces, formally signed the surrender document at 20:30 hours and submitted it to Brig. K.S.Dhillon. OC **4 Sikh L I.** and OC **2 Bihar** witnessed the signing of the surrender document.[110]

TRANSLATION

Instrument of Surrender[111]

I, General MANUEL ANTONIO VASSALO e SILVA, C-in-C of Armed Forces of Portuguese State of India, offer in my capacity as C-in-C, unconditional surrender of Armed forces in Goa at 20 30 hours on 19 Dec 1961.

Accepted	**Manuel Antonio Vassalo e Silva**
K.S.Dhillon	**General**
Brig.	

Formal surrender accepted by **Brig KS Dhillon**, Comdr **63 Inf Bde,** at 20:30 hrs on 19 Dec 61 in our presence
R.B.Nanda. ....Lt.Col. **OC 4 SIKH LI**
K.S. Chadha.........Lt.Col **OC 2 BIHAR**

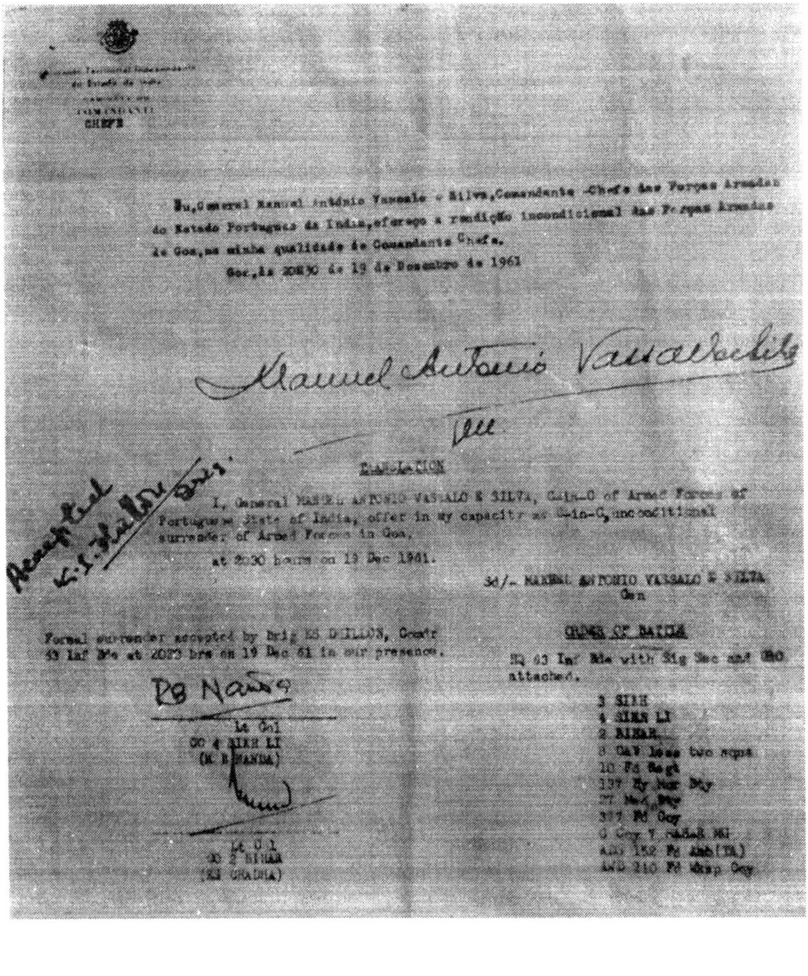

CHEFE

Eu, General Manuel António Vassalo e Silva, Comandante-Chefe das Forças Armadas do Estado Português da India, ofereço a rendição incondicional das Forças Armadas de Goa, na minha qualidade de Comandante Chefe.

Goa, às 20H30 de 19 de Dezembro de 1961

TRANSLATION

I, General MANUEL ANTONIO VASSALO E SILVA, C-in-C of Armed Forces of Portuguese State of India, offer in my capacity as C-in-C, unconditional surrender of Armed Forces in Goa,

at 2030 hours on 19 Dec 1961.

Sd/- MANUEL ANTONIO VASSALO E SILVA
Gen

Formal surrender accepted by Brig KS DHILLON, Comdr 63 Inf Bde at 2025 hrs on 19 Dec 61 in our presence.

Lt Col
CO 4 SIKH LI
(R B NANDA)

Lt Col
CO 2 BIHAR
(RS GHAIMA)

ORDER OF BATTLE

HQ 63 Inf Bde with Sig Sec and [illegible] attached.

3 SIKH
4 SIKH LI
2 BIHAR
8 CAV less two sqns
10 Fd Regt
137 Hy Mor Bty
27 Med Bty
377 Fd Coy
C Coy 7 MAHAR MG
ADS 152 Fd Amb(TA)
AND 210 Fd Wksp Coy

Gen. Thapar with the former Portuguese Governor-General of Goa (on his right) at a POW Camp at Vascó da Gama

Thus within 40 hours of the start of the operations, the task given by the Government was completed by the armed forces of India, and centuries of foreign rule over this bit of Indian territory came to an end.

The other units of the 63rd Brigade, which were active on the 19th and played their part in the thrust from east, were 2 Bihar and 3 Sikh, established on both banks of the Candeapar River. The account of their activities on the 19th completes the operations of the 63rd Brigade.

63rd Brigade Units on 19th December

2 BIHAR

The leading company group had waded across the Candeapar River and established a firm base on the far bank on the night of the 18th. The rest of the battalion[112] had spent the night on the near bank. On the 19th morning, two companies which were on the near bank left by mechanical transport by a lateral route which joined up with the Green route to Ponda, while those who had waded through the river continued their advance to Ponda on foot. The route taken by the vehicle column was bad, and both columns reached Borim ferry at the same time about 09:30 hours. The 4 Sikh had crossed the river from this ferry one hour earlier in a barge. 2 Bihar also crossed the river in a barge at 10:30 hours and pushed forward in civilian vehicles towards Margao which at that time had already been reached by 4 Sikh. The plan was that 2 Bihar would pass through 4 Sikh and take the lead from Margao onwards.

Subsequently, when 2 Bihar arrived near Margao, it found the 4 Sikh Light Infantry lined up on the outskirts of the town. It (2 Bihar) crossed the Sikh position and without going into the town advanced straight towards Verna (about 8 kilometres north of Margao) after which the next objective would be Vasco da Gama, the railway terminus.

The civilians in Verna informed the leading troops that about 500 Portuguese held a position on the high ground north of the village. C company under Capt. N. K. Bhandari was ordered to go from the left flank and cut the road behind the position. When they were about 273 metres away from the enemy, the Portuguese opened up small arms fire on them. The fire was promptly returned and a charge made. The enemy put up some feeble resistance, and then surrendered.

It transpired that the main Portuguese force for protecting Vasco da Gama had been concentrated here, with their Armour, Infantry, Artillery and Engineer elements.

While C Company was clearing from the left side of the enemy position, B Company under Major M. M. Bose charged from the right of the position further in depth and the Portuguese here too surrendered.

The total 'Bag' of the battalion in the two attacks at Verna was 27 officers, 421 other ranks and large quantities of arms, guns, vehicles, tanks and various other equipment.

(As this was going on, the 4 Light Infantry was ordered to pass through 2 Bihar and proceed to Vasco da Gama, which it did at 14:30 hours)

The battalion 2 Bihar, later concentrated 5 kilometres beyond Cortalim at 16:00 hours and stayed there for the night and the next days, and heard the news of the fall of Marmagoa (port and town) to the 4 Sikh light infantry

3 SIKH

The 3 Sikh battalion[113] was at Darbandora on the night of the 18th. On the 19th morning it was put in reserve and divided into two columns — mounted and unmounted. The marching column reached Dabolim airfield at 21:00 hours, only to learn that the Portuguese had surrendered earlier in the evening. The mounted column reached Margao via Sanvordem by last light. Although the surrender document had already been signed, and some Portuguese soldiers had been captured and made prisoners of war, some others had had no opportunity to surrender. In the early hours of 20th December, when Captain R.S. Dahiya was out on a contact patrol, he with his small party rounded up 400 Portuguese soldiers, who were 'hungry and keen to surrender'.

Southern or Deceptive Approach

Apart from the thrusts from the North and East, an approach from the South[114] was also planned along Majali-Canacona-Margao. This was to be made by a very small force, with the main object of drawing off Portuguese forces from other sectors by giving the impression that large forces were moving along this route. To achieve this deception and to effectively mislead the Portuguese forces with regard to the general plan of the Southern Command, the moves of this force of just one company strength aided by some men of the SRP (Special Reserve Police) had to be cunningly devised. Though not intended to be of much tactical advantage, this move was primarily planned for strategic considerations and is of interest as showing the clever measures of deception adopted to give the impression of a brigade operating in that direction. This small force was surprisingly the first to enter Margao.

The officer under whom the force was to operate was instructed to be 'careful not to get embroiled in a battle with the Portuguese armed forces, and should there be signs that such a battle may occur, you are at liberty to withdraw and establish a defensive position or to establish where you are'.

The company selected for this purpose was B Company of the 4 Battalion of the Rajput Regiment, under Captain D. P. Nayar. It left Hyderabad on 4th December and reached its concentration area at Majali on the 15th via Sholapur, Poona, Belgaum, Londa, and Kandra etc.

Immediately after arriving at Majali, contact was made with Mr. Naidu, Assistant Commandant of the SRP there and measures were taken to simulate concentration of a large force in the area for three days before D-Day, to attract the attention of the Portuguese forces. These measures were:

(i) Cookhouse fires were lit in five different places to give the impression that a considerable number of troops had arrived.

(ii) A platoon each was sent to the northeast and southwest of the actual harbour area to a distance of about 1370 to 1830 metres on the 16th to give the idea that fresh troops had arrived.

(iii) False wireless messages were sent purporting to emanate from a Brigade. The force was styled "the 20th infantry Brigade"

(iv) During the night of 16th /17th December, empty vehicles without lights were sent 11 kilometres behind its own position and then brought back with lights on and put in new positions.

(v) A platoon each was sent on the 17th to locations other than those occupied on the 16th, ensuring at the same time that some activity was maintained in previous locations as well.

(vi) Fresh diggings were done at two tactically important places.

(vii) Senior officer's badges of ranks were used to confirm the impression of a large force having arrived.

(viii) Rumours were spread that a force with armour and artillery had formed up.

(ix) 3.5–inch recoilless guns were mounted on ordinary vehicles to give the impression of tanks.

Having adopted the above measures on 15th, 16th and 17th December, the force entered Goan territory at 06:00 hours on the 18th, and sent platoons to the east and west of the road to probe the area up to 182 to 273 metres from the road, and then join up at Poinguinim and move forward. At abut 13:00 hours, at a place called Ardifond, it came across a Portuguese machine-gun post which opened fire on the platoon. The force deployed for attack and returned fire. This failed to silence the enemy guns, but when some troops were sent to attack the gun-post the Portuguese noticing the advancing troops on their left flank, fled in panic. Some arms and ammunition were captured. (3 Portuguese were killed and 5 wounded in the encounter. There were no casualties on the Indian side. The 'Bag' was, one machine gun, one 3-inch mortar, one jeep, two Verey light pistols and a large quantity of ammunition).

After this incident there was no opposition and the advance was continued despite mines and blown up bridges. The force reached and occupied Canacona; and after sending out patrols northwards, decided to stop there for the night. This was because the administrative elements were lagging behind and it was necessary to allow them to come up and reorganise before resuming the advance the next morning.

On the 19th, the marching column moved ahead towards Margao while the unit's own vehicle column lagged behind clearing roadblocks and making diversions for the vehicles. When the foot column learnt on the way that the Portuguese had left Margao, they managed to secure some civilian transport and rushed towards the place. They reached there some time before midday and found that the other Indian troops who were supposed to take charge of Margao had not reached there as yet.

Thus, men of this plucky little force, who were meant only to make a feint, had not only met and overcome opposition, but had finally found themselves in charge of one of the three main objectives of Indian troops in Goa. They busied themselves in restoring law and order in Margao, and sealed all public buildings, such as police stations, post offices, treasury, banks, etc. Efforts were continued to restore public confidence on the 20th and by the evening of that day 70% of the shops were open, cinemas were running and life had more or less returned to normal.

In the Goa operations all troops had acquitted themselves with credit, but the conduct of Captain D.P.Nayar and his small band of men deserves a special praise

Tragic Incident at Aguada[115]

On 18th December, 1961, the 'A' Squadron of the 7th Cavalry, under Major Shivdev Singh Sidhu reached Betim around 18:0 hours, an hour earlier than the main force of 2 Sikh Light Infantry. On reaching the Betim water front Major Sidhu warned the boats not to leave the ferry site, and had to sink one boat, which tried to ignore the warning. On hearing this firing, the Portuguese flag in front of the Governor-General's Secretariat across the river in Panjim was lowered and a white flag was hoisted in its place, which was indicative of surrender.

At 19:30 hours, the 7th Cavalry Squadron moved into night harbour within a kilometre of the ferry towards Aguada Fort side as there were no instructions to cross the river and capture the city.

At about 20:00 hours, a priest (Padre Gregorio Magno e Sousa Antao) from Panjim came in a boat to the Squadron, harbour site with a communication written in Portuguese. This document was understood to be a letter of surrender from the Military Commander in Panjim (Major Acacio Tenreiro) to the commander of the Indian forces in Betim.

Major Sidhu took this letter to Lt. Col. Cherian, CO of 2 Sikh Light Infantry, who, however declined to order the crossing of the creek to accept the surrender of Panjim, as he had not been able to contact the Brigade Commander— Brig. Sagat Singh–to get his orders.

On returning to the squadron harbour, Major Sidhu was informed that his troops had taken two prisoners who were suspected to be Portuguese soldiers. The prisoners claimed to be locals who had been discharged that day from the army and told to go home. Their village called Reis Magos was about two kilometers from the squadron. Thereupon Major Sidhu ordered a Dodge 15 CWT truck to be got ready for reconnaissance up to that village, as the squadron was likely to advance along that route the next day. Also, the suspects could be dropped in that village if the locals recognized them. This was at about 21:45 hours. Five officers and three ORs volunteered to go with him on the patrol. They started in the truck at 22 30 hours. The party consisted of: [116]

Maj. S.S.Sidhu	-7 Cavalry
Capt. V.K.Sehgal	-7 Cavalry
Capt. H.L.Bhat	-'P' Bty. 24 Med Regt.
Lt. Law	-7 Cavalry
2/Lt. Paramjit Singh	-7 Cavalry
2/Lt. Johar	-8 Cavalry
Dafedar Des Raj	-7 Cavalry
L/ Dafedar Dhir Singh	-7 Cavalry
Swr/ Dafedar Pyare Lal	-7 Cavalry

At Reis Magos, the prisoners were recognized by the locals as residents of the village, and thereupon released. But a Goan came up to Maj. Sidhu and told him that there were 5 or 6 Portuguese soldiers guarding about 50 to 60 nationalist prisoners at the Aguada Fort, and that these prisoners might be murdered during the night if they were not rescued immediately.

Without confirming the exact number of soldiers in the Fort and the weapons with them and swayed by the humanitarian impulse to save the prisoners, and hoping that, since the fort had a small garrison, it would surrender easily, Major Sidhu ordered the patrol to proceed to Aguada Fort, about 11 kilometres away, at top speed, so as to be in time to prevent the Portuguese from committing the atrocity. The civilian informer was taken along as guide and interpreter.

The party reached Aguada Fort half an hour before midnight, and got down from the truck, which was taken to within 9 to 14 metres of the fort gate. Through the local guide, the sentry inside the gate was asked to come out, but he refused. He was asked then to call his Commander. The Portuguese inside were then told that Panjim was ready to surrender, and Maj. Sidhu had the letter of surrender in his pocket, and fighting would cause unnecessary casualties.

The Portuguese refused to surrender, and after a silence of about five minutes they opened automatic and rifle fire through the gate. Grenades and mortars also rained down on Maj. Sidhu's party. The Dodge truck caught fire.

The patrol party was taken by surprise. It had only small arms and hand grenades, while the Portuguese inside the fort were using, in addition to rifles and grenades, a 2" mortar, a medium machine gun, and light machine guns. A grenade wounded Captain Sehgal, a member of the patrol. Maj. Sidhu threw his turban towards Sehgal and asked another of his men to tie up his wounds. It was 01:05 hours on 19th December when Maj. Sidhu sent a member of his patrol to go and bring up the tanks. He himself took up a Sten gun and started firing into the gate of the fort from a distance of 55 metres although he himself was wounded. At 01:40 hours, a mortar shell exploded near Maj. Sidhu, causing a severe wound in the back. Within five minutes he was dead.[117]

Two officers and an OR of the patrol, who were not seriously wounded, walked back to the harbour, a distance of about five kilometres, and reached there between 03:30 and 04:00 hours in the morning. One troop of AMX tanks, another of Stuarts and two rifle troops were dispatched. They reached the fort at 05:30 hours.

A few bursts of MMG were fired at the fort. The main guns of the tanks were not used for fear of harming the nationalist prisoners. The Portuguese hoisted the white flag, but did not come out. They came out after a warning, and surrendered outside the gate at 06:0 hours.

The incident resulted in the tragic loss of two good officers. The Commander of the 50th Para Brigade said in his report, "It has to be accepted as an incident of war". There can be two opinions as to the propriety and tactical wisdom of taking an inadequately armed patrol to force the surrender of a fort, but there can be no doubt that Major Sidhu was prompted by honourable humanitarian motives in carrying out this dashing gamble. That it failed was unfortunate, and the gallant officer paid for it with his life.

PORTUGUESE VERSION OF AGUADA FORT INCIDENT [118]

"The garrison at Fort Aguada consisted in December 1961 of Companhia de Cacadores No 8 (C.Cac.8) According to 'Plano Sentinela' it was determined that the company would occupy the positions in the Verna plateau. However the later decision indicated Vasco da Gama as its final destination.

Thus on 12th December the C.Cac 8 with the exception of a platoon left the fort and marched to that city. A platoon commanded by 2nd Lt. of Infantry Jose' Casimiro Pereira Pinto with an effective strength of 36 men remained in the fort.

This platoon was responsible for guarding one hundred and twenty prisoners of which twenty- eight were military and ex-military prisoners and the remaining were civilians sentenced to punishment due to their political activities. The military strength was insufficient to do the double duty of guarding the prisoners as well as defending the Fort in case there was an enemy attack.

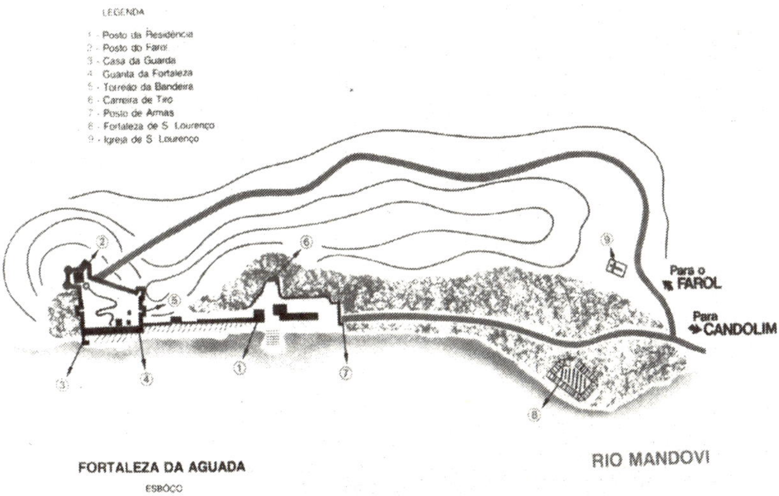

Aguada Fort

Alferes Pereira Pinto immediately introduced many alterations for safety and defence. He mounted patrols in the more sensitive areas, and installed barbed wire nets in the areas susceptible to infiltration. As the effective strength was reduced, he decided to put into practice the plan that he had proposed earlier to his commander that in case of an emergency situation the military and ex-military prisoners should be used for the defence.

So, during the night when C.Cac 8 moved to the city of Vasco da Gama, he went to the cells of the military and ex-military prisoners in order to convey to them the decision he had taken and the required instructions to put them in practice.

Every one of them understood what was required of them and voluntarily came forward to carry out any work, assigned to them. They were ready to take up arms if the situation so demanded.

The Commandant of the fort was touched by this gesture and from then onwards started using them to strengthen the sentry posts and the improvement of defence positions. These men without exception showed an exemplary behaviour both prior and after the attack. They fulfilled all the missions allotted to them.

The defence of Aguada Fort was structured essentially with a base on four posts of combat:

POSTO de RESIDENCIA*—it was occupying the roof of the residence building situated outside the fort. It had a machine gun and an anti-tank grenade thrower 'PIAT'. Its principal direction of observation was the approach street to the fort.*

POSTO do FAROL*—it had complete command on all the remaining installations, as it was located at a higher position. It had a tripod-mounted machine gun BORZIG, a 5 cm grenade thrower, and also a light machine gun DREYSE. Its aim was to cover the Aguada plateau and the hillside around the fort.*

POSTO da CASA da GUARDA*—It had a light machine gun DREYSE, which would try to foil any infiltration from the sea or the hillside.*

POSTO da GUARDA da FORTALEZA*—it had a light machine gun DREYSE that would foil any infiltration from the seaside and take care of Fort of S. Lourenco (unoccupied). It was an alternative position to the Flag Tower.*

The Commandant organized with the remaining personnel several nuclei entrusted with the task of repelling any infiltration that could take place at any moment and also formed a reserve force at his disposal. The Command Post (P.C.) was installed in FAROL (Light House).

On 18th December around 06:30 hours the bombardment of Dabolim Airport was seen from the Fort.

At 10:00 hours the launch 'Quintanilha' reached near the fort. However, it could not come to moor alongside due to the low tide. It was informed that it had come on orders from Captain of Ports Capitao-Tenente Abel de Oliveira to evacuate the garrison of Aguada Fort. Alferes Pinto wanted to ascertain if any written order was sent about this matter. There was no written order. There were also no instructions about the prisoners. In view of the above he sent a soldier who swam to the launch so that he could go to Q.G (Head Quarters) in Panjim, and bring back a written order.

Meanwhile, the garrison of the fort witnessed the beginning of the combat of 'Aviso Afonso de Albuquerque'

When it grew dark, Alferes Pereira Pinto gave orders for taking defensive positions. Thus all the personnel were occupied in their respective posts.

At 00 hours[118] *when the Commandant of the fort was on his way with Sergeant Horacio de Sousa from the fort to his residence he saw a vehicle (half truck) coming down with lights on and off in the direction of the approach road to the fort. When the vehicle drew closer, they went to the gate and the Sergeant Horacio tried to identify the individuals who had arrived and were stationed outside the main gate. They did not answer the password but said that they were from the Police post of Betim, and that they had come with the orders of the Captain of Ports to evacuate the garrison. They even asked to talk to the Commander of the garrison. There was a short dialogue and the persons who had arrived simply said that they were Portuguese and that they should not open fire. When the sound of loading of arms was heard, Alferes Pereira Pinto ordered to open fire. There was an exchange of fire, a hand grenade was thrown from outside which however did not result in any casualty. From our side too a grenade was thrown but it did not explode.*

Our military men immediately went to the installations of the fort. Alferes Pereira Pinto decided to immediately open fire. Meanwhile, Sergeant Horacio remained in the Residence directing the action from that sector and the Commandant moved to his P.C. in the Light House.

Soon after the start of the fire exchange, the 1 º Sergeant of Cavalry Antonio R. Sabino aimed at the enemy vehicle with the Grenade Thrower 'Piat' and destroyed it completely together with its occupants. While the Half truck was burning, the noise of exploding ammunition could be heard.

....

After going to the lighthouse, Alferes Pereira Pinto alerted all his men and asked them to take positions on high ground so as to cover the hillside. Meanwhile, the political prisoners continued to be under guard.

Around 04:00 hours armoured tracked vehicles were heard approaching by road, which connects Candolim to Aguada. Then Alferes Pinto ordered his people not to open fire with light weapons without his permission as there were armoured vehicles in front and the firing could have exposed their position. It was 05:30 when they were observed coming down in the direction of Aguada fort. All of a sudden they machine-gunned the gate with intensity. From the sound produced one could also detect other tracked vehicles in the zone of St. Lourenco Church. As there were no anti-tank weapons, which could be used, it was decided not to use the light weapons. It was expected that there would be infantry troops accompanying the tanks.

Two tanks advanced in the vicinity of the burnt vehicle. Two others stayed behind covering these from the topside of the street. They machine-gunned the gate from this position. There were no infantry troops with the tanks nor did they come from any other sector. It was thought that the enemy would launch an aerial attack.

The Commandant observed that he did not have sufficient means of defence against the armoured vehicles. The ammunition stock was practically exhausted, and there was no chance of replenishment.

After having thought about all the factors, the Commandant of the Fort decided to surrender. The surrender took place at 07:30 hours. At this point the infantry appeared in company strength. At 08:00 hours two jet planes overflew the Aguada Fort. The Portuguese military men were imprisoned. All, including the commander were tied with ropes and were transported in vehicles firstly to Betim and then in a northerly direction. On the way they saw the enormous war material: Armoured vehicles, Amphibious tanks and Recoilless guns.

They spent the night in the vehicles, and on the next day returned to Betim from where they were taken to Messa do Altinho. Here they joined the other prisoners."

There is vast difference between what the Portuguese records say and the Indian army records. There were only nine members in Major Sidhu's party which left in a Dodge Truck. They had no weapons to face the enemy stationed in the Fort. Using Sten gun, a CQB weapon and hand grenades on an enemy fully protected in a fort was an unmilitary action. It had wrong information about the strength and weapons of the enemy. The informer had told them that there were only six soldiers guarding the political prisoners. In fact there was a full strength platoon with machine guns and grenade throwing equipment, as well as some extra manpower in form of military prisoners.

The Portuguese too did not know the strength of the Indian patrol. The report of Alferes Pereira Pinto is exaggerated. It seems he wanted to glorify himself as a great leader of men. With this report he succeeded in getting a medal for himself after his return to Portugal[119]. He received the *'Medalha de Cruz da Guerra de 2ª Classe'*.

Appreciation of 7 Cavalry by Commander 50 Para Brigade

Extract from the DO letter from Brigade Commander to Maj. Gen. Rajinder Singh, MVC, General Officer Commanding 1 Armoured Division[120] on the performance of 7 CAVALRY:

"I have had the good fortune of having your Regiment with the Parachute Brigade during the GOA Operations. The Regiment's operational performance has been excellent. They moved and acted very fast and efficiently.

I wish to offer you my heartfelt condolence on the tragic loss of two very gallant officers Major Sidhu and Captain Sehgal. To us in the Parachute Brigade, their loss has been very personal. We have all felt deeply.

"The loss of these two officers and an unfortunate accident involving an officer and two ORs in a jeep accident has made the Regiment sad and they deserve sympathy."

References

91—Op. Vijay—AppendixVII-p186
92—Ibid-p59
93—Ibid-p61
94—Ibid-p62
95—Ibid-p64
96—Ibid-p64
97—Ibid-p64
98—Ibid-p66
99—Ibid-p68
100—Ibid-p70
101—Ibid-p73
102—Ibid-p75
103—Ibid-p-76
104—Ibid-p-78
105—Op.Vijay-AppendixVIII –p-187
106—Ibid-p80
107—Ibid-p81
108—Ibid-p84
109—Ibid-p-86
110—Surrender Document
111—Ibid—Appendix XV-p-71
112—Ibid-p89
113—Ibid-p90
114—Ibid-p91
115—Ibid-p-71
116—Ibid-p-71
117—Ibid-p-72
118—C.A.Morais-Queda-p-127
119—Ibid-p-388
120—P.N.Khera-Op.Vijay-p-197.

CHAPTER XI

THE PORTUGUESE RETREAT ON 18TH AND 19TH DECEMBER

Action from different **Agrupamentos** reported in the Portuguese documents in the month of December was as follows:[121]

Agrupamento D. Joao de Castro[122]

15th December

In the morning of this day, the Commander of Agrupamento D. Joao de Castro, Major of Cavalry Acacio Tenreiro, went to Mapuca (headquarters of E. Rec.1) in order to contact the local commander and visit later the Police Post at Sinquervale. He was however surprised with the information given by the Captain of Cavalry Jose' Silva Reis, the commander of the Squadron, that the above post had retreated to Doromarogo (Dodamarg) due to strong pressure from the enemy who had attacked it with automatic weapons.

When he went to Dodamarg he came to know about more details of the event as well as some more information about the enemy activity. He came to know also that on the previous day, around thirty-five trucks with troops and war material had arrived at a place twenty kilometres from the border on the Indian side. The enemy had constructed at that place an improvised runway for plane landings.

When he was in Dodamarg Major Tenreiro was called by radio to a meeting at Q.G. (Quartel General), where he went immediately having reached that place by mid-day. The meeting was presided over by the Chief Commander (Governor General).

Major Tenreiro emphasized that the withdrawal of the police post at Sinquervale and yielding around three kilometres to the enemy was a serious matter. General Vassalo e Silva did not consider the matter of yielding the territory to be of special significance.

During this meeting the Group Commander came to know that a few Customs posts also had withdrawn. A message received from Lisbon was read which said that India would attack on the next day. So it was decided that the units would occupy the same evening the positions earmarked in the "Plano Sentinela".

16th December

During the day various news about enemy movements and concentrations near northern borders were being received. However, there was no news about the situation in other groups especially in the southern sector.

17th December

When Chefe do Estado Maior (Chief of General Staff) Tenente Coronel Marques de Andrade and Major Tenreiro were in Assonora they were informed by the local police post commander that there was a fight between Indian forces and E. Rec. 2 and already three soldiers were wounded on our side.

These officers immediately rushed to Bicholim (the headquarters of E. Rec2) and came to know from Squadron Commander, Captain of Cavalry Manuel Engraves Antunes that the General Comandante –Chefe had been at Maulinguem and that two soldiers were missing and one was wounded and already evacuated to the hospital in Mapuca.

In the Palacio do Hidalcao there was a meeting of General Comandante Chefe, Brigadeiro (Brigadier) Comandante Militar and Deputy Chief of E.M (Estado Maior). The commander of Group D. Joao de Castro, Major Tenreiro who had meanwhile arrived was asked about the action he thought should be taken. He said that our troops should counterattack and force the enemy to withdraw from our territory. General Vassalo e Silva did not support the idea saying that the aim of our troops is to withdraw so as to gain time.

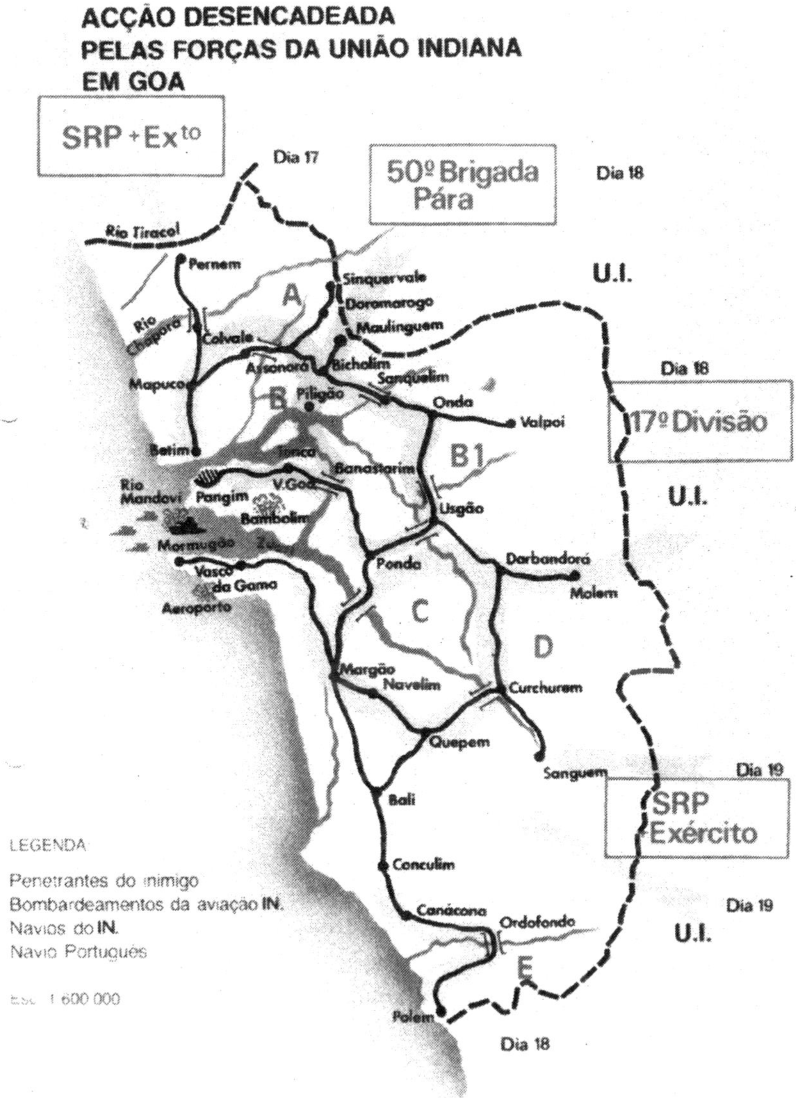

The Military Action
by Armed Forces of India in Goa

Major Tenreiro returned to his group at Velha-Goa where he came to know about the death of two of our soldiers and the wounding of several others besides the loss of a machine gun. He telephoned Major Francisco de Morais at Ponda and informed him of what had happened in the meeting. He added that then onwards the E. Rec. 2 would be coming under his command i.e. Agrupamento Centro.

At 09:45 hours on the 17th the Indian armed forces started the invasion of national territory. Two platoons occupied Maulinguem village and prepared to capture Maulinguem hilltop. At this moment our forces had a platoon to attack and repel the enemy.

The group commander was informed about the matter and his orders were awaited to take suitable action. Meanwhile, the Comandante–Chefe visited these positions in Maulinguem in the company of some journalists and indicated that it would not be proper to attack. However he advised to await orders from the group commander.

Alferes Aguiar was entrusted to prepare an observation post (P.O.) at Maulinguem hill with a section of troops. When he reached the crest with his people he was ambushed by the enemy. This resulted in the death of two soldiers (1° Cabo No 154/60 Antonio Fernando Ferreira da Silva and the soldier no 126/60 Fernando Jose' das Neves Moura Costa) and wounding of three others. So he was forced to withdraw at Maulinguem hill with the help of automatic weapons and light machine gun fire.

At 13:45 hours a negative answer for counterattack was received. It affected the morale of our troops in that sector. Though there was a negative order, E.Rec. 2 decided to counterattack in order to recover the bodies of the soldiers fallen in combat, and forced the enemy to withdraw. This way the Maulinguem hilltop was reoccupied.

Around five o'clock in the evening, a reconnaissance platoon with an automatic gun and a section of troops covering Maulinguem-Bicholim road was installed. The radio message from the Group HQ to E. Rec.2 with a negative reply was the last communication received by the squadron. From then onwards orders were being given directly by the HQ.

Around 21:00 hours, the Deputy Chief of General Staff, Major Matos Correia transmitted telephonically to the commander of E.Rec.1, Captain Silva Reis, the text of the radio message in which he was ordered to move to Assonora. This was due to commencement of 'Plano Sentinela'. A similar message was sent to E. Rec. 2. By 21:30 the commander of E. Rec.1 was at the police post of Assonora.

Through the Police radio, a few messages being sent by Doromarogo post to Bicholim could be heard. The messages said that the enemy had encircled them and that they could hear the noises of vehicles, foreseeing the imminent Indian attack.

18th December

The Commander of E. Rec.1 felt it necessary to know the exact situation at Doromarogo, which is situated seven kilometres from Assonora. He sent to that place a patrol party consisting of section of automatic guns and gunners, commanded by Alferes of Cavalry Barrigas Lacerda. He was ordered to collect the latest information and if necessary help the police personnel to withdraw.

The patrol left around 2 o'clock in the morning with headlights switched off and reached Doromarogo without any incident. Near the post that was already abandoned they found a police guard seriously wounded and a burnt automatic gun belonging to the police. While returning, the wounded police was brought and sent to Mapuca. During the short stay at Doromarogo the area was subjected to heavy enemy artillery fire and our people kept themselves protected in the armoured vehicle. During their return journey they were ambushed. Though they were fired on with machine gun bursts, the patrol counter fired and silenced the enemy.

Later on it came to light, in the prisoner's war camp that there was a company of Indian army in that area. Slightly to the north there were tanks ready to enter into action. This company on hearing the arrival of our patrol thought that the tanks were coming and so decided to withdraw. The fact was that the armoured vehicle had its silencer damaged and hence was making a huge sound similar to the one made by the real tanks.'[123]

When this action was in progress, the noise of approaching tanks could be heard in the area of Maulinguem. Around 4 o'clock the area was being subjected to Indian artillery fire. Our troops were compelled to withdraw to Bicholim. After some time this place saw the effect of this bombardment and E. Rec.2 lost radio contact.

As the 'Plano Sentinela' was already in force, the Bicholim bridge was demolished at 04:40 hours. During the process of demolishing soldier No 109/60 Mario Bernardino dos Santos died due to explosion of an anti-tank mine already planted in that area. Around 5 o'clock in the morning the enemy tanks were approaching the eastern bank of the Assonora rivulet. Soon after, the bridge was demolished as the result of simultaneous explosions of two explosive charges of 2500 kilograms each kept in two trucks in the rivulet bed below the bridge. A detachment was kept behind to cover the obstacle and to send warning of the approaching enemy.

Meanwhile, the 2nd platoon of E. Rec.1 stationed at Colvale had finished the execution of demolishing plan north of Chapora River and was proceeding in the execution of the remaining plan along the delaying axis.

While returning from Colvale the squadron commander was overflown for fifteen minutes by low flying jets. Though they did not open fire, they paralysed the movements of the personnel entrusted with the demolishing plan.

Captain Silva Reis went further to the entrance of Mapuca city in order to inspect the installation of the 3rd platoon and other installations, such as mortar section and automatic guns of the 3rd platoon. Meanwhile, news was received from the 1st platoon that the enemy was turning its direction to the north thus threatening the withdrawal of the 2nd platoon in Colvale.

The 1st platoon informed further that the enemy had crossed the left bank of Assonora rivulet and was moving in the direction of Panjim. Despite bursts of machine gun fire, against the enemy troops it was not possible to stop their advance due to the distance involved.

By this time the Agrupamento Centro was activated as 'Plano Sentinela' was in action.

At 7 O/clock, four enemy planes overflew Velha-Goa. They went in the direction of Bambolim and the airport at Dabolim and bombarded these places. Thick columns of smoke could be seen coming out from these places.

Meanwhile, there was a phone call to Major Tenreiro from the Chief of General Staff asking him what mission was allotted to the platoon at Bambolim. The commander of the same had reported that he did not know what action to take, though Alferes Antonio Abreu Abrantes the platoon commander, was well aware that he had to withdraw to Panjim or in case of impossibility he had to move to Marmagoa Peninsula. Later on it was concluded that the Alferes Abrantes must have died in the bombardment carried out by the Indian Air Force and the enquiry must have been made by his substitute.

***"As there were no transmissions, the governor sent me there to find out what was happening. I went in a black Volkswagen. The centre and the generators had been attacked with bombs and rockets. They killed an ensign - I even saw him, with brains spilling out of his head"** wrote Captain (later general) Azaredo*

The enemy artillery was executing bombardment of areas where the platoons of E. Rec. 1 were engaged in delaying actions. This was to allow its advance troops, which were approaching these areas to proceed ahead. A reconnaissance plane was overflying the region to direct the artillery fire and find out the positions of our troops. (Obviously these were AOP planes or the air force was using cab-rank method).

Two platoons of E. Rec. 1 were ordered to overtake the city of Mapuca and take the following positions: Our four mortars were firing at the bifurcation of roads Mapuca-Colvale and Mapuca-Assonora. As the Indian artillery had stopped the fire, it was suspected that the enemy troops were approaching this area. Unfortunately a large number of bombs and charges did not blow up and the grenades did not come out of the barrels due to the bad state of these ammunitions.

Around 13:00 hours when the squadron commander was ordering the 3rd platoon to withdraw and overtake Mapuca, Furriel Correia informed him that when he was crossing the city many armed individuals had fired on his jeep. He had managed to escape due to the speed of his vehicle and firing from his automatic pistol-gun. He further informed that Indian flags were raised on many buildings and that he had seen an individual climbing a mast to raise an Indian flag, whom he had shot down.[124]

He also informed that near the Hindu temple near the bus stand there were many individuals ready to ambush our troops while moving out from the city.

In view of the above, the retreating column first sent its automatic guns that were installed in the city, with barrels directed at the entrance and departure points. These guns protected the vehicles transporting the personnel. They in turn fired with their automatic guns on both the sides of the roads where the terrorist elements were suspected to be present. In this way the column managed to leave Mapuca without suffering any casualty.

The last round of auto machine gun was fired on the Indian flag raised on the mast of Police Headquarters.

Around the end of the morning hours, the enemy had reached Piligao, after using artillery fire and tanks in the area under control of the platoon of Tonca. This platoon was compelled to abandon its first position. This it did at the right moment, as soon afterwards the abandoned area was machine gunned by the planes.

The group commander came to know meanwhile that the H.Q had retreated to Agacaim. He dispatched a rider with a message communicating the events that had already taken place and asking it to warn the E.Rec.2 urgently the possibility of the bridge at Banastarim being destroyed before it could pass over it to the island of Goa. The rider returned and informed that the message was delivered to Chief of the General Staff who said that he would telephone later and that he would take all necessary measures.

At this moment, Sergeant Carlos Silva de Almeida of E. Rec.3 sent by Agrupamento Centro met Major Tenreiro with a request to delay the demolishing of Banastarim Bridge in order to allow E.Rec.2 to cross it in its retreating action. In view of enemy pressure the Tonca platoon was under, there was hardly any chance of agreeing to this delay.

Meanwhile, Major Tenreiro met Captains Pinto Bras of Police and Costa Macedo of Customs Guards who informed that the personnel which had arrived from the North were disorganized and disoriented.

He went to Palacio de Hidalcao where he met Comandante Abel de Oliveira, the Captain of Ports, who intimated that as per the order of Deputy Chief of Staff, Major Matos Correia, he had sent to search at Aguada fort, the platoon stationed there and 50 prisoners imprisoned in the fort. When Major Tenreiro asked what they intended to do with the prisoners, he replied that he had only received that order. After some time the master of the launch who was entrusted to go to Aguada appeared, and said that he could not bring the personnel as he could not moor the launch. Major Tenreiro requested Comandante Abel de Oliveira to search for the platoon and let the prisoners remain behind. The commander of the fort and also of the platoon, Alferes Pereira Pinto had informed however that he would come with his people only after the receipt of a written order.[125]

Major Tenreiro and Commandante Abel de Oliveira together with Major Garrido Borges, Director of Servicos de Economia analysed the situation and decided to send the Comandante of P E I to talk to Comandante–Chefe, informing him about the prevailing situation. This happened at around 12:30 hours. The answer from General Vassalo e Silva was "it is yet not time to surrender" The Q.G. on its part replied to the radio message that "Mission is to resist. Let God protect".

Meanwhile, the Agrupamento D. Joao de Castro was ignorant of the overall action by E.Rec.2 since the moment it came under its command. Its mission was changed, as it had not occupied the previously determined positions in the regions of Carambolim and Velha-Goa.

Around 12:30 hours the bombardment of "Aviso Afonso de Albuquerque" and its surrender after some time was known. It was also known that the crew was safe.

Major Tenreiro accompanied by Major Silva Carvalho, Captains Mexia Leitao and Roberto Durao went to the Police Headquarters and verified that the personnel had returned the weapons and were refusing to fight. There the documents were being burnt and the weapons were being destroyed. The Commandants of Police and Customs Guards declared that their men had surrendered.

It came to the notice that there were divergent opinions between the command and other officers. The result was that the Military Commandant and the Deputy Chief went to the south of Zuari River and the Chief of General Staff stayed at Agacaim. "Plano Sentinela" had determined that the Q. G. would move to Marmagoa Peninsula and not Agacaim.

General Vassalo e Silva was contacted once again in order to obtain the surrender order. This was the only way of saving the city of Panjim and the lives of its population especially the old and the young, as there were no effective means to offer resistance.

Once again the Governor General did not accede to the request.

E.Rec.2 reached Panjim around 03:00 hours in the evening. It could finally cross Banastarim Bridge. Captain Engracia Antunes informed Major Tenreiro the action of his squadron, the death of three soldiers and wounding of several others and overall state of the troops. They had to move under artillery fire and always under flying aircrafts. They did not attack because they did not want to.

By 15:30 hours as there was danger from advancing enemy to Panjim and possible bombardment from the artillery and the air force, the "Patriarca da India" Dom Jose Vieira Alvernaz accompanied by Captain Pinto Bras appealed to the Governor General to issue the surrender order but this went unheeded.

Action of Reconnaissance Squadron No1 (E. Rec. 1).

While following the manoevre to reach Panjim the squadron commander ordered to install a platoon of C. Cac.9 in the region of

Britona, in order to guarantee the access to the jetty of Betim. With an identical mission a platoon and a section of mortars of the 3rd platoon of E. Rec.1 were already installed. On moving to the jetty of Betim to find out about the arrangement for crossing the Mandavi river, Captain Silva Reis noticed that there was no arrangement for crossing as guaranteed in 'Plano Sentinela'. The squadron could be embarked by means of a ferry boat of S.A.N.I. (Servicos Autonimos da Navegacao de India) and two mine transporting barges after taking necessary safety measures. During this period Captain Silva Reis received an order from the Group Commander not to take any initiative.

"When all the elements had crossed the river, the Squadron Commander embarked with his vehicle. The time was approximately 17:45 hours.

"The ferry boat had just moved a few metres from the jetty when many bursts of machine gun were fired from an enemy position five hundred metres away.

"On disembarking at Panjim Captain Silva Reis was received by Captain Roberto Durao, Information and Operations Officer of the Group. He transmitted the order of the Group Commander asking him not to take any measures indicative of intent to take combat action

"The city presented a picture of total abandonment; practically nobody was being seen–neither the local population nor combatants. Windows and doors were shut and the streets were deserted. It was a desolate panorama. The squadron assembled in the vicinity of building "Casa Internacional' and Captain Silva Reis moved to the Headquarters (Q. G.) Building where the Group Commander was accompanied by various officers of Q.G., Tribunal, Police and others.

"Meanwhile, the enemy Artillery having reached Betim plateau had started firing on Panjim. One shell had fallen in front of Hospital Escolar (Hospital) and the other near the road leading to Altinho. At the same time eight armoured vehicles appeared in Betim and took position along river Mandavi.

"All this could be understood as preparatory for bombardment of the city. The situation was really critical. The Group Commander called a meeting to which all the unit commanders (except the commander of C. Cac.1), the Commandant and Deputy Commandant of Police, the Commandant of Customs Guards and all the officers who had returned to Q.G. were present.

"After studying the situation it was verified that: 'there were no human and material means which would enable us to give fight to a heavily armed enemy who had already taken exceptionally important positions. Equally there were no means to oppose the enemy artillery action as well as action from enemy air force. There were such conditions that would permit the disembarking of Indian troops on this side of Mandovi and on our side there was no possibility of facing them. Our troops were few as compared to the Indian troops. They were already tired during the retreats executed under fire of enemy's artillery. There could be terrorist actions during the night from elements already infiltrated into the city."

"In the face of all these circumstances it was concluded that 'To resist would constitute sacrificing unnecessarily the city, its population and the troops. Accordingly the Group Commander decided to propose to the enemy the surrender of our troops. So a white flag was raised on a tree near Mandavi River."

"Simultaneously the Group Commander sent a message to the Q. G.

"We are encircled. In the evening the enemy Artillery was seen at Alto Betim and many combat vehicles were at the banks of river Mandovi. They have started firing indicating their intention of neutralising any resistance. In order to avoid massacre of the population and having no means to offer any resistance I held a meeting of the officers who concluded that the remembrance of Portuguese will be preserved better in the spirit of the Goans by not compelling them to fall with us. Thus with constraint we request to send negotiators in order to avoid the ruin of the City of Goa. We are awaiting the decision from the enemy."

Then two negotiators were procured from the Patriarcado (Office of Archbishop). Monsignor Antao (Padre Gregorio Magno de Sousa

Antao) volunteered to go to Betim, where he had discussions with the Commander of the Indian Forces. On return he informed Major Acacio Tenreiro that the enemy had guaranteed truce till ten o'clock in the morning of the next day. At this hour the Indian Commander would come to talk to the Commander of the Portuguese forces in Panjim.[126]

"Our troops went to barracks in Altinho where all the armament, radio equipment and automatic guns were made inoperative".

19th December

"At 09:00, the Commander of Group D. Joao de Castro, was contacted by Captain Minas da Piedade Deputy Commandant of Police who informed him about the arrival of Lt. Col. Sucha Singh, Commandant of the Indian Forces Operating in the North, accompanied by a Major and a Captain, at the gate of Altinho Mess The contact was established and soon after the Indian troops appeared. They occupied Altinho and considered that our forces to be the prisoners of Indian Army from that moment onwards.

After some time General Candeth (who later became the Military Governor) a Brigadier and many other Officers, visited the locality."

Action of Agrupamento Centro

Agrupamento Centro[127] *came into existence the moment "Plano Sentinela" was in execution. This plan was activated when the enemy had invaded the territory of Goa. In that eventuality Major Francisco Morais was to assume the role of Group commander.*

On 13th December the following alterations were introduced in the original plan:

C. Cac. 3 (minus 1 platoon) ceased to be an integral part of this Agrupamento and would occupy the position at Mormugao. However it would keep in Usgao and Candeapar a platoon to guard the bridges at those places. It would leave this place only after having been relieved by detachment of E.Rec.2. This platoon would also guard the P C of the Agrupamento.

The E. Rec.2 after crossing the line defined by the Candeapar River (known as the Green Line) would withdraw directly to the Island of Goa. Then it would fall under the command of Agrupamento D. Joao de Castro.

Due to these two alterations the temporary resistance at the Green Line envisaged in the"Plano Sentinela" had ceased to operate.

The E. Rec. 3 when forced to abandon its position at Darbandora, was to rapidly retreat to Sanvordem. It would fall under the command of Agrupamento Afonso de Albuquerque after having demolished the communication centre at Darbandora and the bridge at Dauconda.

There would be a First Aid centre at Ponda, to be started by Health Services. (Actually this centre was never started).

17th December

In the evening there was news that the enemy had bombarded Sinquervale, Doramarogo and Maulinguem.

At night Major Matos Correia telephoned the Agrupamento that E.Rec.2 had counterattacked for reconquering Maulinguem. He transmitted the order that the platoons should limit themselves to opening fire to repel the enemy and delay its advance, but should never counterattack.

18th December

At 04:00 hours the Chefe do E. M. informed telephonically about the artillery bombardment of Bicholim. Thus the 'Plano Sentinela' was to be put in execution.

At dawn, three enemy jets overflew the P. C. However they did not open fire, though they could have aimed at the police vehicles found at that place.

A curious incident occurred at that moment. When the soldiers were ordered to take cover when the planes appeared, they did not obey the order. They replied: "Do not worry. These are our planes which were in Karachi." This was an illusion, which was resultant of the news of planes of TAIP, which were engaged in airlifting of people to Karachi.[128]

Around 07:00 hours AL/E. Rec. Sergeant Augusto Verissimo came to P.C. and informed that the enemy, consisting of infantry units and reinforced with armoured vehicles and strongly supported by artillery, had bombarded Bicholim. The 3rd platoon of E. Rec.2 was forced to retreat to Sanquelim where it suffered one casualty. The remaining platoons occupied the allotted positions. Further he informed that the bridges at Bicholim and Sanquelim had been demolished as per 'Plano Sentinela'.

At 08:00 hours there was information that the enemy was putting strong pressure along the axis of retreat. This had forced the platoons at Sanquelim and Onda to retreat.

Seeing such a rapid advance of Indian troops the group commander informed AL/ E.Rec.3 to communicate to Captain Matias, the order for the platoon at Molem to retreat directly to Darbandora as soon as it established contact with the enemy. At 09:00 hours there was a communication that the enemy was halfway between Onda and Usgao. At this moment the last vehicles carrying police personnel from Valpoi had crossed Usgao Bridge. Its commandant Comissario Teixeira informed that all the personnel from there had been collected.

Around 11:00, the last platoon of E. Rec.2 had crossed the Candeapar Bridge which was covered by the 2nd platoon stationed on the southern bank of that river.

Apprehending that the Banastarim Bridge might be demolished before passage of E. Rec 2 to the Island of Goa, Major Francisco Morais ordered AL/E Rec. (Sergeant Carlos Almeida) that he should go to that Bridge and delay its destruction.

When Sergeant Almeida reached that place, the bridge was ready to be destroyed. Though the personnel responsible for that mission was informed to wait till E. Rec.2 could cross the bridge, they did not show any receptive attitude, as they had received orders for the destruction and the enemy was putting strong pressure on that area. In view of this attitude, Sergeant Carlos Almeida went with his vehicle to the platform of the bridge and declared that they could blow up the bridge with him. This action by him allowed for the necessary delay to permit E. Rec 2 to cross the bridge.

Meanwhile, the bridge at Candeapar was destroyed and E. Rec 2 had retreated to Ponda and from there to the Island of Goa. The Banastarim bridge was destroyed at 13:30 hours.

E. Rec.3 executed the destructions of Darbandora and Dauconda bridges as entrusted to it. During this destruction, Alferes de Engenharia Antonio Lopes Gonsalves Pereira lost his life, being a victim of an explosion.

Agrupamento Centro finished all the missions allotted to it and then moved to Marmagoa peninsula. It did the evacuation of the Police forces, executed the destruction envisaged in the Demolishing Plan, and saw the withdrawal of C. Cac 3 to Marmagoa Peninsula at the right time.

On reaching Borim Bridge, Major Francisco Morais informed the guard that there were no more troops to cross over and hence the demolishing could be executed on receipt of the order to do so. The Borim Bridge was in the zone under the responsibility of Agrupamento Afonso de Albuquerque. Therefore Major Francisco Morais had radio contact with that unit and obtained the order for its destruction. Furriel de Engenharia Joaquim Alcobia executed the order and the bridge was destroyed exactly at 13:00 hours.[129]

Then Major Morais moved with the people under his command to Cortalim where the Q.G. was supposed to be installed. He came to know that the same was at Agacaim. When he together with Captain Couto Leite was crossing the Zuari River they saw the boat carrying Comandante-Chefe, Comandante Militar and the Deputy Chief of E.M going towards Cortalim.

The mission allotted to this agrupamento was completed. The enemy air force did not want to attack our forces but always controlled our movements. All the Commanders of units, which were in Goa, expressed a similar opinion. This preplanned procedure, put into practice in an efficient and disciplined manner created in our forces a demoralizing, frustrating and inferiority sentiment. In all the sectors our units were positively pushed by a gust of a crushing military power.[130]

Around 14 00 hours, the Comandante Chefe, the Comandante Militar and Sub-Chefe do E. M. moved to Marmagoa peninsula.

They established there, an advance P. C. while the Chefe do E. M. remained at Agacaim with an advance echelon. After the receipt of information at around 22:00 hours that the Agrupamento D. Joao de Castro had surrendered, General Vassalo e Silva ordered the advance echelon to move to Marmagoa Peninsula. At the junction of roads to Vasco da Gama and Dabolim there was a crowd of men and vehicles of all types, some of them transporting enormous quantity of explosives. There were military men with dropped weapons, having received orders not to fight. The Chefe do E.M. had ordered Major Pimentel de Oliveira to disperse and move to places they wished to go.

Major Morais went to the building of Estaleiros Navais de Goa, where the Command had taken shelter. He met there the Chefe do E.M. who was sharing the room with Comandante Militar and asked him if it was true the order he gave to Major Pimentel Oliveira. He confirmed it and repeated the same. Four more officers who were accompanying Major Morais witnessed this scene.

Thus, the mission of Agrupamento Centro was over. The elements that had heard the words of Chefe do E.M. decided to move to Q. G. at Agacaim. They were made prisoners around 14:00 hours on the 19th where they came to know about the surrender of the High Command.

They were taken to the Prisoner's camp at Altinho. Major Morais was hospitalized as he was injured in an accident.

Action of Agrupamento Afonso de Albuquerque

People coming from Panjim were saying that one could see ships of the Indian Navy on the horizon, from the Altinho Mess. A week prior to the invasion, an aircraft carrier, two cruisers, many frigates and a support ship of the Indian naval fleet remained in the direction of Mormugao port but outside our territorial waters. In the air its Air Force was violating our air space every day.

There was however a considerable percentage of military men who were in Goa for quite some time who did not believe that there would be an Indian invasion. This was due to the fact that for all these years there would be threats from our neighbour that ultimately would fizzle out. In Portugal, however they were aware of the intentions of the Indians.

On 9th December[131] the police post at Polem was attacked. The patrol party of E.Rec.4, sent to establish contact with the unit in the Butpal area, blew up due to the mine. This resulted in severely wounding the driver, who later on succumbed to his injuries.

On 10th December, around 01:12 hours the headquarters of the platoon at Canacona of E.Rec.4 was attacked by terrorists. There were no casualties due to prompt reaction from our troops.

On 11th December it was informed for the first time that C. Cac.3 would occupy the position at Verna and it would function as the reserve force of the Agrupamento. The C. Cac 10 would occupy the region of Velsao; the E. Rec.4 would occupy the region in front of the island of S. Jacinto; and E. Rec. 4 would look after the region of Alto Dabolim; and finally B. Art.1 would occupy the position near to this unit.

Actually, these positions were in the areas coming under Agrupamento Vasco da Gama and thus were unknown to us. While we were studying and preparing these important positions, once again they were changed two or three days prior to the invasion.

During the night, around 23:45 hours, the terrorists attacked the HQ of E. Rec.4 at Bali. In the firing one terrorist was shot and later imprisoned during combing operations in the morning. He was sent to the hospital at Ribandar as he was badly injured in the throat and the lower jaw. Later on we came to know that he had recovered fully.

18th December 1961

Around 00:00 hours the first news of the invasion of Goa reached us. The Indian Union had launched an attack from the North of our territory.

The Commander of the Agrupamento, Major Rangel de Almeida was called to the telephone of Margao Police around 03:00 hours. He returned at about 06:00 hours with the news of the bombardment of Bicholim. The "Plano Sentinela" came in force for Agrupamentos D. Joao Castro and Centro. There were many worrying radio messages during the nighttime. Some time later there was news of the occupation of Bicholim.

The enemy, in order to disturb our radio communications was transmitting music and noise. This was disrupting the audio reception at our post.

The bombardment of Dabolim airport commenced at 07:00 hours. One could clearly hear the explosions of bombs dropped by the Indian Air Force. Our headquarters vibrated and glass panes broke. Some time later the jets over flew our headquarters. A few jets aimed at it but did not fire.

The soldiers were ordered to lie down and take cover but surprisingly they ran to see them flying.[132]

The transmitting station at Bambolim was bombarded too. We received the news that the Alferes of the Infantry who was posted there had died in the air attack. Around 08:30 hours the enemy attacked the southern frontier (Polem). The personnel from the posts on the frontier retreated to Marmagoa Peninsula.

The "Plano Sentinela" was applicable to Agrupamento Afonso de Albuquerque at 09:00 hours. Orders for the demolishing of Ordonfondo Bridge were given. Orders for the evacuation of the headquarters at Navelim were issued so that we could occupy the positions allotted to us.

We occupied the allotted position near Nuvem church around 10:00 hours. News were received that the first enemy elements had appeared at Ordonofondo around 11:30 hours from the south. The

3rd platoon of E.Rrec.4 together with the platoon of C.Cac. 10 withdrew after heavy firing on the opposite side of the river.

Around 12:00 hours we were informed that the battle between "Aviso Afonso de Albuquerque" and the Indian Naval fleet was in progress. We could clearly hear the artillery firings of the naval ships, and intermittent explosions of bridges being destroyed. After some time we came to know that "Afonso the Albuquerque" had run aground and surrendered after a brief fight.[133]

The bridge at Borim was destroyed at 13:00 hours after the elements of Agrupamento Centro had crossed it.

The Commander of the Agrupamento visited the positions of B. Art 1 and ordered it to retreat to Nuvem. By this time E. Rec 3 had one platoon at Quepem, one at Maina and another at Loutulim.

By this time the Q.G was found situated at the entrance of the city of Vasco da Gama in the office of Estaleiros Navais de Goa. The "Aviso Afonso de Albuquerque" was aground on the right bank of the Zuari River. Smoke billowed out from the ship.

Around 17:00 hours, a section of C. Cac.10 reached Verna and then installed itself on the left side of the position on the Nuvem-Cortalim road. We came to know that though the bridge was destroyed, the enemy had crossed the Zuari River by using ore carrying barges and had moved onwards by civilian transport[134]*. This transport was provided by Firma Chowgule.*

At 23:00 hours Alferes Antunes Rapoula informed Captain Martins Ferreira (Commander of C. Cac. 3) that all the indigenous soldiers of the company had deserted.

At 23:30 hours a message intimating the surrender of Panaji city was received. Contact with other Agrupamentos and Head Quarters could not be established. A jeep coming from the front stopped near the P. C. The occupants revealed that the terrorists were attacking our troops positioned at different places. There were two trucks full of explosives near the P. C. There was a great danger of explosion in case there was any attack. Steps were taken to disperse the explosives and safety precautions were reinforced.

19th December

Around 01:00 hours a jeep appeared with a Sergeant who was responsible for supplying petrol to vehicles. He confirmed that Panjim was occupied by Indian troops.

Around 04:30 hours, Alferes Aresta Branco came to the P. C. with alarming news. He was taken to the Commander of the Agrupamento, Major Rangel de Almeida who was sleeping at the residence of the priest of the Church of Nuvem. Alferes Branco said that the Governor General, the Military Commander, the Chief and Deputy Chief of E. M.were in Vasco da Gama. Other officers of H.Q had returned to Panjim and the Agrupamento D. Joao de Castro had surrendered. The enemy had already occupied the capital and other troops were surrendering.

After hearing news from Alferes Branco, Major Rangel de Almeida drafted the following order and dispatched it to his sub-unit:

"Nuvem 190500DEZ961

"You should collect your Squadrons/Companies and conduct them to Verna plateau. You will be held responsible for any form of indiscipline practiced by elements of your units."[135]

The Commander of the Agrupamento gave order to his P.C. around 05:30 hours to leave Nuvem and proceed in the direction of Verna. We met Bat. Art.1 stationed along the road to Nagoa, during our transit.

After reaching Verna, Major Rangel de Almeida ordered the raising a white flag on the antenna of the transmission vehicle. He further ordered that the weapons should be collected on the ground and then destroyed. The vehicles should be brought down to the areas near the roads and then damaged. C. Cac.10, E. Rec.4, and E. Rec.3 obeyed this order given by the Commander of the Agrupamento.[136]

After some time, a reconnaissance plane overflew the place and signalled that it was acknowledging that our troops had surrendered. A jet flew at low altitude and also overflew two or three times.

Portuguese Troops Withdrawal

Then Major Rangel declared that he was going to Q. G. and talk to the General Comandante Chefe. He left alone in a jeep. After a long time he returned to the plateau and said that the Governor General was aware of what had already taken place, and had ordered that the Agrupamento should concentrate in Marmagoa Peninsula. We felt that the order was very strange, because the white flag had already been raised, and our surrender was also acknowledged

All the captains decided to meet General Vassalo e Silva as they felt it necessary to inform him about the real situation. The Governor was met in the palm groove situated between Cortalim and Vasco da Gama. Brigadier Comandante Militar and Deputy Chief of E.M accompanied him.

The Governor listened to each one of us and agreed that the Agrupamento could not gather in the Marmagoa Peninsula and ordered us to go to our troops.

Around 14:00 hours the Indian troops reached Verna Plateau and we were made prisoners.[137]

Action of Agrupamento Vasco da Gama

It should be noted that the Agrupamento Vasco da Gama[138] never took part in any combat. Major Cardeira da Silva commanded this Agrupamento.

At 06:30 hours on the 18th the Deputy Chief of E. M. intimated on the phone that "Plano Sentinela" was already in action. He also informed that India had started the invasion of Goa from the north after preparing the ground with artillery fire for four hours. It was presumed that the invasion would also take place from the remaining axes as foreseen.

At 07:05 hours the enemy air force suddenly started the bombardment of the airport and ten minutes later that of the transmitter at Bambolim. The entire zone was convulsed with the violence of explosions of the bombs dropped by Indian warplanes.

The Commander of the Agrupamento tried to communicate telephonically to Q. G. about the attacks. As the lines were snapped he sent a radio message.

There was a second bombardment of the airport at 07:40 hours. After a while there was a message from B. Art. 2 that the main runway of the airport was hit at different places. However, they could remain in their positions.

Meanwhile, the various enemy warships, which were seen at a distance, had started moving towards the coast.[139]

Major Cardeira da Silva decided to shift his P.C. earmarked earlier, to the south west of the **Estaleiros Navais de Goa** *(Goa Shipyard), as bombardment of the present area was feared. All the personnel shifted to the new P.C.*

By mid-day three Indian warships, which were approaching the river Zuari bar commenced naval combat with "Aviso Afonso de Albuquerque". A few shells had fallen near Alto de Alparqueiros.

Meanwhile, the vehicles from the front had started arriving. The Police personnel retreating from the frontier were brought by these vehicles. Tenente Canuto Pereira came with eighty men from Bicholim Police. A majority of these were locals. Captain Albuquerque who was in charge of indicating the positions to new arrivals assigned them some positions.

Meanwhile, the combat with "Aviso Afonso de Albuquerque" continued. Three more Indian warships were in sight about five miles from the coast. The third and the most violent bombardment of the airport took place at 11:40 hours.

Captain Fernando Lobo da Costa, the Commander of Bat. Art.2 informed telephonically that a few bombs had fallen in the vicinity of the Command Tower. The advance observer of the Battery was housed in the tower. The glass panes of the building were shattered and the T.S.F instruments were damaged. The petrol pump had already started burning.

The anti-aircraft guns could not be fired as the planes were flying at a very high altitude, beyond range. They could only be detected when they were flying over the positions.

Captain Lobo da Costa informed further that the situation of the positions of anti-aircraft defences of the airport and the Observation Post of the Artillery was untenable. Thus it was not possible to observe the artillery fire due to failure of connection with the Central Post of Fire (P C T). As the telephonic connection with the positions was cut due to the enemy air bombardment, he requested permission to allow the military in the area of the airport to move to the positions of field artillery situated on the north of Cortalim-Airport road.

The movement of vehicles and civilians to Vasco da Gama and vice–versa was increasing and obstructing access to the P. C. Therefore Captain of Artillery Manuel Marrecas Ribeiro and Comissario Jose Jorge Teixeira were entrusted with the duty of policing the roads with their personnel. They stopped the transit of civilian vehicles, thus securing the safety of "Posto do Comando".

After some time Lieutenant Maximo arrived with his Police from Colem. He was entrusted with the work of beefing up the Police stationed in Vasco da Gama.

As the forces entrusted with defense in the vicinity of airport were withdrawn, they were asked to augment the unit of gunners positioned on Bogmalo beach. It was feared that the enemy might disembark and appear in the rearguard causing danger to the unit installed in that area as well as to the forces on the land above.

As the result of the aerial bombardment the following military personnel had lost their lives: 1o Cabo 16/61 Joaquim Luis Duarte; Soldiers; 66/61 Manuel Jordao Carreira; 91/61 Afonso Carlos Ferreira and 121/61 Armelindo Pereira Soares. All these belonged to C.Cac.7 and formed the garrison of A. A. 20 mm gun detachment.

Meanwhile, the naval bombardment was in progress. A few shells were falling near Alto de Alparqueiros. ***The "Aviso Afonso de Albuquerque" was hit at 12:20 hours and had started listing in the region of Dona Paula. The enemy ships were continuing to fire on it. After some time it ran aground and raised the white flag. The Indian ships were continuing to fire on the ground area where the crew was taking shelter after abandoning the ship.***[140]

Around 15:30, the "Patriarca das Indias" Dom Jose Alvernaz, accompanied by Capitao Pinto Bras contacted the Governor near the Police positions in order to request him to give the order of surrender. The Governor however did not agrèe to the proposal.

The General Comandante Chefe arrived at the P.C. of the Agrupamento accompanied by Brigadeiro Comandante Militar and Captain Albuquerque.He decided to stay near the P.C. of Agrupamento. He called Captain Lobo Costa and evaluated whether the B. Art. 2 could be used as field artillery. As there was no communication between the command and observation post the idea was given up and the battery unit was assigned the infantry role. It was asked to take position to the east of the chapel in Vadem.

At seven o'clock in the evening there was news from "All India Radio" that the city of Vasco da Gama and petrol installations of Burmah Shell were to be bombarded. There was also the rumour spread by civilians that the city of Panaji had already surrendered.

Around 21:45 hours. Capitao-Tenente Abel de Oliveira who had disembarked at Major Bunder appeared near the P. C and enquired whether the naval personnel had arrived there. He was bringing the news of the fall of Panaji city. He informed further that he had seen the disarmed Portuguese troops in formation along the avenue on the riverbank. He said further that already the Indian flag was found raised on one of the masts. He was taken to the General Comandante Chefe and Brigadeiro Comandante Militar where he conveyed the news, which he had passed on earlier.

At 22:30 hours, a boat carrying Commodore Raul Ventura, the naval commander, together with officers and the personnel of this command arrived at the jetty of the shipyard. They moved to the area of the Command post where they stayed. At this moment a rider sent by Comandante of Agrupamento Joao de Castro at around 19:30 hours arrived with a message asking for the exchange of representatives.

Around 22:45 hours, Major Cardeira da Silva ordered his adjutant, Captain Portela Ribeiro to change the location of the P. C. of the Agrupamento as by now it would have been zeroed in by the enemy, due to the large number of troops and vehicles which had arrived there in the evening. During the night one could hear the planes flying at high altitude in the sector of the Agrupamento.

The movement of vehicles transporting the retreating troops was continuing unabated. It could not be controlled despite the policing of the area.

19th December

Around 01:30 one could hear the bombardment at a distance on the terrestrial front. After some time a message arrived informing that the garrison in the Aguada Fort that had fought for several hours was going to surrender.

The Commandant of C. Cac 7 Captain Sousa Alves informed around 04:15 hours that the groups of disarmed and disoriented military men, who could not be identified, were trying to enter the city of Vasco da Gama. They were spreading demoralizing news. When the General Comandante Chefe was informed about this matter, he decided to move to the city of Vasco da Gama together with Comandante Militar and Deputy Chief of E. M to verify the matter. On his return the Comandante Chefe informed Major Cardeira da Silva that he was going to the positions at Dabolim where the Q. G was situated and thereafter he would return to the P.C. of Agrupamento. Meanwhile he was informed that the P.C would be shifted at 04:45 hours to a new location in the region to the west of Vadem.

Captain Portela Ribeiro went to the positions of the sub-units under this Agrupamento to inform them about the new location of the P.C. The Comandante of the Agrupamento went to the different positions and found all the personnel calm, though they were visited by groups of military, the majority being indigenous (naturais). They were coming from the front with alarming news that could have affected the morale of the troops.

Around 08:45 hours, the Comandante Chefe arrived at the P.C. accompanied by Comandante Militar, Deputy Chief of E. M, Captain Silva Ramos and Major Rangel de Almeida, Comandante of Agrupamento Afonso de Albuquerque who had come to discuss matters with General Vassalo e Silva.

The enemy jet planes meanwhile were overflying the city of Vasco da Gama and the Naval Shipyard.

Around 11:00 hours, the Adjutant of Agrupamento Afonso de Albuquerque and the commanders of its sub-units came to the P.C. in order to discuss matters with the Comandante Chefe. He heard each one of them individually. At 12:15 hours, General Vassalo e Silva informed that in view of the surrender of Agrupamento Afonso de Albuquerque and after analysing the situation of our forces still in position, he had decided to surrender. He entrusted the Deputy Chief of E.M.to move to the position of C.Cac.6 in Cortalim and to the Command of Agrupamento in order to call all the commanders of the sub-units of that sector.

At 12:45 hours the decision taken by the Comandante Chefe to surrender was conveyed to all the commanders in one of the residences of the Goa Naval Shipyard.

The Deputy Chief of E. M. Tenente Coronel Marques de Andrade, in the company of 'Patriarca das Indias Orientais' D. Jose Vieira Alvernaz and an interpreter, Captain (graduado medico) Garcia da Silva were entrusted to contact the commander of the Indian forces. He was entrusted to carry the following message:

Nos termos do comunicado que junto a V.Ex.ª e de acordo com a competencia que me e conferida pela carta de Comando do Governo Central, solicito a V. Ex ª suspensao de fogo entre as nossas Forcas, a partir deste momento.

Quartel General em Vasco da Gama as 14:00 do dia 19 de Dezembro de 1961.

O General Comandante –Chefe
Manuel Antonio Vassalo e Silva
General[141]

As per the terms which I send along with to your Excellency, and as per the competency conferred on me by the letter of Command from the Central Government, I request your Excellency for the suspension of fire between our Forces with immediate effect.

The General Commanding-in-Chief
Manuel Antonio Vassalo e Silva.
General

The final official communication said:

Tendo a defesa da peninsula de Mormugao reduto final da defesa —como base a ocupacao pelas nossas forcas de posicoes que pusessem a cidade de Vasco da Gama a coberto dos fogos aereos, terrestres e maritimos do inimigo e das consequencias inevitaveis da luta proxima e tendo ainda em atencao a desproporcao das forces e meios em presenca, e que nao permitem continuar a luta sem grande sacrificio de vidas de habitantes da cidade de Vasco da Gama, decidi, com espirito bem constrangido e o sentimento patrio bem presente, entrar em contacto com o inimigo na altura em que a sua aproximacao faz perigar a populacao daquela cidade que desejo poupar, para se conseguir treguas de acordo com competencia que me e conferida pela Carta de Comando. Nesta conformidade determino a todas as forcas sob o meu Comando a suspencao do fogo.

E oportuno salientar a forma calma e ordeira como toda a populacao da Provincia se tem mantido desde que se iniciou a invasao como continuidade daquela que sempre patenteou anteriormente.

Nesto momento presto homenagem aos que ja tombaram no campo da honra.

Quartel General em Vasco da Gama as 14:00 do dia 19 de Dezembro de 1961.

O General Comandante –Chefe
Manuel Antonio Vassalo e Silva
General[142]

Official statement of C-in-C of the Portuguese India Army

"Having the defence of the Peninsula of MARMAGOA –the final stronghold of our defence as a base for the occupation by our forces of positions which could make the city of Vasco da Gama as the target of aerial, ground and naval fire of the enemy and inevitable consequences on the vicinity and having considered the big difference between the forces and the resources between the two, it does not allow us to continue the fight without great sacrifice to the lives of the inhabitants of the city of Vasco da Gama, I have decided with my spirits well in control and with patriotic spirit present, to contact the enemy whose approach is endangering the population of that city, that I intend to save, in order to attain peace by virtue of the powers conferred on me by the letter of the Command. By virtue of this power I order all the forces under my Command to ceasefire.

I take this opportunity to emphasize the calm and orderly behaviour of all the population of the province since the beginning of the invasion as the continuation of the one, which it has shown always in earlier times

At this moment, I offer homage to those who have fallen on the battlefield.

HQ, VASCO da GAMA,
14:00 hours of 19 th December 1961

Sd/-
General C-in-C
Manuel Antonio Vassalo e Silva.
General

A copy of this communication was sent, at a later date to the Secretary General of National Defence with the report of the Governor, dated 22nd December 1961.

The General suggested to proceed to the HQ at Alparqueiros where he reached around 14 45 hours, with the officers of the Q. G. and the Commander of Agrupamento Vasco da Gama.

After an hour, the first troops of the Indian Army appeared in the area of Goa Shipyard. A Major and later on a Colonel with their respective bodyguards came to the Alparqueiros establishment and met the General Comandante Chefe.

After discussions, the Adjutant of the Command Captain Portela Ribeiro was ordered to accompany an Indian Officer in order to gather some of our forces still occupying positions, and other isolated groups that made part of the Agrupamento. Major Cardeira da Silva also participated in this mission.

On the 20th General Chaudhury, Commander-in-Chief of operating forces came to HQ of Alparqueiros to talk to General Vassalo e Silva. The Indian General had arrived by helicopter. The Governor was awaiting him in a room, where Captain Carlos Azeredo was also present as official interpreter. When General Chaudhury appeared at the door, the General Vassalo e Silva moved to stand up. However he was not allowed to do so, pressing him down after putting his hand on his shoulder and forcing him to remain seated. He pulled a chair and sat before him. The conversation was short. He started it by saying that he had come to wish him and to know if he needed anything or he wanted any special treatment. The Governor thanked him and said that he wished to be treated like his other men.

General Chaudhury in the course of the talk revealed that the wife of General Vassalo e Silva was well and safe and that the Indian Government was trying its best to send her to Lisbon on the coming Thursday. He added further that he wanted to congratulate him for the combats that had taken place in Mapuca, Bicholim, Diu and Daman. Despite the scarce means the Portuguese had reacted well against the action by the Indian Troops. Further he said that he had ordered the prisoners from Diu to be evacuated to Goa. He

ended the meeting saying that if he wanted anything he could request the Indian Official- the Camp Commander. At the end, when he was already on his feet, General Chaudhury cordially shook the hand of General Vassalo e Silva and left the room. [143]

Captured Portuguese Troops

Summary of the action set off by Indian forces in Goa (Portuguese Version)

It is not possible to indicate with exactness the strength of the Indian armed forces that took part in the invasion of Goa, nor that of units that constituted it and the means used by them. However the information was gathered from the clippings in the Indian newspapers, from the direct observation of facts and from contacts with the Indian Officers in the Prisoner's Camp.[144]

1- The effective strength and commands

It is understood that the effective strength used against Goa had been around 45000 men and 25000 reserves, with the support of men of 'State Reserve Police' (SRP), Naval and Air forces.

The Command of operating troops was under the following officers:

—Commander-in-Chief of all the operations—Lt. General J. N. Chaudhury.

—Commander of the Air Force—Air Vice Marshal E. W.Pinto (Rosario.)

—Commander of Naval Forces—Rear Admiral R. S. Soman.

—Commander of Land Forces—Major General K. P. Candeth

2-The units used

(A) Air Force

Used helicopters; reconnaissance planes; fighter planes and fighter-bombers.

It was found that Canberra bombers, Vampire and Mystere. fighters were used

(B) Naval Force

Participated in the direct action against Goa the following naval units:

—Command ship INS MYSORE under the command of Capt. Cameron.

—Frigate Trishul

—3 frigates and 3 Destroyers not identified. The first two units were used for the bombardment and conquest of the Island of Angediv.

(C) Land Forces

Northern front

50th Parachute Brigade, consisting of four battalions acting as Infantry troops, under the command of Brigadier Sagat Singh, reinforced with units of Armoured Corps, Artillery and Amphibious Vehicles

—Forces of SRP (Strength unknown)

Eastern Front

—17th Infantry Division of which the following brigades were identified:

—63rd Brigade of Infantry (Sikh Light Infantry Brigade) under the command of Brigadier Kulwant Singh.

—48th Brigade of Infantry (48th Brigade of Guards)

Southern Front

—Motorised and mechanized units of unknown strength.

—Also the following units were noticed, however it is not known from which front they entered our territory:

—8th Cavalry

—Machine Gun Regiment

—Kumaon Regiment

—Bihar Regiment

3- Weapons

From the variety of weapons used the following were identified:

—Smith Wesson Revolvers

—Lee-Enfield Rifles and Carbines

—Sten Guns

—Grenade throwing attachment Mills for rifles–2 per section

—Anti –tank grenade throwing attachment –2 per section

—Telescopic attachment for sniper guns-1 per section

—LMG guns

—Heavy machine gun –Browning

—Mortars 60.81 and 10.7cm

—Bazookas 1 per section

—Recoilless guns 10.6 cm, mounted on jeeps

—Units of AMX and SHERMAN tanks

—Artillery units 8.8 and heavy

—Units of amphibious tanks

4—Enemy Operations in Goa[145]

(A) Preliminary operations.

Movements of reconnaissance patrols, which penetrated in our territory from the northern frontier in the evening of 16th December around 22:00 hours and on 17th, especially in the region of Sinquervale, Maulinguem, Patardeu and Foquirpato' (these two in the extreme north of the district), preceded the attack

These territorial violations were limited to old posts close to the frontier. Their garrisons had abandoned these posts to retreat to easily defendable positions, as ordered. The posts of Doromarogo and Maulinguem B were attacked on 17th around 14:00 hours. Thus the first encounters took place with the Portuguese Police forces defending the post at Maulinguem B.

The enemy invaded the territory of Goa from the North, East and South, during the early hours of 18th.

The Operations Conducted On 18th December

Around 02:00 hours the enemy forces attacked and destroyed the Doromarogo post and withdrew thereafter[146]*. This was verified and reported by the platoon of E. Rec.1, which was sent there for reconnaissance.*

The main attack started at 04:00 hours with the support of heavy artillery fire on the towns of Bicholim and Assonora.

The 50 Para Brigade augmented with units of armoured vehicles artillery, amphibious vehicles and support from the air force continued the advance, attacking the axis: Maulinguem-Bicholim.

COLUMN "A" *with a strength of a reinforced battalion turned to the east and continued its advance along the axis Bicholim-Mapuca-Betim (opposite Panjim). It went around Assonora from the north threatening to cut the withdrawal of the platoon of E. Rec.1, which was installed in that area and was forced to abandon that position. The attack on Mapuca was pressed on, and it was occupied around 14:00 hours.*

The column reached' Betim by 18:00 hours. The artillery was installed at Alto de Betim and the armoured vehicles took position along Mandovi River, taking advantage of the non-existence of weapons that could have targeted them.

COLUMN "B" *with the strength around a brigade, once Bicholim was occupied, and where the bridge was demolished by our troops at 04:40 hours, continued its advance on Panjim by the axis Bicholim-Piligao-Tonca-Banastarim-Velha Goa and Panjim, reaching Piligao before 12: 00 hours. By 14:00 hours, after bombarding Tonca with artillery and armoured tanks, a part of the column began the river crossing by amphibious vehicles. It installed itself in that region, ready to proceed with the attack on Panjim.*

COLUMN "B" with the elements of 50 Para Brigade, operated by axis Bicholim-Sanquelim-Onda-Usgao in order to join the forces of 17th Division coming from the east, penetrated in the island of Goa by way of Banastarim where the bridge was already destroyed

In coordination with the attack on Bicholim, the SRP forces supported by elements of Army attacked in the early hours, the entire border of Pernem. It had to conduct clean-up operation, occupy this 'concelho' and pin down the platoon of E. Rec 1 in the north of Chapora River. It wanted to prevent the reunion of this platoon with the squadron at Mapuca, but could not do so.

While this was happening in the northern frontier, the following was taking place in the east:

By the virtue of volume of the attacking forces and the declaration to the Indian Press by General Candeth himself, the attack from this front represented the main thrust. It characterized as an important factor –the surprise factor-which the attack from the north did not pretend to assume.

In fact, the concentration of troops in the north and south during the days preceding the invasion was easily known. This could be known from the news given by Goans coming from India, as well as from the noise coming from armoured vehicles and movement of troops near the border, observed by the personnel of our border posts. There was no effort there to hide the preparations for invasion.

On the contrary, the first news received about the arrival of troops in the east did not indicate its importance, its strength, its weapons etc. The later reports only indicated a major military movement in the areas adjacent to the rail lines from Tinai to Londa.

The forces of 17th Division went to their respective bases for attack, only after nightfall on the 17th. The forward elements began the crossing of the frontier some time after 05:00 hours on 18th.

COLUMN "C" *moved along the axis ONOMOD (in India)-Molem-Darbandora-Ponda.*

With the first units of the column there were units of Engineers (miners and sappers), equipped with modern material and prepared to effect rapid clearance of obstacles created by the Portuguese forces. This column reached Candeapar River, 6 kilometres from Ponda around 14:00 hours

COLUMN"D" *moved by the same axis up to Darbandora, and then it moved to the south, to Sanvordem where it harboured in order to attack from the Quepem-Margao route and then, in coordination with Column C, conquer Marmagoa*

COLUMN "E"*moved along axis Polem-Ordonofondo-Canacona-Cuncolim. After reaching Polem around 07:00 hours and arriving at Ordonofondo, it was stopped by forces of E. Rec.4 which caused it some casualties. The platoon was forced to retreat due to bombardment, and moved to Canacona and thereafter to Bali with the remaining elements of E.Rec.4 and a support platoon of C.Cac.10. The enemy continued its advance up to Cuncolim and then it stopped.*

In cooperation and complementing with the attacks carried out by land forces, which invaded Goa from north, east, and south the following operations were executed by naval and air forces:

—At 06:30 hours on 18th, the Cruiser Mysore and Frigate Trishul bombarded Angediv Island where they landed troops and occupied it after suffering considerable casualties.

—On the same day, between 07:00 and 08:00 hours, a squadron of 'Canberra' attacked Dabolim airport, bombarded the runway from a height of approximately 3000 metres. This height was beyond the range of the 4 cm anti- aircraft guns trying to protect the airport

—At the same time, jet fighter planes bombarded the radio station at Bambolim and put it out of order.

—The attack on 'Aviso Afonso de Albuquerque' anchored in the port of Marmagoa commenced just before 12:00 hours. Three frigates impeded it as it came out of the port. The Portuguese Aviso answered and hit two enemy frigates, which abandoned the combat. However, it surrendered later on.

The Enemy Situation at the End of Day 18

—In the north, the 50 Para occupied the right bank of Mandavi River with positions at Betim, Piligao and Tonca,[147] and was preparing to begin the bombardment of Panjim with aircraft, artillery and armoured vehicles and launch thereafter an attack from the north and east on the Island of Goa

—In the centre, the 17th Division occupied the region of Ponda and Sanvordem, and was preparing itself to cross the Zuari River at Borim and Sanvordem.

—In the South, column E had retired to a position to the south of Cuncolim and had harboured there.

—Absolute air and naval control completed the encirclement of Portuguese forces.

Operations Conducted On Day 19 December

On Day 19 December it was observed that[148]

On the Northern front

—Around 08:00 hours the first elements of 50 Para Brigade, supported by air force, began the crossing of Mandavi River and occupied Panjim, followed by the Island of Goa.

On the eastern front, which by now had moved to the centre of the territory the following was observed:

—During the night of 18/19 the "All India Radio" Transmitting Station announced the threat of bombardment of the city of Vasco da Gama in case the resistance continued.

—Around 11:00 hours, the column C began the crossing of Zuari River at Borim, where the bridge was destroyed by Portuguese forces. The firm 'Chowgule' provided their ore transporting barges for these crossings. They also provided on the left bank their trucks for transporting the attacking forces. Then the column continued their advance towards Margao.

—The column D consisting mainly of artillery and armoured vehicles of the Division, crossed during this morning the Zuari River at Sanvordem and continued its progress via Quepem, in the direction of Margao

—From the early hours of the morning of the 19th the foot columns of army and SRP had entered from the south east, and begun clean-up operations and occupation of conquered territory.

—In this way the conditions were created for launching the final assault on the defensive nucleus concentrated in Marmagoa, once the Agrupamento Afonso de Albuquerque had surrendered by the middle of the morning of this day.

—Around 15:45 hours the first Indian troops arrived in the Vasco da Gama zone and the Portuguese troops installed in that area surrendered to them.

The official Portuguese surrender was conducted in a formal ceremony held at 2030 on 19 December when Governor General Manuel

António Vassalo e Silva signed the instrument of surrender bringing to an end 451 years of Portuguese Rule in Goa.

In all, 4668 personnel were taken prisoner by the Indians - a figure which included military and civilian personnel, Portuguese, Africans and Indians (Goans). This comprised 3412 prisoners in Goa, 853 in Daman and 403 in Diu.

The war had lasted two days. India lost 34 killed and 51 wounded. Portugal lost 31 killed, 57 wounded, and 4668 captured.

Those Indian forces who served within the disputed territories for 48 hours, or flew at least one operational sortie during the conflict, received a General Service Medal 1947 with the *Goa 1961* bar.

References:

121—C.A.Morais-Queda da India Portuguesa-p-74
122—Ibid-p-74
123—Ibid-p-81
124—Ibid-p-84
125—Ibid-p-86
126—Ibid-p-89
127—Ibid-p-90
128—Ibid-p-98
129—Ibid-p-100
130—Ibid-p-102
131—Ibid-p-104
132—Ibid-p-120
133—Ibid-p-121
134—Ibid-p-124
135—Ibid-p-125
136—Ibid-p-126
137—Ibid-p-127
138—Ibid-p-136
139—Ibid-p-141

140—Ibid-p-144
141—Ibid-p-149
142—Ibid-p-150
143—Ibid-p-151
144—Ibid-p-173
145—Ibid-p-177
146—Ibid-p-178
147—Ibid-p-180
148—Ibid-p-181

CHAPTER XII

OPERATIONS IN DAMAN AND DIU

Preparations

The original plan had been to begin the operations in Daman some time after the operations in Goa had started or were over, so the morale effect of the Portuguese defeat in Goa could be exploited. However, it was decided finally to have the same D-Day and the same H-Hour for starting the operations in all the three sectors–Goa, Daman and Diu.[149] This was because it was felt that with the confusion that would occur at the Portuguese Army Headquarters if all the enclaves were attacked at the same time, an advantage would accrue to the attacking Indian Forces. This was the reason responsible for the change of decision. First Battalion of the Maratha Light Infantry, also known as "*JUNGI PALTAN*" was selected for operations in Daman.

This unit was stationed in Poona when Lt. Gen. Chaudhury issued the warning order on 30th November, 1961, to the CO of the battalion to get ready for operations in Daman. The news was received with great enthusiasm, men were recalled from leave and preparations begun for the task allotted. The task at this stage, and even till some days later, was merely to "contain Daman" and occupy it if possible. An advance party of the battalion was ordered to move out to Vapi area southeast of Daman in Indian Territory by road on 11th December. The rest of the battalion traveled by train in the afternoon of 12th December. After passing through Bombay the special train arrived at Vapi in the early hours of 13th December, and the troops detrained silently in order not to alarm the people, particularly the Portuguese agents in Vapi.

By using the order " contain" it was hoped that even if the order leaked out to the Portuguese, they would think that no immediate attack was intended and would not therefore intensify their defence preparations.

When the decision to start simultaneous operations in all Portuguese enclaves was taken, the task of the battalion was consequently changed from "containing" to "occupation" of Daman. Since the advance party had no information of this change, the place selected by them for camping of the battalion was an exposed one. The earlier idea was to merely make a "show" of force and threaten the enemy from the border areas where the Portuguese could see the concentration of the force. With the change in plan, now it was necessary to maintain secrecy to achieve surprise regarding the point and time of entry into Portuguese territory. That was the reason why the troops detrained silently and moved to an area six kilometres on the Nagar-Haveli road during the dark hours before daybreak on the 13th morning.

The battalion was to function directly under the command of the Headquarters Southern Command, and certain other troops like a battery of artillery, an Air Control team etc., were put under its command to make it a full fledged battalion group.

Reconnaissance was started the same day and it was revealed that apart from 18 or 20 outposts established along the border, the Portuguese had taken adequate measures in Nani Daman and Moti Daman to meet the threat from the Indian side. No exact information regarding the defensive positions in and around the town was available.

The Portuguese dispositions for the defence of Daman as revealed later by the Governor of Daman were as follows:

(i) Four rifle platoons were guarding the approaches leading to Nani Daman from the north and north-east;

(ii) Two rifle platoons were guarding the approach from the south to Moti Daman and there were two more rifle platoons and artillery batteries in the big fort in Moti Daman where the Governor had his headquarters;

(iii) Road Kunta-Wadkund and the airfield area was heavily mined;

(iv) 81 mm mortars were deployed in the small fort and Nani Daman and later shifted to a temple area in the heart of the town.

There was a hill on the border called Hill 365, the western slopes of which were in Daman area and were of tactical importance as they dominated the airfield, which was one of the first two objectives of the battalion group. The eastern slopes of the hill, being in Indian Territory, afforded cover to move up to the border and facilitated reconnaissance from vantage points. A suitable "forming up" place for the troops before launching the attack was also selected in the area of the eastern slopes.

The Plan

Based on the information gathered from reconnaissance and other sources, a plan of operations[150] in four phases was prepared.

The salient features of this plan were as under:

(a) A rumour was to be spread through our police and other civilian officials that the force that had arrived was only an advance party of a brigade that was expected to arrive any day. This was done successfully, and, as later ascertained from the enemy, they believed that a force of approximately 5000 and some tanks had finally assembled.

(b) A deception party of about 30 or 40 infantry soldiers and State Reserve Police with one section of 3-inch mortars were to threaten Moti Daman from the south and destroy all Portuguese border outposts on that side in the first phase.

(c) The four phases of the real attack and occupation were as follows:

Phase 1: Hill 365 was to be reached in darkness on the night of the 17th. From the forming up place here, the main thrust was to be launched by A and D Companies, also in darkness, to capture Dudetha grove (NR 835895), post-175 (NR 857901) and to secure the Flight Control Tower and the airfield.

Phase 2: After completion of Phase I, the force was to swing southward and capture the northern edge of the garden north of Nani Daman by first light.

Phase 3: Capture of Nani Daman or the north fort.

Phase 4: Once Nani Daman was secured and if the Portuguese decided to fight from Moti Daman, the town and fort on the south bank, two companies of the battalion were to be moved by mechanical transport via Vapi, Pathar Punj and Bhamti to take the Moti Daman fort from the south.

(d) The artillery and Air Force were to come into action only after first light when surprise was lost.

It will be seen that the smooth execution of the Plan depended largely on two factors:

1—Complete surprise up to the completion of the second phase and

2— Very little or -no opposition by the enemy. The plan thus erred slightly on the optimistic side, but this was due no doubt to faulty intelligence which had underestimated the Portuguese strength and preparedness.

The Portuguese strength in Daman was estimated, on the basis of intelligence reports, at about 360 all ranks in addition to some police and customs personnel along the border. This was an underestimation, as actually they had 23 officers and 544 other ranks (white). The Portuguese had also some 25-pounder guns, mortars and many medium machine guns, all of which they used. The defending ground forces of the Portuguese were thus almost at par with the attacking forces of the Maratha Group. Added to this was the natural advantage enjoyed by a defender fighting on his own ground. Moreover, the Portuguese Commanders in Daman and Diu put up a much stiffer opposition.

Fort of Daman

THE DETAILED PLAN OF ATTACK

1 Maratha 00 No 1, 15 Dec 61
(No change from verbal orders issued on 14 Dec 61)[151]

Maps: Bombay-Daman Map line to a mile Sheet No 46 D/15 and D/11

INFO

1(a) Enemy

Approximately 3 Coys (360 Portuguese) strength located in DAMAN. In addition there are approx 200 police and 30 customs guards living in the outposts along the border. The outposts are suspected to be mined. Enemy is lightly equipped and does not seem to have organised defense. Some families have been evacuated from GOA and DAMAN recently. There is no info about special arms.

(i) Own troops have been concentrated for occupation of Goa and Diu
(ii) IN will be blockading the port of DAMAN but will not support our operations
(iii) Four Mysteres ex BOMBAY will be available in the form of arranged sorties,
(iv) The following troops have been placed under comd 1MARATHA:
-23 Bty 9 Field Regt
-Two Otter aircraft
-One ad hoc Lt (light) ADS
One ACT (Air Control Team)
SRP (if allotted).

Intention

2. 1 MARATHA and attached tps will capture DAMAN by...(date/ time to be notified later)

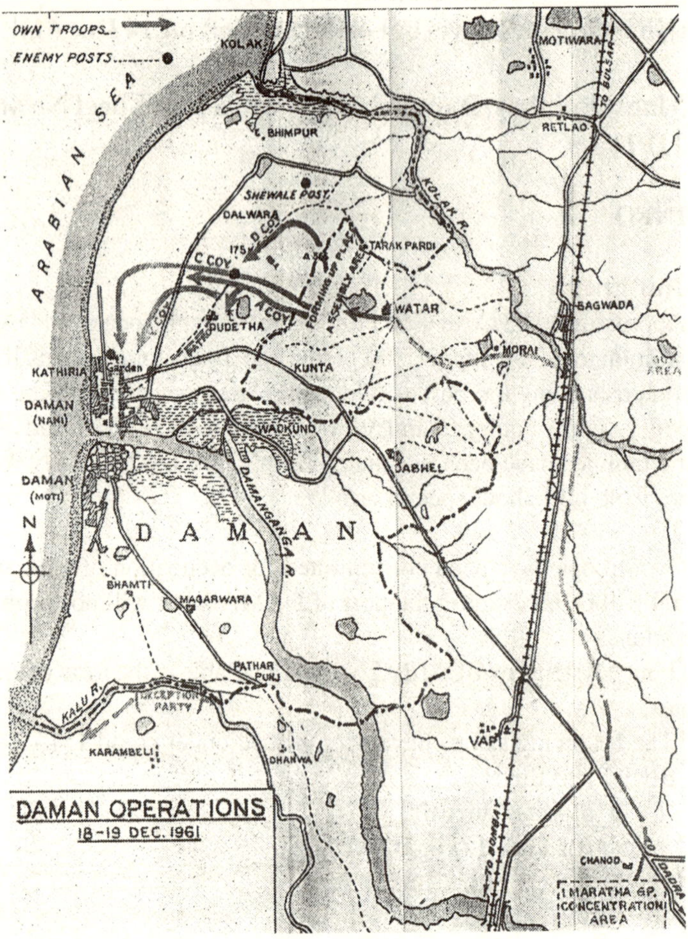

The Map showing the plan of attack on Daman

Lt. Col. S.J.S. Bhonsale, Commander of 1 Maratha at Daman

METHOD

Gen outline

3 Attack will be carried out in four phases.

Phase I

4 Capture of DUDETHA grove NR 855895 incl flight control tower and post175 NR 857001 by A and D Coys.

Phase II

5 Capture of the northern edge of garden SOUTH of the airfd from NR 832885 to NR 840886 by C Coy.

Phase III

6 Capture of NANI DAMAN by Y and C Coys

Phase IV

7 Capture of MOTI DAMAN by A and Y Coys.

Phase I

8 **Tps**

Left	A Coy
	Under Comd

FOO
MFC
Det A tank 6 per gun
Detachment sniper

9 **OBJECTIVE**

A Coy	DUDETHA grove NR 852892 incl flight control tower.
D Coy	post NR 857901.

10 RESERVE

Left	Y Coy

Right C Coy

11 BOUNDARY

HANUMAN post NR 864888 to flying Control NR 844898 to A Coy

12 AA

Mango grove WEST of WATER lake sq 8989

13 FUP (forming up place)

Hill 365 (own side) NR 872904. Protection by SRP.

14 ROUTE

Present posn to cross rd NR 931810 thence to MORAI and along trench to Mango grove on to Hill 365 NR 872904.

15 SL

International boundary from Nr 864888 to 872907.

16 AXIS

D Coy along right spur sq 8690 to obj.

A Coy from international boundary on to depression sq 8689 to objective.

17 Rate of advance

100 yds in 4 min (subject to confirmation depending on H hr)

18 Obstacles

No maj obstacles known in the area except wire and mines near outposts.

19 Reserve

a. Tps
   Y Coy
   C Coy.
b. Doc
   F UP.

(C) Tasks

Reinforce assaulting Coys if required and capture objs

20 **Action on capture of obj**

(a) Reorg in

Reorganise in areas captured. Exploit area upto airfd. Hold the ground until further orders.

(b) Move of reorg stores and supporting arm

F echelon vehicles can be called for from Bn HQ when required.

21 **Success Sig**

Green over green over green Verey lt. Codeword GANPAT on wrls.

22 **Time**

H hr—codeword 'SHIVAJI' followed by time

Phase II

23 **Troops**

C Coy with under comd FOO and det sniper.

24 **Objective**

Northern edge of the garden SOUTH of the airfd.

25 **Reserve**

Y Coy

26 **BOUNDARY**

Main airstrip excl 'C' Coy

27 AA

KUNTA sq 8688.

28 **FUP** (Forming up place)

DUDETHA grove

29 **SL**

Rd DAMAN-DALWARA.

30 **AXIS**

HANUMAN post NR 864888 to lake and thence to rd and across the strip to ob

31 **Rate of adv**

100 yds in 4 min

32 **Reserve**

(a) Tps

Y Coy

(b) Loc

KUNTA thence mov to DUDETHA grove on order from the CO

(c) Tasks

Reinforce C Coy if required

33 **Action on capture of obj**

(a) Reorg

Reorg in area captured. Exploit area upto 500 yds of the town.

(b) Move of Reorg stores and supporting arms

F ech vehs can be called for from Bn HQ when required.

34 **Success sig**

Green over red over green. Codeword GITA on wrls.

35 **Time**

H hr not before H+60 on codeword CUBBY followed by time.

PHASE III

36 **Tps**

Left ...Y Coy

Right ...C Coy

37 **Obj**

Y Coy ...Area Camp sq 8387

C Coy ...Fort NR 83187

38 **Res**
Left ...A Coy
Right ...D Coy les

39 **Bdv**
Rd running from NORTH to SOUTH sq 8489

40 **AA**
Y Coy ...DUDHETA grove
C Coy ...Northern edge of the garden.

41 **FUP**
Southern edge of the airfield.

42 **SL**
Fwd edge of FUP.

43 **Axis**
Straight from NORTH to SOUTH

44 **Rate of advance**
100 yds in 2 min.

45 **Ras**

(a) **Tps**
A Coy
D Coy less one pl.

(b) **Loc**
A Coy—DUDETHA grove.
D Coy less one pl to mov to northern edge of the garden on codeword ‘PENY’. Move to be carried by smoke provided by A and C Coys. A tank detachment will move with Coy.

(c) **Tasks**
SP attack and reinforce if required.

46 **Action on capture of obj**
a. Reorg

Reorg in areas captured.
b. Mov of reorg stores and supporting arms
F ech vehs will mov fwd on call/receipt of success sig.
(C) Exploitation
Exploit upto north bank of river DAMAN GANGA.

47 **Success sig**
Red over red over red Verey lt. Codeword GOURI on wrls.

48 **Time**
H hr not before H+240 on codeword TANAJI followed by time

PHASE IV

49 **Tps**
Left—A Coy
Right—Y Coy.

50 **Obj**
FORT MOTI DAMAN

51 **Res**
D Coy less one pl.

52 **Bdv**
Rd

53 **FUP**
WEST of BHAMTI sq 8384.

54 **SL**
Fwd edge of BHAMTI sq 8384

55 **Axis**
SOUTH to NRTH along with coastal garden of Khaji trees.

56 **Rate of adv**
100 yds in 2 min.

57 **Res**
a.Tps
D Coy less one pl.
b.Task
Reinforce.

58 **Action on capture of obj**
(a) Reorg
Area FORT MOTI DAMAN.
(b)Exploitation
(c) Exploitation area upto South bank of the river DAMANGANGA.

59 **Success Sig**
Red over green over red verey lt. Codeword GAJANAN on wrls.

60 **Time**
H hr not before H+360. Codeword SHAHAJI followed by time

Gen all phases

61 **Flank Protection**
SRP if allotted to protect eastern flank

62 **Pioneers**
Phase I
One pnr aslt sec each with A and D Coys. Destroy outpost NR 854898 on orders from Co.

Phase II
One pnr aslt sec with C Coy.

Phase III
One pnr aslt sec each Y and C Coys.

Phase IV
One pnr aslt sec each A and Y Coys.

63 **Mortars**

Loc

(a) Pl less one sec—sq 8789. Should be prepared to mov to post 175.

(b) One section under comd deception force comdr in area INDRAGAD FORT.

(C) One MFC each with A and D Coys for phase I.

64 **A Tank Platoon**

Loc

TARAK PARDI NR 883907.

Task

One det each to mov to post 175 and DUDETHA grove on capture and thence accompany D Coy.

65 **Artillery**

(a) Gun areas

(i) Phase I, II and III

Area E 9215 N 9050 ht 350 ft sq 9290.

(ii) Phase IV

Sq 8780.

(b) Task

Timed programme and concs n call on known and likely enemy posns. To engage both forts (NANI and MOTI).

(c) Fire plan

66 **AIR**

(a) **Task**

On call engagement of both FORTS, military barracks, troops and vehicle concentrations. Fighter aircrafts will fly over the area at 0700 hrs and thereafter every two hrs.

(b) **Method of demand**

ACT will accompany CO's party. Request from fwd coy comdrs to be made to CO.

67 **H Hr**

Codeword SHIVAJI followed by time.

68 **Deception**

(a) **Comdr**

Lt. RM BISWAS

(b) **Tps**

One Pl incl one sec 3 inch Mor.
One Coy SRP (if allotted).

(c) **Task**

(i) Destroy posts JAMPUR NR 817822 KADU sq 8382 and JHARI NR 8682 by 1st lt D-day.

(ii) Prepare for a point attack on MOTI DAMAN.

(iii) Dominate the southern border by active patrolling.

(iv) Hold northern and western slopes of INDRAGAD Fort.

69 **Movement**

For mov of tps and timing from conc area to AA.

ADM

70 **RAP**

LOC

Phase I and II ...KUNTA sq 8688

Phase III ...post 175

Phase IV ...PALSAT sq 8582

71 **CP**

Loc

Phase I, II, III ...NR 925878

Phase IV ...NR 906764

72 **Lt ADS**

Loc area IB VAPI NR 920820.

73 **Evac f casualties**

Evac of cas from R.P. t Lt ADS NR 920820 by jeep/amb car. An Auster airstrip has been constr in area sq 9179 for evac of casualties. Arrangements have been made to evac casualties by rail beyond ADS

74 **Rations**

One meal and two tea rations will be carried in haversack.

75 **Water**

Water bottles will be filled. Water sterilizing tablets will be carried under sec arrangements.

76 **Transport**

Will be allotted

77 **Ammunition**

(a) **Pouch**

Pouch amn will be carried on person/with weapon.

(b) **Unit reserve**

Auth scale from unit res will be carried in 'F' ech tpt. The remaining unit res will be carried in 'A' ech tpt.

(c) Second line amn
Will be kept in adm Base or 'B' ech.

78 **Special points**

(a) Treatment of all Portuguese forces captured/surrendered will be under the normal usage f war.
(b) PW will be sent to Bn HQ and if in large nos will be kept in the same area under guard. Adjt will segregate the PW into three groups: Portuguese, Africans, and Indo-Portuguese.
(c) Women and children will be protected
(d) Wanton killing/looting will be avoided/prevented.
(e) Political parties will be avoided.
(f) Poor and innocent people may have t be given protection and safegd their interest from the hooligans and any other interested parties/people.
(g) On capture of DAMAN, it will be adm by Army until handed over to the civ auth.

INTERCOMN

(h) Loc HQ

Bn HQ. ...	......MORAI sq 9188
CO's Party	... ...Phase I and II.... FUP post NR 871897
	Phase III......... Post NR 857901
	Phase IV..........PALSAT sq 8582.
Adm base	NR 951774. On capture of DAMAN mov to CHALA sq 9083.

79 **Method of intercomn**

(a) Line

Line will be laid from Bn HQ to FUP hill and post NR 857901

(b) Wrls

The Offensive

By 14th December, all the units which were to take part in Daman operations, had arrived in the concentration area. On 17th December, D-Day (18th December) was intimated, followed by permission to launch the offensive[152]. The same evening, the battalion moved to the assembly area near Watar, and from there, after a little rest, to the forming up place. Exactly two hours after midnight, A and D Companies crossed the border and advanced towards their objectives; A Company toward the Flight Control Tower (FCT) and 'D' Company to post –175. Both were expected to capture their objectives by 04:00 hours.

As A Company closed in on the FCT, it met with stiff resistance in the vicinity of the tower. After a brief action in which one Portuguese was killed, A Company captured the tower at 04:00 hours, and with it a few prisoners, guns and a considerable quantity of ammunition. Leaving one platoon in control of the tower, the company moved into the Dudetha Grove. The brief action near the FCT had alerted the Portuguese, the surprise was gone and the enemy posts all along the border opened up with rifle and medium machine gun fire. Since surprise was lost, the battery of 9 Field regiment opened fire on the Big Fort at 04:10 hours with high explosives, and fired 150 rounds, which completely disrupted the enemy's wireless communications with the rest of the world. D Company which had been moving somewhat slowly towards its objective, now quickened its pace and attacked and captured post-175 at 05:15 hours. This action completed the Phase I of the operations.

Phase II began immediately after first light when two Mystere aircraft of the Indian Air Force arrived and fired rockets on the Big Fort directed by the air control team (ACT) on the ground. Their targets were the gun and mortar positions from which flashes had been seen when the firing had begun early in the morning. Meanwhile A and D Companies were firming up in their positions preparatory to further moves in pursuance of Phase II.

Once A and D Companies had consolidated and the latter had relieved the platoon of A Company at Flight Control Tower, 'C' Company was ordered to move forward through the area between A and D Companies and cross the airstrip for the subsequent advance southward. By 09:00

hours this company had reached the Flight Control Tower and having cleared a small enemy pocket near the airfield, the men crossed the airfield one by one and commenced their advance southwards on to the garden north of Nani Daman. The advance was very slow, as the enemy MMGs and mortars from the garden as well as the coastal area were firing at this company effectively. However the advance continued inch by inch.

Meanwhile, a small group consisting of the Battalion Commander's party, the Battery Commander and the air control team moved across the country in three jeeps to get to post 175 where D Company had consolidated. When these jeeps had entered approximately 1.6 kilometres inside enemy territory and were driving along the northern edge of Hill 365, an unknown post from NR 871919 fired upon them. Intense fire was directed on this small party, with two of the bullets hitting the CO's jeep. Considering it unwise to expose them in the open any longer, these jeeps followed a small dry nullah bed, climbed on to the northern slopes of Hill 365 and reached post-175 by a hazardous route on which normally a jeep would not ply.

Meanwhile, the Mystere aircraft were flying at regular intervals of two hours with intensive strafing and rocket firing. A total of 14 sorties were flown and tactical targets attacked in the north and south forts, barracks, gun positions, MMG bunkers and strong points adjacent to the airfield.

After C Company had crossed the airfield, Y Company, which had meanwhile reached Dudetha grove, was moving forward and began to advance with the road (control tower –Daman) on its left and airfield on the right. This was at about 11:30 hours. A Company, which saw this move of Y Company, sent a strong platoon patrol forward in the direction of road-junction 841884 to protect the left flank of Y Company. When this platoon was exposed, the enemy brought down MMG and mortar fire on it and thus inflicted many casualties. Due to heavy small arms and MMG fire pouring from the gun-post at NR 831888 Y and C companies were held up and could not make much progress towards the garden. Thereupon the guns of the Indian battery (9 Field Regiment) engaged this gun-post from two directions and neutralized it by 12:00 hours. After this bombardment both Y and C Companies resumed their advance at 13:00 hours. When fire began to emerge from another enemy post located at NR 839884 it too was engaged by the Indian battery.

The opposition before the Indian troops began to weaken after 14:00 hours, as a result of artillery action and aerial strafing of the gun-posts. Y and C Companies started advancing again and finally reached the garden area south of the airfield between 16:00 and 17:00 hours. Once again the advance was halted due to 81 mm mortars and heavy machine gun fire from the town area.

By this time all the companies were tired and badly needed water and ammunition. The artillery's wireless communication with the forward observation officers was not working satisfactorily as the batteries had gone down, and there was only about an hour and half of daylight left. The Battalion Commander had to decide whether to:

(a) Withdraw the two forward companies to the safe area of post-175 for the night and lose the ground gained during the day's fighting or

(b) Move up the remaining two companies closer to the forward companies and remain somewhat exposed to enemy attack at night.

After careful deliberation, the Co made his decision in favour of course (b),

The Commanding Officer visited the two forward companies and ordered them to firm in for the night in the garden. The rear companies were moved up to the Flight Control tower Area. The telephone line was brought up to the forward position and plans were made for the advance next morning. Hot meals were served to the troops, casualties evacuated and treated and the night was spent in patrolling and making other preparations.

The deception force that had operated south of Moti Daman, and done a good job in creating the false impression of attack coming from the south, was also recalled to join the main force. This small force

Surrender document

I, Major Antonio Jose da Costa Pinto, Governor of Daman, hereby surrender unconditionally to the Indian Forces at 08:30 hrs on 19th Dec. 1961, at the outskirts of Nani Daman[154]

Major
Governor of Daman

Received on 19th Dec 61 at 08:30 hours personally

Commander Task Force Daman

(S.J.S.BHONSALE)
Lt Col

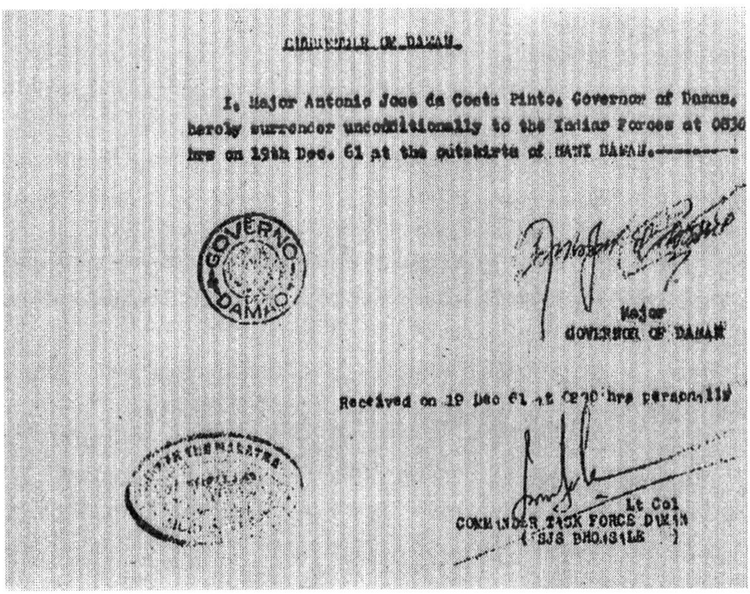
I, Major Antonio Jose da Costa Pinto, Governor of Daman, hereby surrender unconditionally to the Indian Forces at 0830 hrs on 19th Dec. 61 at the outskirts of NANI DAMAN.---------

Major
GOVERNOR OF DAMAN

Received on 19 Dec 61 at 0830 hrs personally

Lt Col
COMMANDER TASK FORCE DAMAN
(SJS BHONSLE)

Surrender Document

came in very handy during the night for patrolling and similar duties.

Later on the Portuguese Governor of Daman confirmed that he believed even after the aerodrome and post-175 in the north had been lost to the Indian forces that the main thrust was to come from the south on Moti Daman. The occasional shelling of the Big Fort and the constant harassment deceived them from guessing the direction of the main thrust.

19 December—Surrender

On the morning of the 19th, however, there was no fighting. It seems the Portuguese had had enough and perhaps the news had reached them that no opposition was being offered in Goa. This news might have demoralized them considerably. Two Mystere aircrafts came up at 07:45 hours and fired rockets at the Big Fort and at the guns in the area of a temple inside the town. The Portuguese in Daman surrendered half an hour later just when a ground attack was about to be launched.

The Governor, Major Antonio Jose da Costa Pinto, who himself was wounded, signed an unconditional surrender at 08:30 hours.[153.] He was stretchered to the airfield as Indians were only willing to accept the surrender from him·

Approximately 600 Portuguese soldiers (including 24 officers) were taken prisoner. The Indians suffered 4 dead and 14 wounded, while the Portuguese suffered 10 dead and 2 wounded.

The 1st Light Maratha Infantry was decorated for the battle with one VSM for the CO, two Sena Medals and five Mentioned in Dispatches.[[50]

By 11:00 hours on 19th December, the town of Daman was occupied by the Indian troops, and approximately 600 white soldiers, seven 25-pounder guns, eight 81-mm mortars, many MMGs small arms and ammunition were captured. The people of Daman had, unlike the people of Goa, passed through two very anxious days during which they had witnessed intense exchange of artillery, mortar and machine gun fire, in addition to the flying warplanes coming above their town at regular intervals. Due to these events they might have been shaken a bit. A few civilians had also suffered in the bombardment of the Portuguese gun positions. When they saw their lords and masters of several centuries defeated, they were so stupefied that they were frightened of the Indian army men. They did not come out of their houses to greet their liberators, as was the case in Goa. The army, however, promptly took up the work of supplying the daily and immediate needs of the public by bringing in supply of fresh vegetables, fruits, etc., from Vapi. One by one the shops began to open and the transport services between Vapi and Daman began to operate.

It was noticed that the Portuguese garrison in Daman were made of sterner stuff than their counterparts in Goa, and were determined to put up as much resistance as they could. They were helped in this by the open nature of the country in which they could see the movements of the Indian troops from a distance. The Portuguese Governor revealed that their original instructions were "to fight to the last man and round". The wireless link with Goa having been destroyed on the morning of the 18th, Daman received no fresh instructions either from Goa or Lisbon.

The factors contributing to their demoralization and capitulation were no doubt the accurate air strikes and artillery shoots, and also the feeble opposition their compatriots put up during the first day's fighting in Goa. They must have heard on the radio on the evening of the 18th or morning of the 19th.

The Maratha advance was slow; firstly owing to the considerable opposition and secondly due to the fact that the enemy strength had been underestimated. The Maratha battalion had limited air support, and had to move through open country. Despite the odds it had reached the outskirts of the town by the evening of the first day, and the Portuguese must have realized that it was poised for a decisive attack the next morning.

The casualties on both sides were as under;

INDIAN

	JCO	Soldiers
Killed	1	3
Wounded	1	13
Total	2	16

PORTUGUESE

	Officers	Soldiers
Killed	1	7
Wounded	-	9
Total	1	16

PRISONERS

Portuguese Officers	24
Portuguese Soldiers	544
Portuguese Police	9
Local Police	268
Portuguese Civilians	8
TOTAL	853

The Defence Of Daman

(Portuguese Version)

After the annexation of our territory of Dadra and Nagar Haveli by the Indian Union, in 1954, the district of Daman, situated near to the coast in the Bay of Cambay, 160 kilometres to the north of Bombay, was reduced to an area of around 50 square kilometres, with a population of approximately 22300 inhabitants.

In the north it is bound by the river Coileque, in the south by river Calem and to the east by the Indian Union. It is divided into

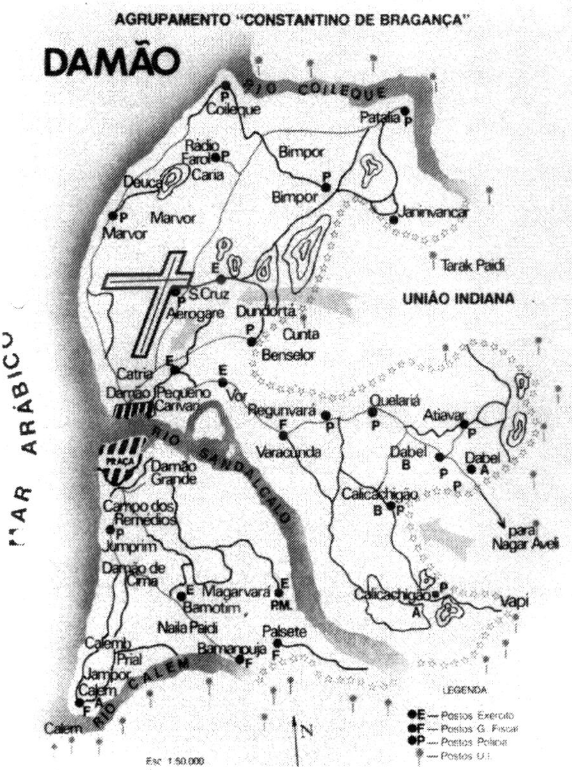

AGRUPAMENTO
"CONSTANTINO DE BRAGANCA"

two distinct zones by the river Sandalcalo or Damanganga. The one at the north is known as Damao-Pequeno and the one in the south is Damao-Grande[155]

AGRUPAMENTO "CONSTANTINO de BRAGANCA"

The Agrupamento of Daman designated as "Constantino de Braganca"[156] *was commanded by the Major of infantry Antonio Jose da Costa Pinto who was also the Governor of the district*

a) Effective Strength

It comprised the following:

—The Command H Q

—Companhia de Cacadores No 11 (C. Cac. 11)

—Companhia de Cacadores No 12 (C.Cac.12)

—Bateria de Artilharia No 3(Bat. Art. 3)

It was reinforced with the Police Forces (PEI), and Customs Guards (G.F.) with effective strengths of 200 and 33 men respectively.

The Police occupied 13 posts, which were allotted to them

A-(Coileque—Patalia—Bimpor—Bensel—Regunvara—QuelariaAtiavar—Dabel—CalicachigaoA-Calicachigao

B—Marvor Praia—Radio Farol and Aerogare) with an effective strength of 130 men, and the remaining 70 distributed to the city posts or employed in patrolling in Damao-Grande and Damao-Pequeno.

The Customs Guard occupied the posts in the southern frontier (Jampor—Bamanpuja—Palsete) having only five men in the headquarters.

The Army, which had anti-terrorist duty, had six posts, distributed as follows:

—C.Cac.11: -Serra da Cruz—Bamotim—Posto Militar

—C. Cac.12: -Catria—Vor—Varacunda

Two companies and their respective commands were barracked in Damao-Pequeno

The Battery of Artillery and two platoons of C. Cac 11 were stationed in Damao-Grande.

b) Various Materials, Ammunition and Training:

The weapons were old and heavily used. However the matter of great worry was the availability of ammunition. The hand grenades were not in working condition and were required to be changed. Some were of 1953 vintage and thus were beyond their useful life. The 9 mm ammunition were not good for firing and therefore there were instructions from Q.G. to fire five rounds before the departures of patrols.[157]

Many of the grenades and 80mm mortars would not explode due to the poor condition of firing mechanisms. The ammunition for 'instalaza' rocket launchers was never received despite several requests.

The communication equipment was not in proper condition. The radio link with Goa was by means of the civilian postal station (CTT), from the Police post belonging to the PEI network and from the launch "Antares" belonging to Naval Command network. All these were unreliable and could not meet military requirements.

As far as training was concerned the situation was alarming. The units forming the garrison had not done any exercise before their departure to India. Some personnel did not know the weapons, which were distributed just before the beginning of the invasion. They learnt the functioning just then and opened fire. Only the Battery of Artillery 3 had done live firing in the month of November.

c) Normal Organization:

The territory was divided into three sectors[158]

1.Damao-Grande: it was commanded by Captain Felgueiras e Sousa, commandant of Bat.Art.3. There were also two platoons of C.Cac.11, which were guarding the Bamotim bridges and the Posto Militar. They were doing all the garrison service.

2.Eastern Sector of Damao-Pequeno: It was commanded by Captain Gustavo Rebelo de Sousa Commandant of C. Cac 12. This company guarded the posts of Catria, Vor, and Varacunda., and kept watch on the bridges of the same name..

3. Western Sector of Damao-Pequeno: It was commanded by Captain Jose Simoes Faria, Commandant of C. Cac 11. It was guarding the post of Serra da Cruz.

There were three Customs posts (G F) and thirteen police posts (P E I), which would come under the respective commands whenever required.

The Battery of Artillery and two detached platoons were barracked in the buildings inside the 'Praca'. The infantry units were installed in private buildings in the city (Damao-Pequeno), dispersed and without meeting any safety norms.

The Agrupamento 'Constantino de Braganca' had the following mission[159] in case of invasion:

—To retard the enemy advance along the national territory;

—To occupy and defend, at any cost, the last defence posts-Fort of Praca and S. Jeronimo.

In order to fulfill these missions two defensive lines were established. One was at Damao-Grande and the other at Damao-Pequeno, after including in the same some already existing posts looking after anti-terrorist defenses.

A second line was established in Damao-Pequeno, in order to cover the retreat of the former and its move to Damao-Grande.

In this way the defence posts of Praca and S. Jeronimo were occupied- the former by the Army and the latter by elements of PEI.

In Damao-Pequeno, the following points defined the first defensive line:

Praia—Posto de Catria—Posto de Vor—Posto de Varacunda.

The left flank of this line was occupied by two platoons of C. Cac.11 and the right flank by two platoons of C. Cac.12. These forces would retreat only when ordered to and would occupy later on the bulwark of Praca.

However, the forces of the second line installed along the periphery of the city would cover this retreat. It would be constituted of the Police forces on the left flank and by troops of C.Cac.12 in the right flank. The former would retreat to S. Jeronimo Fort when ordered to do so or under pressure and the latter to the Fort of Praca in Damao-Grande.

Here the defensive line was formed from the posts of Jumprim—Water Tank—Mangueiral (mango orchard) –to Sandalcalo River. This means that it followed from Jumprim to the river. This line was occupied by two platoons of C. Cac. 11, one platoon of Bat. Art. (with the infantry role), and the remaining elements of P.E.I.

The remaining forces from B. Art.3 would occupy the fort looking after the previously prepared gunfire plan. It will have two gun positions for anti-tank mission in the Praca, and other two positions in the Cais de Trapiche.

The elements of the border forces of P.E.I. and G.F. would retreat when ordered to do so or in its absence till the ammunition limitations and would concentrate at the previously decided places.

The Command Post (P.C.) will be situated in the Fort of Praca.

These were the general lines of manouevre conceived to face the invasion of the territory.

The violations of airspace by Indian aircrafts began in early December. The reconnaissance planes were overflying our territory at lower heights twice daily without respecting our sovereignty. Meanwhile three helicopters were doing daily reconnaissance along the frontier[160].

At some point of time, an Indian aircraft overflew the runway of our airport. It lowered down the landing gear and remained airborne approximately at a height of thirty metres from the ground. Later on after the invasion, we came to know that it was carrying the Commander and his officer of General Staff who were on reconnaissance mission.

When this incident was referred to the Q. G. in Goa, we were told that we should open fire only when fired upon or whenever there is an attempt at landing. Accordingly one Breda machine gun was mounted on the Airport Tower and the other in the police post situated in that place. Similarly machine guns for anti-aircraft fire were installed on the walls of S. Jeronimo Fort.

News was received on the 8th about the landings of a considerable number of Indian troops at Vapi and Sanjan railway stations. From that date onwards, our patrols and beats to the frontier were intensified. Also visits to the highest points from where the activities in the enemy territory could be observed were undertaken.

It was known that there were 4000 men concentrated around Daman, comprising of elements of the Indian Army and forces of S.R.P. It was also known that the police force in the neiboughering area was reinforced substantially. No uniformed military personnel were seen but it was known later that they were in civilian clothes or in S.R.P. uniform. The enemy was using the posts of Calem and Kunta for observations

On 8th December itself, an anti-aircraft machine gun with thousand rounds of 20 mm caliber bullets was received in Daman. As this weapon was not familiar to the men concerned, a rapid lesson about its functioning was given to them and it was installed in the Praca in order to protect the Artillery positions.

The posts of P.E.I were carefully organized. They had trenches for the personnel in case of an attack and also a small minefield. Due to these security measures organized by the commandant of P.E.I of Daman, Tenente Alberto Ferreira, there were reduced numbers of casualties during the Indian attack.

On 12th and 15th December men wearing khaki uniforms were seen to the south of Bamanpuja at the fort in Indian Territory. It seemed that they were in the process of installing some weapons. Also in the region of Cunta some elements were observed targeting some heavy weapons.

Thus, there were many indications that the enemy was preparing to attack. On the 15th an order was received from Q.G. of Goa that all forces of Agrupamento "Constantino de Braganca" should be on alert. Measures were taken to improve the ground organization and all sensitive access points were closed.

On the same day a message was received from Comandante-Chefe that the diplomatic measures being taken by the Central Government in order to avoid the imminent invasion of our territories had failed. Therefore one could expect an attack from the Indian Union at any moment. That message expressed faith in the responsible behaviour of the military men of the Agrupamento.

The District Governor replied, "All are in their posts, and know to honour the traditions and names of illustrious Portuguese, and with their eyes directed towards these heroes, if required they would wet the soil of the homeland with their blood".

On 16th the Commandant of the Agrupamento together with his deputy, Captain Francisco Soares Ogando made some adjustment in the positions in Damao-Grande. A meeting of officers was called in which the subject of discipline in the face of eminent enemy attack was discussed.

The teams of P.E.I. were placing mines around their posts at the nightfall, and removing them at the daybreak. The hospitals were clearly marked to avoid strafing by Indian aircrafts. The area around ammunition dumps was cleaned to avoid spreading of fires.

4—Action of Agrupamento "Constantino de Braganca"

On 18th December, at two o'clock in the early morning the Indian troops crossed the frontier between the post of Benselor and the village of Janivancar, without having been noticed by our troops. Around 04 00 hours, all the enemy posts located along the frontier, simultaneously opened fire on our positions.[161]

Three Indian companies advanced along our territory and achieved rapidly the line defined by Airport—Dundorta and Benselor. The personnel in the post of the Air Station thought that the approaching troops were elements of P.E.I on a mine laying mission and thus were surprised by the enemy after a small exchange of fire. In this exchange guards Joao Paulo de Noronha and Jovian da Fonseca died while 1° Cabo from C. Cac.11 Francisco Ramos Taveira, and police guards Narciso do Rosario; Joaquim de Albuquerque, Jesus Pereira; Teorico Fernandes; Agostinho Pereira and also a Goan civilian who was meteorologist at the airport were made prisoners. Two guards managed to run away.

While this incident was taking place, the Indian troops were entering our territory by the route of Calicachigao and occupying our post of the agricultural zone.

In view of the above, the Commandant of the Agrupamento immediately rushed to his P.C. and called all the posts by phone and radio. As there was no concrete information about the invasion of the territory, it was believed to be an incident on the border.

Meanwhile, the post of Serra da Cruz informed that it was hearing firing in the neiboughrhood, and was asking for the order to retreat. It was told to stand fast.

The first bombardment of Damao-Grande by the artillery started around 04:30 hours. The bombardment lasted for thirty minutes and it hit 'Palacio do Governo', the barracks of the Battery, the Command centre and telegraph station. The aim of the attack was the neutralization of sensitive points that once destroyed could influence the conduct of operations. It was appraised that the battery units stationed in Cunta and Vapi were executing the bombardment.

1º Cabos Antonio Rodrigues da Cruz and Domingos Caldeira Feixeira and the soldier Antonio Piedade dos Reis were hit by shrapnel during this bombardment

As soon as the bombardment started, Alferes Miliciano Francisco E. Rodrigues Baptista who was commanding the gun placements in the Cais de Trapiche was ordered to fire on Cunta in the Indian Union. This order was promptly executed and sections under his command carried out twenty-eight shots.

The Commandant of the Agrupamento ordered the civil radio station and P.E.I radio post to inform Goa that the invasion of the territory of Daman had started at 04:00 hours. There was no reply. It was verified that the antennas of both the posts were hit and destroyed. As decided earlier, the personnel of the coding section began immediately destroying classified documents and coding material.

In our three territories the Indians took care to destroy all the points of extreme sensitivity. This shows that it knew the perfect place of these points and therefore had made a careful preparation.

Major Costa Pinto went to the hospital around 06:30 hours to see the wounded. He met there Captain Felgueiras e Sousa, the Commandant of the Battery unit, visibly demoralised and conceding that he was down due to the blowing of the shell in his vicinity. This officer requested the Commandant of the Agrupamento to surrender. The answer was negative and he advised him to leave the hospital.

Meanwhile, the situation in Damao-Grande had not altered. In Damao-Pequeno at 7:00 hours, Tenente Alberto Ferreira, the Commandant of P.E.I. together with Alferes Alberto Santiago de Carvalho, Furriel Silva and other two soldiers moved in a vehicle in the direction of the airport to check the situation as the radio post was not answering the call. They were stopped in the neighborhood of the airport by firing from an Indian company, which had already occupied that post. They jumped out of the vehicle on to the roadside. Alferes Santiago de Carvalho could not take proper cover and thus he was shot dead. The remaining elements rapidly retreated making use of the ground features so as to not being shot. They saw while returning the soldier Abel Araujo Bastos hiding below a culvert. He belonged to the machine gun garrison installed in the airport. Later on he was identified among the dead.

By 07:30 hours two jets overflew the region at a low altitude, and after a light reconnaissance attacked the forts, using bombs, rockets, and machine guns.

In S.Jeronimo Fort the parish priest's residence was hit and the battery, the Institute of 'Nossa Senhora da Fatima', the Government Palace, the See, the Tribunal, the Cold Storage Plant, and the Radio Station were hit in the Praca. The attack lasted around half –an-hour.

Meanwhile, our two companies installed in Damao-Pequeno succeeded in locating the enemy in the region of the airport and initiated mortar fire. When this succeeded the elements of P.E.I. and the European civilians raised the barricades in the streets of the city in order to arrest the advance of the enemy.

After the enemy air attack, the Commandant of the Agrupamento travelled all along the Praca and ordered the evacuation of civilians whose houses were situated in the area subjected to enemy fire.

He decided to change the location of his P.C. to a place near the Municipal Council and went to the posts along the wall, giving his instructions. Around 08:20 hours when he reached the artillery position he ordered Alferes C. de Sousa to open fire towards Cunta region. However he came to know later on that the firing was not executed due to unknown reasons.

Meanwhile, he received communication from frontier posts in Damao-Grande that they were being fired upon by the enemy. However till that moment there were no casualties or any enemy entrance in our territory. They were ordered to fall back to defensive positions previously decided on.

After our mortar fire, the enemy started to scorch our positions in Damao-Pequeno with artillery and mortars. Around 09:00 hours a dispatch rider from C.Cac.12, handed over a message to the Commandant of Agrupamento informing him about the attacks being launched against that defensive position, without however giving the enemy strength. The order was transmitted to continue with the resistance.

Soon afterwards there was a second air attack. Once again two jets bombarded and hit the Praca, the Naval house and other buildings previously bombed. The barracks of C. Cac. 12 were hit in Damao-Pequeno, damaging its radio post. Due to flying shrapnel, Furriel Rogerio da Silva, 1º Cabo Pedro Esteves dos Santos and the soldier Ramiro Rosa de Oliveira were wounded.

Around 10:00 hours the Commandant of the Agrupamento, Major Costa Pinto decided to cross the river and go to Damao-Pequeno, as there was no news about the situation on the other side. He went to the riverbank in the company of his adjutant and the officer of transmissions but saw that the crew had abandoned the launch 'Aniceto Rosario' and the ferryboat 'Lautem'

Meanwhile, Major Costa Pinto met Captain Gustavo Rebelo de Sousa, Commandant of C. Cac. 12 and Tenente Alberto Ferreira, P.E.I. Commandant, who informed that all defensive positions were being attacked with infantry soldiers from close distances. Our mortars were changing the locations as their positions were being detected. The enemy artillery and mortar fire was however not very accurate. Paulo Pedro do Rosario, the guard of P.E.I., died when the post at Catria was attacked.

By 11:00 hours the enemy air force executed the third bombardment, causing fire to the combat positions in the front, P.E.I. headquarters, and S. Jeronimo Fort. The planes also attacked the Bimpor post, as its personnel were responsible for obstructing the enemy advance route. The post was razed to the ground but there were no casualties as the garrison was in the trenches. This post resisted for two hours and then retreated to Marvor after the post was destroyed.

Meanwhile, there was no ammunition left in the post of Varacunda. Furriel Antonio Calado da Cruz Semedo of C.Cac.12 offered to supply the ammunition. Though his vehicle was aimed at, he managed to fulfill his mission under enemy fire.

The Commandant of Agrupamento sent a message to the battery unit asking Alferes C. de Sousa to direct the fire on Cunta as our front was being subjected to heavy fire with 8 cm mortars.

The post of Benselor was forced to retreat under fire as ammunitions were exhausted. After replenishment it went to reinforce the post of Catria. As the post of Benselor had disappeared the access to our defensive positions was open to the enemy. This was the reason for aiming fire on Cunta.

The rider, who was carrying the message of Major Costa Pinto, returned after some time, informing that there was no boat to enable him to cross the river. Therefore the commandant of the Agrupamento decided to send his adjutant Captain Soares Ogando back to the Praca so that the orders were followed. However within a short time, Captain Ogando returned with the news that the white flags had been raised in the Praca and that the boat for his transport had stayed on the southern bank. When the message was delivered after a lot of effort, he received the reply from the Commandant of the Battery that he had surrendered and that he had ordered the raising of white flags and destruction of weapons.

Major Costa Pinto in the company of Tenente Ferreira went in the direction of the beach with the intention of crossing the river but could not achieve this purpose. Finally they shouted across the opposite bank ordering to continue firing and to remove the white flags.

Meanwhile, the Commandant of Battery ordered the forces situated in the Praca to come together and destroy the weapons. Alferes C. da Silva, who was carrying out the decision of surrender and placing the white flags, informed Alferes Rodrigues Baptista, who was in the Cais de Trapiche, that he should also take similar steps and destroy the weapons. He however declined to obey these instructions saying that the Commander of Agrupamento who was presently in Damao-Pequeno had not given them. He further said that he needed written orders to obey them.

Alferes C.da Silva sent written messages on behalf of the Battery Commandant to the platoons of 'Cacadores' who were manning the defensive positions to surrender. A similar message was also sent to the post of Varacunda in Damao-Pequeno who insisted that it would accept orders only from the Commandant of Agrupamento.

Around 14:00 hours, there was the fourth bombardment by enemy aircraft. It hit our positions in Damao-Pequeno, the forts and the barracks of two companies located in the city.

Meanwhile, the posts of P.E.I. at Calicachigao, Dabel, Ataviar and Regunvara retreated to Damao-Grande through previously designated routes, as the ammunition was exhausted. The P.E.I guard Tiburcio Machado died during the fight at Dabel.

In view of incessant mortar and artillery fire from the enemy on the positions in Damao-Pequeno, the troops were ordered to retreat and occupy the zone near the market. The time was around 16 00 hours.

At 16:30 hours there was the fifth air bombardment, in which the post of Catria was razed to the ground. The retreating personnel used the compound wall of the Police barracks as cover while occupying new positions.

Major Costa Pinto, Captain Soares Orgando and a civilian tried to locate the enemy forces in the sector near the sea, as they had already reached the Garden of Maneckji, which was in the central area, and situated at the entrance of the city.

Around 17:30 hours the Indian Air force carried out the sixth bombardment. They used incendiary bombs that engulfed the market and the Godown of the Corporation of External Trade. Two civilians died and many others were wounded.

Some of our forces who were trying to retreat to Damao-Grande were surprised by the air raid in the middle of the river with the resultant loss of weapons which fell in the water.

In Damao-Grande, the soldier Leonel Milhanas was hit on the back and fell dead. The situation worsened appreciably. The last bombardment demoralised a sizeable number of military men who tried to reach Damao-Grande where the white flags were flying since 11:00 hours.

The Commandant of the Agrupamento after having examined a part of the second line of defence where there remained a few elements, met Alferes Americo Maltez Soares who accompanied him in the direction of enemy positions to analyse the situation better. When they were moving through one of the city streets, Major Costa Pinto was hit on his right hip and fell wounded. He tried to open fire with his weapon but it was jammed.

Alferes Maltez Soares, who was on other side of the road, immediately ran to help his Commandant after providing covering fire with his automatic gun. He then carried Major Costa Pinto to the first aid post, where he was taken care of by doctors Tenentes Luis Leite Noronha and Mateus Marques.

Around 19:00 hours, the Commandant of the Agrupamento was visited by Captain Soares Ogando, and both of them studied the situation. Recognising that there was no sufficient manpower and other means to face the Indian forces, the Commandant decided to arrange to contact the adversary in order to establish negotiations. Captain Soares Ogando was given charge of this mission. He left with Alferes Maltez Soares, a soldier and a police guard in the direction of the enemy. They were met however with fire when they were in the process of establishing contact. The soldier Jacinto Joao Guerreiro was hit and fell dead.

Meanwhile, it was growing dark, and the firing had stopped from both sides. On 19th December the enemy launched the seventh aerial bombardment that hit a great number of houses in the city, in Damao-Pequeno and in Praca.

Major Costa Pinto, due to the prevailing situation decided that the negotiations be started with the enemy forces. They however did not accept the contact established by the Adjutant, who explained that the Commandant could not be present as he was wounded. Even then the Indian Command insisted that Major Costa Pinto, the Commandant of the Agrupamento, should remain present at the site. At 09:00 hours he was then carried on a stretcher to Maneckji Garden where the Indian Commandant Lt. Col. Bhonsale accepted the surrender of the Portuguese troops.

However, at some places resistance was still being offered. The post of Varacunda commanded by Furriel Manuel Camelo Dias was the last to surrender. It surrendered at 16:00 hours on the 19th after Alferes Maltez Soares found his way with great risk to the post and informed its occupants about the surrender order given by the Portuguese Command.

After the surrender the Indian Command decided to evacuate the wounded by helicopter to Bombay. Major Costa Pinto did not accept the evacuation and preferred to remain in the hospital in Daman where he received treatment from our two doctors. It should be pointed out that the Indian wounded troops were transported by rail.

Our forces suffered seven dead and nine wounded. The Indian casualties were eighteen in number.

At the place, near Maneckji Garden where the surrender took place the Indians displayed a plaque with the following words:

“Major Antonio Jose da Costa Pinto
The Portuguese Governor of Daman
Surrendered to Lt. Col. S J S Bhonsale
Commanding officer 1st BN
The Maratha Light Infantry (Jangi Paltan)
On 19 DEC 1961 at 08.30 HRS
After 36 hours of gruelling fighting

5-The enemy which acted against Daman

a) The Strength

It is not possible to indicate exactly the strength of the Indian troops which invaded the territory of Daman. The news received during the days prior to the operations and confirmed later, estimated the strength of 4000 men that included the elements of army and S.R.P.

Evidently, all these men and material did not participate in the operations. The major portion was kept in reserve, as it happened in the case of the light tanks and Breda vehicles.

The composition of the effective strength, which could be verified, was as follows:

- *1st battalion of Maratha Light Infantry, with headquarters in Poona, under the command of Lt. Col. S.J.S.Bhonsale, reinforced with*
- *2 Batteries of Artillery,*
- *Heavy weapons,*
- *Personnel of Signals, Medical Corps and Engineers,*
- *Personnel from S.R.P.*

These troops were assisted by four Jet planes type ' Mystere'

- *The battalion had 4 to 6 companies with a strength of 150 men each.*
- *The personnel from Signals, Medical Corps and Engineers had a total strength of 200 men.*
- *The batteries of Artillery had around 100 men each.*
- *The 33 posts of S.R.P. located along the frontier were reinforced with 8 guards each, with the total addition of 264 men, besides 200 who are estimated to have participated in the operations.*
- *The Engineers personnel of unknown strength prepared the roads for assembly of invading troops and the landing runways for planes for observation and of evacuation of casualties, sent to Vapi.*

The enemy knew perfectly our strength, and the axes of approach and all the details necessary for execution of manouevres. It should be clarified that each section of the Indian Companies had maps of scale 1/25000 of Daman, material that we ourselves did not possess.

b. The method

The strength used initially is not known.

The Indian army invaded the territory of Daman between the Police post of Benselor and the village of Janivancar with four companies in the front and two in reserve.

The Indian artillery had a battery in the region of Vapi and the other at the base of the mountain to the east of the Indian village of Udwada, around two kms to the north-east of the police post of Patalia. It also had heavy mortars in the region of Cunta and in the Fort to the east of the Customs post of Bamanpuja.

To begin the attack on our defensive positions in Damao-Pequeno, the enemy used its two companies in the front along the line defined by the Air Station, region of Dundorta and zone of Benselor. The reserve companies did not cross the Serra da Cruz heights. A reinforced platoon stayed in the southern zone between Calem and the region of Palsete, without entering into our territory

C. Material

From the different types of material used it was possible to identify the following:

—Rifles and carbines type Lee-Enfield
—Revolvers Smith Wesson
—Machine carbines Sten
—Attachments Mills for grenade firing on the rifles
—Attachments for anti-tank grenades firing
—Telescopic sights on some arms for snipers
—Light machine guns Bren
—Light and medium mortars
—Heavy machine-guns Browning
—Bazookas
—Artillery with 8.8 cm howitzers

The jet planes, type fighter-bombers, were armed with machine-guns and attachments for firing rockets.

The uniform used by the troops was of the English model m/43 of canvas of 'jungle green' colour, having straitjackets for carrying magazines for light machine guns and bands of 50 rounds.

The Indian army used many types of vehicles: jeeps, GMC, Breakdown recovery vehicles all of them in excellent state.

Regarding Signals equipment, it had:

- *—Radios CPRC 26 per section;*
- *—Posts of long range mounted on jeeps, for connection with artillery and aviation;*
- *—Posts Dc 1000 for connection Battalion-Company;*
- *—Posts type P 21, carried by two men that are supposed to be earmarked for connection with echelons that have moved back.*
- *—One post mounted in 'WAGON' for connection with the Chief Commander*
- *—Various telephones, types DEE 8 of English make.*

Besides this material, personnel from Engineers, Medical Corps, Admininistration and others utilized various equipment while carrying out their missions.

It should be emphasized that it was observed in all the three districts that the Indian troops were perfectly trained to use the material effectively.

6—The Captivity

After the surrender all the Europeans (Military, elements of Customs Guards, Police, and five civilians who were working in the hospital in Daman and airport), the police inspector, Manuel Pegado and a civilian-the chief of radio post of Daman, Edmundo Castro- both Goans but who refused to sign the declaration of loyalty to the Indian Nation, were made prisoners. All the personnel of G.F. and P.E.I. naturals of India were handed over to the Civilian Administration. The Alferes Graduates Voicunta Naique and Braulio Fernandes, doctor and pharmacist respectively, enjoyed special privileges and were set free and stayed back in India. Alferes Miliciano Arnaldo Ferreira, natural of Cabo Verde who initially did not accept the proposal of the Indian military of setting him free and absorption in the Indian Army, accepted it during his stay in Goa during the days prior to repatriation. He was the only person who deserted from the officer ranks in the entire territory of Portuguese India

Bombed ATC at Daman Air Port

The Portuguese Military personnel received advance salary according to their ranks. The prisoners left Daman and were transferred to Goa on 1st February 1962.They traveled on board the Cruiser "INS DELHI" which reached Marmagoa on the same day. The Portuguese prisoners who belonged to the Daman garrison left on board 'Paquete Vera Cruz' for Portugal in the beginning of May.

ACTION IN DIU

The Portuguese colony of Diu, situated in the middle of the south coast of Kathiawar (Gujarat) at a distance of about 196 kilometres by sea from Daman, was the smallest of their possessions in India. It had an area of 38.49 square kilometres and a population of 14,280 according to the census of 1960. The colony consisted chiefly of the island of Diu, but included also a small area on the mainland to the northeast of the island, and the island of Panikota.

According to intelligence reports, the enemy strength in Diu consisted only of three companies (360 all ranks) of infantry. This proved later an underestimation.[165] There were some police and customs guards manning posts along the land border and along the northern shores of the island. The area around some of these places was believed to have been mined with anti-tank and anti-personnel mines. The Portuguese were not supposed to have any armour on the island, but there were several light and medium machine guns, particularly in the fort area. They had also 3.7" AA guns.

It was expected that the lightly equipped Portuguese forces would initially offer coordinated resistance and that certain portions of roads on the mainland and on the island would be either demolished or prepared for demolition. Their Air Force might possibly operate in close support of the ground forces, with its modern jet aircraft, but this was not very likely. Some naval action was also expected, as one cruiser was reported to be located in the vicinity of the island. Stiff opposition was not expected as the morale of the garrison was reported to be "not very high'.

Plan of Action in Diu

Diu Operations

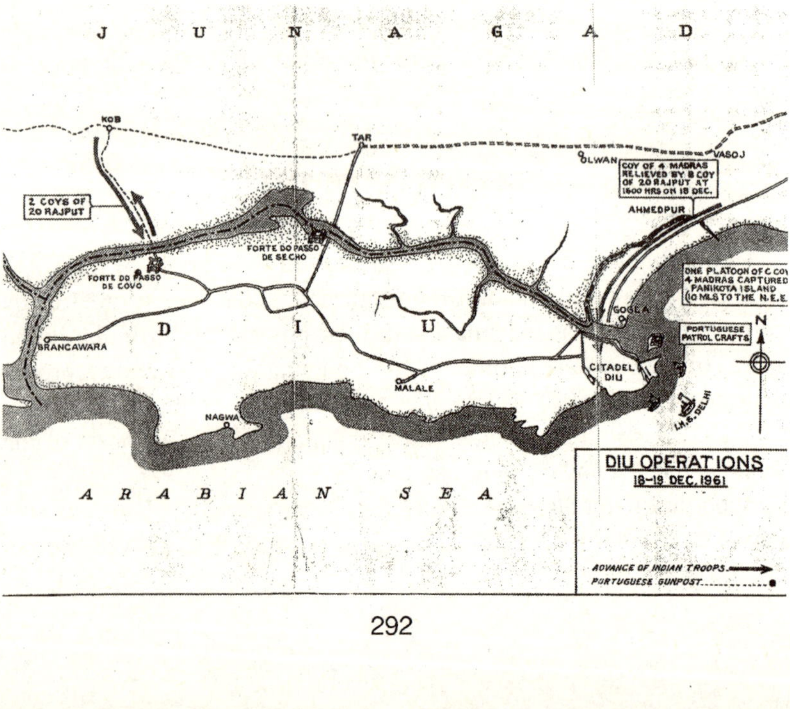

The Indian plan provided for ground, air and naval actions to occupy Diu with utmost speed. [166] As in Daman, here too, the original plan was to start the operations after awaiting the result of action in Goa. However, it was decided later to begin all operations simultaneously.

For ground operations, the 20th Battalion of the Rajput Regiment was chosen. It was to be commanded by Lt.Col. Bhupinder Singh and to act under the direction of Brigadier Jaswant Singh, Commander of the 112th Infantry Brigade. One company of 4 Madras was also to take part in the Diu operations under Major P.W.Curtis.

The naval part of the operations was entrusted to the cruiser INS Delhi, which was to appear in close vicinity of the island one hour before the time of commencement of operations. The cruiser would be prepared to engage targets, if required by the army units, but its guns would not fire in close support of the troops. An army liaison signals unit with its own wireless sets was embarked on the cruiser for communication between land forces and INS DELHI. On completion of these tasks, INS DELHI was to capture Simbhor fort (Panikota), approximately thirteen kilometres to the east of Diu.

Panikota (Simbhor)

Limited air support was to be given from IAF Station Jamnagar, but only in the form of a few pre-arranged sorties, as no signals link between the forward troops and Jamnagar was available.

The task of 20 Rajput was first to carry out an assault crossing of the tidal creek at low tide at a point south of Kob during the hours of darkness, and then move on to capture Diu airfield on the island as quickly as possible, and thereafter occupy the town of Diu. One hour before the assault crossing by 20 Rajput, the company of 4 Madras was to capture Gogla on the mainland, near the eastern border of Diu and opposite the Citadel.

At 01:30 hours on 18th December, the 4 Madras Company attacked the village of Gogla on the mainland, but met with heavy opposition and had to withdraw by 04:00 hours. A second attack at 06:30 hours was also unsuccessful and fourteen men were wounded. Gogla capitulated without resistance the same night when a third attack was made about 12 hours after the second.

The attempt to cross

20 Rajput was attempting an assault crossing of the creek from the northwest to capture the airfield.[167] It had to make a long approach march from the side of Kob across very soft and marshy ground. This took considerable time, the surprise was lost, and the Portuguese put themselves in readiness to meet the assault crossing.

Nevertheless, two of its companies launched their boats in the water and started the crossing at 02:30 hours, exactly one hour after the unsuccessful attempt on Gogla by 4 Madras about 10 or 11 kilometres to the east. Their task after crossing was to move forward a few hundred metres and establish an initial bridgehead for the battalion. Although they had received a few regular assault boats from the 112th brigade, the major portion of the crossing equipment had been improvised from its own resources. One such improvised item was the simple, almost primitive type of boat called 'charpoy boat', of which there were twenty.

As both the companies reached the middle of the creek opposite Fort of 'Passo do Covo', the enemy medium machine guns and two light machine guns opened up across the creek. Most of the boats including the assault boats, capsized. It was impossible to advance in the face of such fire. However a Major and five jawans made a desperate attempt to cross over and silence the LMG in the area of Forte de Covo. This gun was doing more damage to the men and boats than the other guns.

They fired from the boat with such good aim that they were partly able to neutralize the LMG fire. Then they pushed ahead in an effort to reach the other bank. Just as they were to land, a burst from another enemy LMG from the Fort area wounded the Major and two jawans. The other uninjured jawans tried to return the fire, but now another gun, a MMG opened up (from the area GR 455657) and forced them to turn back. They managed to put the Major and two jawans inside the boat and brought them back to the near bank.

The 3-inch mortars of 20 Rajput now took on the positions from where the Portuguese were firing, but were unable to silence them fully. Due to the marsh and heavy slush, the barrels of the weapons were blocked with mud and were rendered unusable. With the coming of daylight, the intensity and volume of the enemy fire was increasing, and there were not enough boats to attempt another crossing. Therefore it was decided at 05:30 hours that the battalion should fall back upon Kob.

In this failed operation, one Major and some other ranks were wounded and a few were found missing. Of the missing, some returned the same day and some the next morning. A few were killed and their bodies were found later. Some daring men had even crossed over in an attempt to move forward and silence the guns, but on finding impossible odds against them, they had either crossed back or taken shelter in a field from where they were brought back the next day by a patrol of their unit.

The failure emphasized the need for better planning and the importance of preliminary bombardment of strong points on the opposite bank, as well as close fire support in the initial stages of a landing of this type. In this case, such support could not be provided as the crossing was to be made in darkness for considerations of surprise, and aerial or naval bombardment would need daylight for accuracy.

The fact remains that the enemy could see you coming and you were advancing without forcing him to lower his sight. The result was failure and casualties.

In the afternoon, the third company (B Company) of 20 Rajput, which had not taken part in the unsuccessful crossing, was sent towards Gogla. It relieved the 4 Madras company at 16:00 hours. Soon after, it went into action and blew off the Portuguese check post and Mandavi (GR 6467) and another stronghold with the help of 3.5 inch Recoilless and 6-pounder guns. This telling blow to the Portuguese defences opened the route to Gogla and as B Company got ready to advance into town, the garrison showed a white flag and surrendered.

The air force and the navy were meanwhile shelling the Fort and the airfield on the island. This convinced the Portuguese that further resistance was futile.

Air Operations in Diu

The primary aim of air operations[168] originally envisaged the neutralization of the Portuguese air arm in the three territories on the first day of operations and thereby gaining air supremacy over the entire theatre. The secondary aim was to provide close air support to the ground forces. The airfields in Daman and Diu were not to be bombed, but to be kept under observation by fighter patrols, and their use denied to enemy planes. (Though no bombing of Diu and Daman airfields was envisaged, tactical bombing of Diu airfield had to be carried out after failure of the ground advance)

It became known that the Portuguese had no air opposition to offer. The only opposition was from anti-aircraft defences in and around vital areas and targets. However, it was considered possible that after the start of operations by India, the Portuguese might send distress messages by wireless to countries unfriendly to India and request for Fighter reinforcements. The contingency was remote, but to provide against it the primary objective set for the air force was to destroy the wireless stations in Goa and Diu and to preempt the three territories from receiving reinforcements by air while the land battles were in progress.

The clear directive for Diu was that no offensive air action was to be taken without guidance from the air control team (ACT) accompanying the battalion on the ground. This was necessary in order to avoid hitting any non-military positions and causing loss of civilian life. Pre-arranged targets such as the airfield, Forte do Passo Seco, the Citadel etc., were also selected but they could not be targeted as the contact between the Air Training Wing in Jamnagar and the ACT with the battalion in Diu could not be established in the morning of the 18th due to the confused

Brig. Jaswant Singh, Commander, 112th Infantry Brigade in charge of Operations against Diu

situation of the land battle. The raid on Diu airfield could take place only at 14:00 hours in the afternoon of that day.

Earlier, on that day a wave of four Toofanis sent to raid at 11:00 hours had returned without completing the mission due to misunderstanding of a message it had heard in the air. The air force tactical headquarters at Poona, therefore ordered a second raid to be made on Diu airfield at 14:00 hours. Two Toofanis bombed the intersection of the two runways and scored direct hits.

Further attacks were made by other aircraft against the airfield installations and wireless station. The airfield control tower, meteorological office and wireless station were completely destroyed within one hour. Another full scale raid by 16 Canberras (in two waves of eight aircraft) was planned and flown out in the evening, but was recalled shortly before it reached the target area on learning that the land forces had put in an attack and it would be dangerous to carry out a bombing close to our own army positions on the ground. Also, a confirmation of the Diu airfield having been put out of commission by the Toofanis was received from Jamnagar.

In Diu, as many as 35 strike sorties were flown on 18th December, using rockets and bombs. Many other targets in the two main forts within Diu, not known previously but which were sighted during the flights were successfully neutralized. One Portuguese patrol vessel, which opened fire on Indian aircraft, was 'appropriately dealt with and sunk'. It has to be accepted that the Diu garrison surrendered without the army even having stepped ashore on the island.

On the 19th also, 32 sorties of armed reconnaissance and patrol were flown, but no ammunition was expended as the 'battle' was practically over, and only the formal surrender ceremony remained to take place.

There is no doubt that the impact of air operations on the attainment of the overall aim of the armed intervention in the Portuguese territories, particularly in Daman and Diu, where the Portuguese did offer stout resistance, was very great. The army's debt to the air force was handsomely acknowledged by Gen, Chaudhury in a special congratulatory message.

Role of the Navy

I. N. S. Delhi

The navy too played a significant role[169] in the capitulation of Diu. The cruiser INS DELHI had been allotted to Diu with the duty of supporting the army moving on to the island, but was meant to act in a show- of -force role. However when 20 Rajput and the company of 4 Madras failed to achieve their objectives in the morning of the 18th, a call for support was made to INS DELHI, which was in position since the early morning. In response to the Army's call, INS DELHI provided naval gunfire support by engaging the Citadel and the control tower at the airfield, around midday on the 18th. As a result of this gunfire, the Citadel was silenced and numerous white flags were hoisted in and around it. The Citadel surrendered a little later.

The formal surrender of Diu, however, came the next day at 18:30 hours when the Portuguese laid down arms, and our troops moved into the island to occupy various important places and installations. 18 officers, 43 Sergeants and 342 other ranks of the Portuguese were taken prisoners.

About 16 kilometres east north east of Diu is the small island of Panikota where the Portuguese had also a few soldiers in charge of a fort. On the 19th, C Company of 4 Madras was ordered to send one platoon with a section of 3-inch mortars to capture the island and the fort. By last light the platoon completed this task. It took one officer and twelve other ranks as prisoners, bringing these operations to an end.

Defence of Diu

(The Portuguese version)

1—The District of DIU

The district of Diu is situated in the extreme south of Gujarat peninsula, exactly at the vertex of the angle, which divides the waters of the Arabian Sea between the gulfs of Persia and Cambay.

The total area of the district was 37.49 Kms^2, divided into three distinct portions of the territory: The island of Diu was the district headquarters, with an age old Fort, and various villages; The territory of Gogola, with an area of two square kilometres and situated on the mainland and separated by the Chassi Channel; and finally the territory of Simbhor, at a distance of roughly 25 kilometres to the east of Diu

Simbhor consisted of an islet and two strips of land intercepted by a rivulet known as "Rio Vancoso". The Portuguese occupation dates from the year 1722. A small fort was built called by locals as 'Pani Kota' or the fort on sea as it was on the bank of the sea.

The district of Diu had a total population of 21,000 inhabitants. It had a small airport situated at around six kilometres from the city and a small port with reduced traffic. The defence[170] of Diu was to be carried out as per the plan.

Citadel of Diu

2—The Agrupamento " Antonio da Silveira"

The Agrupamento de Diu designated with the name "Antonio de Silveira"[171] was commanded by Major of General Staff, Fernando Alberto de Almeida e Vasconcelos, who was also the Governor of the district. It consisted of:

—Command;

—'Companhia de Cacadores de Diu';

—'Battery of Artillery No 4.

From the operational point of view the Police force and the Customs guards were under the command of Agrupamento. There were 33 police and 50 customs guards. These personnel were guarding the posts existing throughout the district practically situated along the border. These were: Brancavara, Passo Covo, Passo Seco, Bunxivara, Radio Farol, Gogola A and Gogola B.

The plan of defence of the island of Diu was very simple due to the small size of the territory and the scarce means at its disposal for its defence. Its last place of final resistance was the Fort. The plan consisted essentially of the followings points:

A—Resistance by the posts of Police and Customs Guards as long as possible.

B—Occupying of the position of Malala and vigilance over Airport and Nagoa and Armatia beaches.

C—Defence of outer wall of the city under the charge of 'Companhia de Cacadores' minus one platoon detached in Malala and the mortars of the platoon for defence situated in the Fort. This consisted the firepower force.

D—The final defence was to be carried in the Fort with reduced means, with even the Battery of Artillery operating in the role of Infantry.

The retreat by the platoon at Malala, which was functioning as the advance post in the defensive position, could only take place after the order of the Commandant of the Agrupamento. It would then become the reserve force of the Agrupamento. The 'Companhia de Cacadores would also retreat only after the Command order.

The Battery of Artillery had a platoon with four guns, which were installed on the external terrace of the Fort and the other in the inside. The posts of command of Battery and the Agrupamento were also inside the Fort.

In short this was the defence plan of the island of Diu.

3—The period before the invasion

It can be said that there were strong signals of the Indian invasion right from the month of November. On 12th November there was news that India was preparing to attack Diu.[172] *For this purpose a sand model was prepared at he military school in Ahmedabad. A detailed study was being done with projected operations. An Indian officer born in Diu was present during these studies. The radio message had also hinted that the enemy might airdrop the forces The Commandant of the Agrupamento therefore ordered that the soldiers reinforced with heavy weapons should occupy the airport and a section of the artillery battery be installed on the bulwark of Fort S. Sebastiao.*

Besides, he requested for reinforcement of forces and sending of a naval unit for the defence of Diu. However, his request was declined as the major brunt of attack would fall on Goa and there was no spare force available. From 3rd December the Indian union began the daily reconnaissance flights over Diu. These flights continued up to the eve of the invasion.

On 15th December a message was received at 12:00 hours from Governor General that there was no hope of foreign powers intervening in order to dissuade Indian Union from attacking Portuguese India. The attack was earmarked for that date. The radio message had ordered that they should take defensive positions as previously established. It was exhorting further that the troops in that district should obey the mission entrusted to them.

Gauging the seriousness of the message, Major Fernando de Vasconcelos immediately ordered emergency measures to be taken and to occupy the positions by nightfall. The detachment that was at the airport till then was transferred to the zone of Malala Radio Station, with the task of keeping watch on the airport and beaches of Nagoa and Armatia. It was given a 20 mm Anti-Aircraft Machine Gun.

During this period there was no concrete information from High Command about the enemy, its strength and aim. Nothing was known on what was happening in the island of Angediv. Based on these aspects measures were taken to fulfill the mission.

During the night of 15th /16th December, cries of children could be heard at the Mandvi border. This incident made us conclude that the Indian population was being evacuated from the border area. On 17th morning a 'Vampire' jet plane overflew the regions in the neibhourhood of our territory. Around the same time news was received about the evacuation from the villages near our frontiers. It also came to the notice of the Command of the Agrupamento that the trains transporting war material and men had reached Una, a town near Mandvi. These were moved around Diu. The total strength was estimated to be 4500 men.

4—Action from Agrupamento " Antonio da Silveira"

Agrupamento "Antonio Da Silveira"

Around 1-30 hours in the morning, the Police Post at the frontier in Gogola was attacked by troops of the Indian army.[173]

[17]The Portuguese defences repulsed the attack backed by 87.6mm artillery and mortars, inflicting heavy losses on the Indians. The first attack was made by the 4 Madras on a police post at 0130 on December

18 at Gogol and was repulsed by 13 Portuguese soldiers. Another attempt by the 4 Madras at 0200 was again repulsed, this time backed with Portuguese 87.5mm artillery and mortar which suffered due to poor quality of munitions. By 0400, ten of the original 13 defending Portuguese soldiers at Gogol had been wounded and were evacuated to a hospital. At 0530, the Portuguese artillery launched a fresh attack on the 4 Madras assaulting Gogol and forced their retreat.

It was known later that it consisted of an infantry company. The attack was launched with grenades and automatic weapons. It wounded a guard who was on sentry duty. Though the attackers had reached the vicinity of the post the garrison reacted energetically.[173] *Its commandant 'Sub-Chefe' Joao Pereira de Sousa, who was wounded, handled the machine gun with courage and cold-blooded determination. The enemy was forced to retreat.*

Around 02:00 hours the post at Gogola at the frontier was attacked again. The Commandant ordered the battery of artillery to open fire in the region of the saltpans in order to ease the pressure on Gogola post. Due to this measure the Indian troops withdrew and moved to its territory.

Around 02:00 hours the Customs post at 'Passo Covo' informed the Command of having heard noise from a large number of flying birds, followed by the sound of somebody crossing through the mud in the canal and the voice of command. They were told to open fire only in case it was confirmed that the canal was being crossed.

At 03:00 hours two landing crafts, coming from Indian territory crossed the canal in the zone of 'Passo Covo', moored on our bank and disembarked some elements. When they were ordered to halt, they answered with fire from their guns. An exchange of fire took place, which ended with the confused flight of the enemy to its territory.

As the Rajput reached the middle of the creek the Portuguese in Diu opened fire with two MMGs and two LMGs, capsizing some of the rafts. **Major Mal Singh** of the Indian army along with five men pressed on his advance and crossed the creek. On reaching the far bank he and his men assaulted the LMG trenches at Fort-De-Cova and silenced them. The Portuguese MMG fire from another position wounded the officer and two of his men. However, with the efforts of company **Havildar Major Mohan Singh** and two other men, the three wounded were evacuated back across the creek to safety. As dawn approached the Portuguese increased the intensity of fire and the battalion's water crossing equipment suffered extensive damage. As a result the Indian battalion was ordered to fall back to Kob village by first light

The telephonic connection between Command and the Posts of Passo Seco, Bunchivara, Passo Covo and Brancavara was lost around 03:15 hours. From that moment onwards they were left to their own fate.

Meanwhile, the Post of Passo Covo continued to be subjected to enemy fire. At 03:30 hours, the Commandant of Agrupamento ordered that the 20 mm A.A. machine gun allotted to the detachment at the airport should be returned to the Fort and the section which was stationed there should go to reinforce the detachment at Malala. At 04:00 hours a patrol confirmed the attack on the Passo Covo post.

By this time a patrol left the fort to reinforce the Gogola garrison and search and retrieve the wounded. The telephonic link with that post was cut since 02:15 hours. However, the fight was continuing at that place. The mission of the patrol was very risky, but after an hour- and- half Furriel of Artillery Joao da Costa Rita and the soldier Ilidio Marques Nogueira succeeded in reaching the post. The remaining three soldiers lost their way in the darkness but reached later the village of Gogola.

In the post, which had an effective strength of thirteen, only three men were in action. The remaining ten were wounded. Due to the courageous action and resistance by Furriel Rita and Sub-Chefe Pereira de Sousa, the remaining personnel could retreat. Furriel Rita was wounded in the chest by shrapnel. During the resistance offered, the guards Antonio M. Ferreira Spinola and Domingos de Nascimento Robalo also stood out. Subsequently both of them were seriously wounded.

Around 05:00 hours the post of Passo Covo was attacked once again from two directions. However, once again the enemy was forced to withdraw. During the attack the enemy was aided by

intense artillery and mortar fire but it did not hit the post. Curiously our garrison thought the fire was coming from our artillery. The A. A. machine gun was installed with great difficulty on the bulwark of S. Domingos in the Fort. At 05:30 hours the battery of artillery under the command of Capitao Mario Pinto Rodrigues de Almeida was ordered to fire at the place in the Indian territory near Gogola. Due to this fire and the prompt reaction from the post the enemy had to withdraw.

At 06:00 hours radio contact with Goa (Bambolim) was tried once again but it was not successful. The communication about the Indian attack was sent through the Police radio. There was no guarantee about its reception. During this time the launch "VEGA" anchored between the Fort and the Fortim do Mar.

Meanwhile, four cannons, which were on the external terrace, were ordered to be brought to the Castelo. At daybreak a warship appeared before the Fort. Immediately, it was ordered that an 8.8 cm howitzer be lifted and placed on the platform on the bulwark of Sta Luzia, in order to hit the enemy ship directly. The initial order to open fire was suspended rapidly as a flag was raised on board, thought to be Portuguese. It was known much later that the flag was black and red, which was the signal for the start of combat. Thus an only opportunity to hit a naval unit was lost. The warship happened to be the Cruiser INS DELHI of Indian Navy.

At 06:30 hours, a guard of Posto do Covo went with great caution to the canal where there were many abandoned canoes and improvised boats. He saw inside the boats many rifles with grenade launching devices, small mortars, ammunition, radios and material used by engineers, which he threw into the water. Near by he saw a wounded Indian soldier. He was treated and a flag was planted to show his position. During this time he saw a few dead bodies of Indian soldiers washed by the current, floating in the waters of the canal towards Bunxivara.

At 07:00 hours, the first enemy planes flying at low altitude were seen. Soon after, in two waves of four planes each, they started the bombardment of our territory. It started from Pass Seco and followed to Passo Covo, Radio Farol— which was soon destroyed, — Queuri, Palacio de Malala and the Radio telegraphic station.

The "Emissora de Goa" which began its regular transmission at 07:00 hours, ceased to be heard after ten minutes of its transmission. It could be concluded that the District of Goa too was being attacked.

The post of Passo do Covo consisted of 1º Cabo of Customs, Jose Domingos Cartaxo da Assuncao, and guards Manuel Martinho Rebocho, Manuel Fernandes Junior, Joao Maria Narciso, Antonio Joaquim Perdigao, Armando R. Pais Avo, and Domingos Aquiles dos Santos and Anibal Pereira. It had heroically resisted various attacks from the Indian army, with a very small force of eight men They set the post on fire and evacuated The Fortim of Passo Seco was partially destroyed in the air attack.

At 07:30 hours the detachment of Malala which had also suffered from enemy air attack started its withdrawal towards Diu via Podamo. Moments thereafter the Fort suffered its first air attack. The areas recently evacuated were hit. The positions of Battery were directly machine gunned and bombed, with the personnel scurrying for shelter. Till that moment the battery had fired around 2500 shots.

The anti aircraft defence of the fort was done by the patrol launch "VEGA", stationed near Fortim do Mar, by A.A 20 machine gun installed on the bulwark of S. Domingos, and by twin 7.7 Bren machine guns installed on the bulwark of S. Filipe. It happened that the launch was hit immediately after the first attack; the A.A.20 machine gun jammed up after the third shot and some time afterwards was hit by enemy aircraft; and the Bren machine gun also jammed up after the fifth shot. The anti- aircraft defence, already insufficient was practically out of action within a few minutes of action. Our troops were left to the mercy of the enemy aircraft, which bombarded and machine-gunned the Fort till 15:00 hours in successive waves which were sporadically interrupted for intervals of ten minutes.

After 10:15 hours, the air attacks were alternating with bombardments from the Cruiser INS DELHI.

Inside the fortified enclosure it was impossible to move. The troops barracked there had to face painful moments, as they were impotent to face the action from the enemy who was enjoying the liberty of air space. Soon after the first attack, the cells of the 'penitentiary' were opened allowing the inmates to take shelter in more protected places. This was an appropriate decision as, soon afterwards the installations previously occupied by them, were hit.

Around 09:00 hours the patrol launch VEGA was destroyed and sunk by air action.

It was only at this time that the two men who still occupied the post of Gogola—its commandant Sub-Chefe Pereira de Sousa and Furriel Costa Rita—both wounded, abandoned the post after having set it on fire.

Meanwhile, due to incessant enemy bombardment, the Fort was left with no communications.

By 12:45 hours, a rocket hit a mortar, provoking a big fire which engulfed the positions and obstructed movement between the ramparts of 1st and 2nd enclosures. It was feared that the ammunitions of mortars, which were in its vicinity, might explode.

The roof of the "Cisterna do Rei"under which more than one hundred men had taken shelter was hit and pierced by enemy fire. After some time, a vehicle, which contained the Verey light rockets and ammunition for light weapons was hit, causing an explosion and obstructing the movement in the courtyard of the Fort and access to the outgoing gate.

In view of this situation, an explosion in the depot of the battery was feared. An order for evacuation of the Fort was given and the personnel were regrouped in the hospital and the city. This evacuation was carried out in a very difficult situation. The personnel had to jump from high walls about six metres high.

Meanwhile, it was feared that the Comandante do Agrupamento and other officers in the fort might have died, as the search party sent to check up had not returned. By this time some civilians informed the battery that they had heard on the radio that the bomber aircrafts would raze the city in case the Portuguese did not surrender.

Around 15:00 hours the aerial and naval attacks had stopped but the Cruiser INS DELHI stayed alongside and the planes continued to overfly the island. The attack on the Fort started again at 17:00 hours, and it continued till nightfall. Similarly the airport was heavily bombarded with runways and buildings destroyed.

Major Fernando Vasconcelos had managed to leave the fort and reach the P.C of Companhia de Cacadores installed near the dispensary of Dr. Aminchande Rupchande. He then analysed the situation and got the confirmation that the launch VEGA had been sunk. He had no news about the situation at the posts at the borders, except about Gogola whose men had been admitted to the hospital. He did not know the number of casualties suffered in the Fort. A greater part of the personnel who were subjected to intense naval and aerial bombardment in the Fort had lost the capacity to fight.

After weighing the circumstances and taking into consideration that the resistance might create great difficulties to the civilian population with casualties and the fires, the Commandant of the Agrupamento concluded that after having done whatever was humanly possible, there was no point in prolonging the resistance. As it was getting dark, there was no possibility of sending a patrol on foot (it was impossible to use a vehicle due to the constant overflight of enemy planes) and expect them back with information about the situation in the island before nightfall. The attacks by the Indian forces were not showing signs of declining and the Companhia de Cacadores was not in a position to face the impact of an attack on the city. As he had no contact whatsoever with the outside world, he assumed full responsibility and decided to surrender. The Commandant communicated his decision to his officers. His decision was also influenced by the time factor. There was no possibility of sending delegates to contact the enemy once there was nightfall.

Later on he met persons of high standing in the place and informed them about his decision, and asked them if anybody from them wanted to go with the delegation that was to meet the enemy, in order to finalise the terms of surrender. Adjutant of the Command, Captain Rodrigo Peres Pinto Soares led the delegation, which included Messers Cantilal Premchande, Professor Ramnicrai Deussancar and Caxinata Sinai Mulgaocar who were well acquainted with the English language. The delegation which was composed of five members were fully explained about the terms, which were as follows:

"—The surrender will be exclusively military and the information of Portuguese prisoners will be communicated to the Brasilian Embassy in New Delhi."

The delegation went in the direction of Gogola. During the crossing of the river it was overflown by the Indian planes that dipped their wings in recognition of the white flag that was being carried.

It was known later that the presence of the delegation avoided the departure of bomber planes that were to carry out heavy bombardment during the evening hours. It was also known that the enemy had conveyed this intention to the civilian population.

After reaching the frontier, the delegation went in a vehicle of the Indian army in the direction of Una where the Headquarters of Brigadier Jaswant Singh, the Commandant of Indian Forces was located.

Our delegation returned to Diu around 23:00 hours. It brought back the following conditions accepted by the Indians:

- *The Indian forces will suspend operations till 08:00 hours on the next day, provided the Portuguese side did not open fire.*
- *The operations would resume from this time if the Adjutant of Command did not appear in Gogola in order to meet Lt. Col. Upendra Singh.*
- *The surrender will be military and the prisoners will not be subjected to violence, and they will be treated according to international laws.*
- *The Government of India will be informed about the taking of prisoners, and will be requested to inform the same to the Brasilian Embassy.*
- *There will not be any destruction and that the weapons should be deposited during the surrender. (The adjutant*

> *clarified that the major part of the armament was not in working condition and already there has been destruction).*

The members of the delegation informed, after their return, that they had come to know in Una that the garrison in Daman had already surrendered and the one in Goa was ready to do the same.

By daybreak on the 19th, the Indian jets over flew Diu at a low height, without however resorting to fire. At 08:00 hours the adjutant of the Command was at the frontier with Lt. Col. Upendra Singh who informed him that the Brigadier Commandant of the Indian forces would land at Diu at 11:00 hours, and will be in the front of Government Palace, the place chosen for the surrender ceremony.

In this way once the surrender was accepted there would not be any military action on Simbhor. The place of surrender was changed later on to a place near the officer's mess as the Palace was already destroyed. The Governor of the district and the Commandant of the Agrupamento surrendered to the Indian troops in the presence of Brigadier Jaswant Singh.

The Indians took 403 prisoners, which included the Lt. Governor of the island along with 18 officers and 43 sergeants. The Indian air force was also present at the ceremony and was represented by Gp Capt Godkhindi, Wing Cmdr Micky Blake and Sqn Ldr Nobby Clarke.

In the evening of the 19th, the adjutant accompanied the Indian platoon armed with mortars, which went to occupy Simbhor. The cruiser INS DELHI also moved to that place. The garrison of that small territory, which consisted of only twelve men, reached Diu in the evening of the 20th.

Major Mal Singh and Sepoy Hakam Singh of the Indian army were awarded Ashok Chakra (Class III).

In this way the action of Portuguese troops came to an end. They offered resistance worthy of greatest praise.

References:

149—P.N.Khera-Op.Vijay-p-94
150—Ibid-p-96
151—Ibid-Appendix-XVII-p-202
152—Ibid-p-97
153—Ibid-p-101
154—Ibid-Original Surrender Document
155—C.A.Morais-Queda da India Portuguesa-p-185
156—Ibid-p-187
157—Ibid-p-190
158—Ibid-p-191
159—Ibid-p-192
160—Ibid-p-193
161—Ibid-p-197
162—Ibid-p-209
163—Ibid-p-210
164—Ibid-p-213
165—P.N.Khera-Op.Vijay-p-103
166—Ibid-p-104
167—Ibid-p-105
168—Ibid-p-107
169—Ibid-p-110
170—C.A.Morais—Queda-p-219
171—Ibid-p-222
172—Ibid-p-223
173—Ibid-p-233

CHAPTER XIII

THE NAVAL FORCES IN OPERATION

Naval Operations Off Goa[174]

NAVAL OPERATION ORDERS

(Office of the Flag Officer Commanding, Indian Fleet at: Bombay)

(SHORT TITLE SAG 1)

INFORMATION

AS A RESULT OF PROVOCATIVE ACTION AGAINST OUR OWN NATIONALS IN THE VICINITY OF **ANGEDIV ISLAND** BY THE PORTUGUESE OUR GOVERNMENT HAS DECIDED TO TAKE RETALIATORY ACTION AGAINST THE PORTUGUESE.

Code Word

*The code name of the operation is **VIJAY***

Command and Control

Overall command and Control—the Chiefs of Staff Committee, New Delhi, will control the operations. The flag Officer Commanding, Indian Fleet will be the Naval task Commander and necessary orders will be issued to him by the Naval Headquarters

Maritime Operations Room

The naval Operations will be conducted through the Maritime Operations Room at Bombay.

Army and Air Command

The army units will be under the command of Force Commander, who will operate under the command of General Officer, Commanding -in-Chief, Southern Command. The air element will be under the command of Air Officer Commanding-in-Chief, Operational Command; his Headquarters will be alongside that of G.O.C. Southern Command. The Air Force has set up a tactical Air Centre alongside the army Force Commander.

Liaison Officers

A Naval Liaison Officer will be attached to G.O.C-in-C, Southern Command. The Naval Officer is to maintain a wireless link with F.O.C.I.F. through Maritime Operations Room, Bombay. All communications between the G.O.C.-in-C, A.O.C.-in-C and F.O.C.I.F. will be passed on this route. One Air Force Officer is attached to F.O.C.I.F's Staff for Liaison duties within the Air Force if required.

Naval Task

The Naval Task is to gain effective control of the seaward approaches to the Portuguese Territory of Goa (including the harbour of **MORMUGAO** bay and **ENSEADA (small port) da AGUADA, DIU,** and the capture of **ANGEDIV** Island. Further the task is to prevent hostile action by the Portuguese Warships against Indian Territory.

ARMY AND AIR FORCE Tasks

ARMY—Army's task is the occupation of the Portuguese territories of **GOA**, **DAMAN** and **DIU** with the utmost speed.

AIR FORCE—Air Force's task is the neutralization of Portuguese airfields and wireless stations at **GOA** on the first day of operations with the object of gaining air superiority in this area. They will also gain air superiority over **DAMAN** and **DIU.** Subsequently they will provide air support to the land forces and exceptionally also to the Naval Forces.

ENEMY FORCES

Surface Force—the following Portuguese Frigates are now based at **GOA:**

(a) ALPHONSE (Afonso) DE ALBUQUERQUE
(b) BART (H) OLOMEU DIAS
(c) GONSALVES ZARCO
(d) JOAO DE LISBOA

(Actually only the Aviso *Afonso de Albuquerque* and the patrol Boat *Sirius* were in the Goan waters).

AIRCRAFT—Upto a squadron of transonic jet fighters may be operating from **DABOLIM** airfield in **MARMAGOA** area. Transport aircraft fitted to carry bombs have been reported. (These are unconfirmed reports).

SUBMARINES—the Portuguese Navy possesses three 'S' Class submarines. There is no evidence however, of any submarines operating in Indian Waters.

OWN FORCES

The Naval Task Force (TF 332) is organized into two task groups as follows:

(a) *The Surface Action Group (TG.332.1).* This group will consist of I.N. Ships **MYSORE** (FOCIF), **TRISHUL** (F15) **BETWA, BEAS** and **CAUVERY.**

(b) *The Carrier Task Group (TG.332.2.* The group will consist of I.N Ships **VIKRANT, DELHI, KUTHAR (F14) KIRPAN, KHUKRI** and **RAJPUT (D11).**

(c) *Minesweeping Group (TG.332.3)* The Minesweepers KARWAR (MS149) CANNANORE, KAKINADA and BIMLIPATAM.

TASK FORCE ORGANISATION

The detailed Task Force Organisation is shown in the following chart

THE NAVAL FORCE

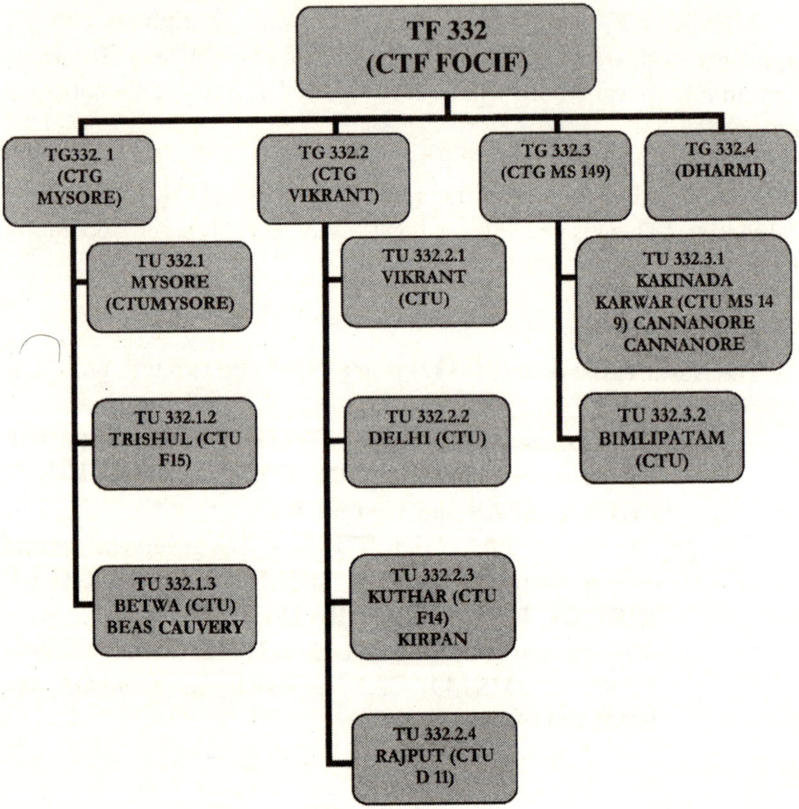

Vice-Admiral R. D. Katari, Chief of Naval Staff in 1961

Rear-Admiral B. S. Soman, Theatre Naval Commander

INTELLIGENCE

Up-to-date intelligence regarding Portuguese forces and their activities is given ***separately.***

INTENTIONS

(a) To operate TG. 332.1(Surface Action Group) off the Portuguese territory of Goa and Angediv Island in order

(i) To capture **ANGEDIV** Island.

(ii) To deny the entrance of all shipping into **GOA** harbour

(iii)To land a party of Naval personnel to administer the port of **PANJIM (GOA)**, if required by the Army after the Portuguese have surrendered

(b) To operate TG.332.2

(i) To provide air support to search and strike if necessary any Portuguese men-of-war slipping through the patrol of surface ships off GOA.

(ii) To prevent any Portuguese warships reaching within gun range of Bombay

METHOD OF EXECUTION[175]

Reference Positions

For this operation the following lettered positions are established:

(a) FF—20° 00' NORTH 71° 00' EAST

(b) GG—15° 20' NORTH 73°30' EAST

(c) JJ—15° 05' NORTH 73° 40' EAST

(d) KK—14° 40' NORTH 74° 00' EAST

(e) MM—18° 35' NORTH 72° 30' EAST

(f) NN—19° NORTH 71° 00' EAST

(g) PP—14° 00' NORTH 70° 40' EAST

(h) SS—17° 00' NORTH 72° 00' EAST

(i) TT—15° 30' NORTH 73° 35' EAST

Initial Deployments[176]

TG.332.1 (Surface Action Group)

(a) T.U.332.1 (***MYSORE***) and 332.1.2 (***TRISHUL***) are to operate within 20 miles radius of position PP—on D-1. At H-10, they are to commence transiting so as to be in position 012 KK 8 miles at H hour.

(b) On D-1, T.U.332.1.3 (***BETWA, BEAS and CAUVERI***) to be on a linear patrol 8 miles off the coast between latitudes 15° 30' N 14° 50' N.

G.332.2 (Carrier Task Group)

(a) Initially TG. 332.2 to operate between the latitudes of Bombay and Northern limits of Portuguese Goa at a distance of not less than 50 miles from the coast.

(b) From D-1, TG.332.2 (to operate to seaward between two arcs radius 70 miles and 120 miles with centre as **AGUADA** light keeping 50 miles off the coast, remaining northward in this area. The westward limit of operation to be 71° 30'E

(c) At H-10 TU 332.2.2 (***DELHI***) is to be in position NN and commence transiting for positioning 8 miles South of DIU for H hour. CTG 332.2 is to detach TU 332.2 accordingly.

(d) On D-2 TU 332.2.4 (***RAJPUT***) is to RV TG 332.2 in area at (b) above.

(e) TG. 332.3(**Mine Sweeping Group**) is to be sailed from Bombay so as to be in position TT at H+4

TASKS on D-DAY

The D-day and H hour will be signalled. Details of action to be taken by various Task Groups from H-hour are enumerated below. At 00 01 EF on 'D' day ships employed in Operation **Chutney** will form part of Operation **VIJAY** and operation **Chutney** will be deemed to have terminated from that time.

CAPTURE OF ANGEDIV ISLAND

TU.332.1.1 and 332.1.2 are to ensure speedy capture of **ANGEDIV** Island[177] with minimum loss to life and property. Detailed orders are contained in Appendix 'C' In the event of a Portuguese frigate being present at **ANJEDIV**, appropriate action be taken to neutralize and capture her. After capturing her, *MYSORE* is to place a boarding party on the frigate and escort her to Karwar harbour.

Anti-shipping patrol off Goa harbour

TU.332.1.3 **(Betwa, Beas and Cauvery)** is to re-establish a linear patrol 10 miles off the coast between latitudes 15° 10' and 15° 40'N moving into 8 miles subject to no opposition from the shore batteries so as to deny the entrance of all shipping into Goa and advise foreign ships not to enter harbour for their own safety, but allowing the free egress of all merchant ships there from. Action to be taken against Portuguese Naval ships is dealt separately in these orders. On successful completion of their allotted task TU.332.1.1 **(*MYSORE*)** and TU.332.1.2 **(*TRISHUL*)** are to join TU.332.1.3 **(*BETWA, BEAS* and *CAUVERY*)** to further tighten the ring round Goa. It is possible that Portuguese warships may masquerade by hoisting foreign naval ensigns. Once operation VIJAY starts all shipping into Goa is to be denied. Except for Portuguese merchant ships, egress of all merchant shipping is to be permitted. Portuguese ships should not be allowed to leave harbour.

Operations by Carrier Task group.

TG. 332.2 to perform the following tasks[178]**:**

Prevent any Portuguese warship from reaching within gun range of Bombay by use of ***ALIZEs*** for recce and ***SEA HAWKs*** for strikes. With ***ALIZEs*** establish and maintain a continuous area search in area bounded by line joining points:

(i) 18° 05' N 72° 50' E

(ii) 18° 05' N 71° 20' E

(iii) 19° 35' N 72° 35' E.

(a) Keep in readiness during daylight hours one strike of three Sea Hawks for strikes against any Portuguese warship that may break through the patrol line off Goa. In order to avoid indiscretion the strike will be ordered by me.

(b) Keep in readiness during daylight hours a second strike of the three Sea Hawks to be used against any Portuguese warship detected by the air search proceeding towards Indian Territory. This strike is to be used at the discretion of CTG.332.2.

(c) At H-hour report to CTG 332 if an ***ALIZE*** could be made available for any extraneous searches that may become necessary.

(d) TU.332.2.2 (***DELHI***) to provide necessary support as required to Army units operating off **DIU** from H-hour to H+5 after which she is to return to RV TG 332.2 (CTG ***VIKRANT***) in position 345 SS 60 by H 14. (Special orders for ***DELHI***).

(e) TU 332.2.2 (***DELHI***) and TU 332.2.4 (***RAJPUT***) to provide necessary gun support to TG. 332.2 (**The Carrier Task Group**) as ordered by C.T.G. 332.2.

Operations by Minesweepers

TG.332.3 (Minesweeping Group) may be required to sweep the entrance to **Panjim** and **Mormugao** harbours after hostilities are terminated. In addition they may be required to embark from TG.332.1 (Surface Action Group) earmarked naval personnel for temporary administration of captured ports if such a request should materialize from the Army Authorities.

SPECIAL INSTRUCTIONS

Action against Portuguese Naval Ships[179]:

All Portuguese Naval ships taking hostile action are to be neutralized and where feasible captured. For this purpose, the term hostile action will include condition when Portuguese warships are found to be steering courses, which will adversely affect the intentions. Any other Portuguese warships met with are to be called upon to surrender and escorted to Bombay/Karwar, whichever is nearer. Refusal to surrender is to be considered as hostile action.

Air and Anti-Submarine threats

Portuguese Air A/S threats at no time should be discounted. All task group and task unit commanders are to take necessary material and tactical counter-measures until such time as these threats are positively known to have been eliminated.

Degree of Readiness

Ships addressed are to assume full wartime degree of weapon and other readiness as will be ordered from time to time.

Self Defence of VIKRANT

TG. 332.2 is to take all necessary precautions against Air and Anti-Submarine threats using his discretions for CAP and Air A/S searches as required by him

Requests for strikes

Request for Air Strikes by aircraft from VIKRANT are to be made to me to avoid indiscretion on part of various Task Units.

Night operations by TG.332.2

After day light hours TG.332.2 may operate to the Northwards of the area of operations to facilitate interception by surface gun support ships of possible Portuguese Naval Ships detected by air search in hours of darkness.

Administration of Ports of MARMAGOA and PANJIM by Naval Personnel

An organisation for taking over administration of the ports of Marmagoa and Panjim by the naval personnel after hostilities have ceased is under preparation and orders will be issued later. Some personnel from Fleet Ships will have to be made available for this purpose.

Operating Speeds

After H Hour until further orders TG.332.2 (Career Task Group) is to operate as far as practicable at as high a speed as possible.

Submarine Contacts

Until further orders all confirmed underwater contacts are to be attacked with a view to destruction.

Attacks by Surface and Air Units

With immediate effect, if engaged by any surface or air units, ships are to retaliate with necessary force.

ADMINISTRATION

Fuel

After receipt of these orders it may not be possible for ships already at sea to return to harbour for fuelling. Senior Officers of groups are to ensure that smaller ships in company are not allowed to fall below 70% of their total fuel carrying capacity before D-Day. Every opportunity is to be taken to fuel the smaller ships from the Carrier and Cruisers. **BETWA** and **BEAS** from now on are to exercise the greatest economy in the use of fuel to extend their endurance at sea to the maximum.

Provisions

Prior to every sailing, ships are to ensure that a sea stock of 15 days provisions is embarked.

Mail

In view of uncertain future movements of ships, mail may be disrupted in the near future. However, every endeavour will be made to collect and dispatch mail whenever opportunity affords

COMMUNICATION and RADIO POLICY

Radio Policy: Complete radio silence below 30 mos, VHF and UHF may be used with signal security policy No 2.

(i) **RADAR**: *No restrictions*

(ii) In the event of our own frequencies being jammed the following principles shall apply:

(a) Tactical primary (1) jammed
TG 332.1 use 04A
TG332.2 use 04B
In the event of further jamming, use Tactical secondary of the appropriate plan in use.

(b) TF/TG Common Primary (09) jammed
Use Circuit 08 on CW

(c) CIP Primary (13) jammed
Use Circuit 15

(d) AA Gun Co-ordination (18) jammed
Use Circuit 19

At the first indication of jamming all ships set watch on 3180 K/cs, this net is then to be used for short messages connected with shifting frequencies etc.

COMPLAN

The three plans in the Interim Complan (INTCAN) are forwarded along with these orders

This Complan is to be used by TF 332 as follows:

(iii)Plan A by TG 332.1
Plan B by TG 332.2
Plan C by TG 332.3

Detailed instructions were also issued regarding,

- **Cryptography**
- **Signal Traffic**
- **Authentication**
- **Recognition and Identification**
- **Ship-Shore**
- **Call Signs**
- **Electronic Warfare**
- **Joint Communication and**
- **Assault Landing Party Communication**

INTELLIGENCE[180]

The following information regarding the activities connected with the Goa situation is enumerated below:

SURFACE FORCES

(a) **Warships:** ***AFONSO ALBUQUERQUE's*** presence has been established. She has been observed anchored off **ANGEDIV** Island bearing 065^0 3 to 4 cables from the Flag Staff. At regular intervals the ship goes into **GOA** but returns to her station within 24 hours. The ship has awnings spread and is fully lit up at night.

(b) It is probable that two more unidentified warships are in **GOA** harbour. These two were tracked by **BEAS** and **BETWA** on the 2nd and 4th December respectively. This is nevertheless confirmed by the Police wireless which states that apart from these two, there are two other warships at Vasco and one more which has been moving in and out of harbour. (In fact the Portuguese had only *Aviso* ***AFONSO*** **de** ***ALBUQUERQUE*** and the patrol boat ***SIRIUS*** in Goan waters).

(c) Own Reconnaissance aircraft have reported that there are no ships at **DAMAN** and **DIU**. (There were however patrol boats ***VEGA, FOLQUE*** and ***ANTERA*** at DIU)

(d) Motor trawlers/fishing trawlers have been active in and out of GOA harbour.

SHIPPING

(a) A considerable amount of shipping has also been observed, a large proportion of these been Japanese tankers.

(b) The volume of shipping traffic in Goa can be gauged from extracts of ship's reports. These are as follows: on 7th Dec D11 (RAJPUT) observed 16 merchantmen and 4 tankers in harbour. On 6th Dec. F15 (TRISHUL) observed 8 merchantmen and 2 tankers in harbour. On 5th Dec. BETWA reported seeing 14 merchantmen at anchor.

AIR ACTIVITY

There is no confirmation to date about the availability of any air power with the Portuguese in Goa. Military 4 engined planes with Portuguese markings have however been observed on reconnaissance over Goa. Portuguese commercial aircraft on scheduled flights from Goa to Karachi have been sighted. On one such occasion, on 8th Dec. a 4-engined Skymaster approached VIKRANT and flew over her at a height of 5000 ft.

SUBMARINE

There is no definite information whether any submarines are operating in Indian waters. **KUTHAR** did however report a possible submarine contact on our main patrol line off Goa at 08 15 on 7th Dec. At 15 30 the same day **KUTHAR** again obtained a confirmed contact of a possible submarine and fired one live projectile without any results. It is however unlikely that this could have been a submarine as its position on two different occasions in the space of 7 hours would appear more or less on our patrol line. Nevertheless the probabilities of a submarine operating in the vicinity cannot be entirely ruled out (These could be dolphins which are found in these waters. The sonar experts call them biological objects).

LAND FORCES

The Garrison at **ANGEDIV** is believed to have been reinforced and the number of troops on the island may be anywhere between 30 and 100 men.

MINING THREAT

There are some unconfirmed reports that the entrance to Mormugao port and Enseada de Aguada are mined. The approaches to the landing beaches on **ANGEDIV** Island may also be mined.

NAVAL OPERATIONS OFF GOA
ORDERS FOR CAPTURE OF ANGEDIV

The following orders are for the capture of Angediv Island: [181]

Action if the Portuguese frigate is not present.

At H-hour TRISHUL is to pass between the northern point of ANGEDIV and BINGE point, keeping as close to BINGE point as is navigationally possible. The Island is to be kept covered with TRISHUL's Bofors. TRISHUL is to anchor in BINGE Bay and lower her boats, watching for opposition from the island. After one burst on the beaches with close range weapons the landing party is to be sent in. A motorboat with an LMG mounted in the bows and towing a whaler is to be used for the landing party. MYSORE at this time is to lie off the North East shore of the Island and afford gunfire support to the landing party if necessary. If the situation is favourable MYSORE is to provide to TRISHUL a motor cutter and whaler to expedite landing.

Action if a Portuguese frigate is present

At H-hour MYSORE is to close the Frigate from the North and engage her while still outside the frigate's gun range, signalling to her surrender. **TRISHUL** is to cover the Southern sector of the Island to prevent her escape to the southward.

TRISHUL is to act as instructed in the previous eventuality, when ordered by CTF 332(Command Task Force)

Orders for removing personnel captured on the Island to Karwar will be issued by FOCIF (Flag Officer Commanding in Fleet)

In all events, personnel landing (the sailors for landing were selected from I.N.S. Vendurathi) are to use their weapons in extreme necessity only. Trigger happiness is to be avoided at all costs. Treatment of all Portuguese armed forces personnel captured or surrendering is to be under the normal usages of war. Behavior of our personnel is to be exemplary.

A minimum of four days provisions is to be landed ashore once the Island is captured.

MOVEMENTS on COMPLETION

On completion of the task **MYSORE** will be ordered to proceed and join TU 332.1.3 (**BETWA, BEAS and CAUVERY**), which will be patrolling at the time. **TRISHUL**'s future employment will depend on the prevailing situation at ANGEDIV Island and instruction will be signalled to **TRISHUL** by me (Rear Admiral Soman).

The island is to remain under Naval control until otherwise ordered by NHQ (Naval Head Quarters).

NAVAL OPERATIONS OFF GOA

Instruction number two
(Short title –NOG 2)

Naval Headquarters
New Delhi,

14th December, 1961

With a lapse of time certain changes have taken place in the conception of the operations as contained in NOG 1 dated 5th December 1961. You are fully in the picture on the detailed thinking of the operations as on 11th December 1961. Certain revised instructions for the naval aspects of the operation are given in subsequent paragraphs [182]. The instructions contained in NOG 1 should be considered as amended wherever it conflicts with the instructions contained herein

Intention

In addition to that contained at para 8 of NOG 1, you shall also be required to assist the land forces as necessary to enable them to accomplish their task with expedition.

Army's TASK

In addition to the occupation of Portuguese territory of GOA with utmost speed, the Army will also occupy Portuguese territories of DAMAN and DIU simultaneously, commencing operations on early hours of D-Day.

AIR Force's TASK

Air Force's task is the same as that contained as para 6 of NOG 1 except that Air Force will not bomb any installations at DAMAN and DIU. Air Force will however maintain a fighter patrol over DAMAN and probably also over DIU, to ensure that the use of the respective airfields is denied to the enemy. For operations over DIU, if fighters are not detailed for patrol, aircraft will be on call at **JAMNAGAR**.

NAVAL FORCE ORGANISATION

Naval Task Force organisation will be the same as that shown in NOG 1 except that **RAJPUT** will now form part of the *Carrier Task Group* instead of the *Surface Action Group.*

NAVAL SUPPORT at DIU

DELHI is to be made available off DIU at 'D' day H-1 hour to support the land operations on the Island, if required. If at all possible, DELHI should rejoin the CARRIER TASK GROUP the same day by nightfall.

PORTUGUESE WARSHIPS

In amplification of the instructions contained in NOG 1 it is desired to emphasize, that every Portuguese Warship, which is in a position to interfere with the operation, must be neutralized, or preferably captured and brought to the nearest Indian Port without undue delay. The possibility, however, slight it may be, of Portuguese warships masquerading as warships of other nations by hoisting foreign naval Ensigns, must not be overlooked.

CONTROL of SHIPPING

After the start of operations, endeavour is to be made to deny the entrance of all shipping into GOA. Egress of all merchant shipping, except Portuguese ships, is to be permitted. Portuguese ships should not however be allowed to leave harbour

ANGEDIV ISLAND

It is necessary that full naval control is established on ANGEDIV Island as quickly as possible after H- hour, by physical occupation of the Island by Naval personnel. The island is to remain under naval control until otherwise ordered by Naval Headquarters.

LIAISON OFFICERS

In addition to the Naval and Air Force Liaison Officers mentioned I NOG 1, you may consider it desirable to embark on board DELHI an Army and Air Force Liaison Officer. Arrangements for obtaining these officers are to be finalised by you direct with GOC-in -, Southern Command and AOC-in-C Operational Command.

OPERATION CHUTNEY

At 0001 EF on D-Day, ships employed on operation CHUTNEY will form part of operation **VIJAY** force and Operation **CHUTNEY** will be deemed to have terminated as from that time.

NAVAL TASK

Naval task will be as contained at NOG 1 except that coastal batteries are not to be engaged unless they open fire first.

NOIC GOA (Designate)

Captain H.A.Agate, I.N. has been earmarked as Naval Officer- in-Charge (designate). A detailed scheme of personnel and equipment required for taking complete charge of the harbours of **MARMAGAO** and **PANJIM** is to be worked out. Personnel and equipment are to be kept ready at Bombay for embarkation at short notice, for passage to Goa.

ALIZE RECONNAISSANCE

Alize Recce will not be flown from **BELGAUM**. You may, however authorize Alize Recce to be flown from **VIKRANT** as necessary for Naval Operations. The Recce should be flown under control of **VIKRANT** keeping Maritime Operations Room Bombay fully informed.

(R.D.KATARI)

VICE ADMIRAL

Chief of the Naval Staff

SPECIAL ORDERS to MYSORE

On capture of Portuguese ships [183]

In the event of Portuguese warship surrendering off Angediv Island, *MYSORE* is to take action as enumerated below:

(a) Contact S.R.P. (Police Unit) at Karwar and inform them to have guards ready.

(b) Send a Boarding party to the warship.

(c) Immediately on boarding the Boarding party is to

(i) Immobilize all armaments

(ii) Post sentries to prevent scuttling and damage to machinery.

(d) Escort the ship to Karwar harbour.

(e) Police guard will board ship and take over security duties on board.

(f) Mysore to leave behind essential personnel on board to supervise the normal running of machinery by the crew in harbour.

NAVAL TASK

The political decision to take action against all the Portuguese territories was taken on 30th November, after which it was decided that the control and direction of all ships of the fleet should be exercised by Naval Headquarters and not delegated to the Flag Officer Commanding Indian Fleet [184].

However, the patrol as per the "**Operation Chutney**" was established on 1st December 1961 by **INS** ***BETWA*** and **INS** ***BEAS*** and continued to observe and signal useful information till after D-Day. From the observations of the patrol ships it was clear that there was no other airfield in Goa apart from Dabolim airfield. Also it was noticed that the Portuguese had only a few transport aircraft and no combat aircraft. Their only man-of-war *Afonso de Albuquerque* kept moving between Angediv and Marmagoa. No other man-of-war of similar or larger size was observed.

When it was decided that the retaliatory measures against the Portuguese were to be taken it was also decided that the same would be in the form of combined operations by three Services.

The operations were to be controlled by the Chiefs of Staff Committee from New Delhi but their own respective headquarters issued the necessary orders to the three theatre commanders. The Flag Officer Commanding the Indian Fleet-**Rear-Admiral B.S. Soman** was appointed the naval task force Commander, and was given the task of gaining "effective control of the seaward approaches to the Portuguese territory of Goa, including the harbours of Marmagoa and Enseada da Aguada and of Angediv Island, and also to prevent hostile action by the Portuguese warships against Indian Territory."

To achieve this objective, which was in effect to blockade Portuguese ports, it was ordered, "On the morning of D-Day, he should bombard Angediv Island, neutralise Portuguese coast batteries and control all shipping movement in and out of Goa". It was realized soon after the plan was made that neutralisation of these batteries was not essential either to the army or to the naval plan and this task could be modified, as there was no intention of resorting to indiscriminate bombing or bombardment. After due modification the task meant "while the Navy should lay on the plans for neutralisation of the coastal guns, it should hold fire until fired upon first by enemy." On 14th December one more item was added namely "Required to assist the land forces as necessary, to enable them accomplish their task expeditiously." To summarise, the naval task which emerged finally was that the Navy should:

(i) Enforce a blockade of Portuguese ports in India,
(ii) Be ready to neutralise Portuguese coastal batteries but should hold fire till the necessity for this arose, or the enemy opened fire first,
(iii) Bombard Angediv Island and capture it,
(iv) Help the land forces where necessary to accomplish their task quickly.

Naval Headquarters commented later on "the naval role envisaged was essentially one of gaining effective control of the seaward approaches to and bays of Marmagoa and Aguada, and to prevent interference by

Portuguese naval units; the occupation of Angediv Island and gunfire support to Army taking over Diu".

Capture of Angediv Island

Since the Portuguese activities from Angediv were the primary reason for **OPERATION VIJAY**, the first action by the Navy was aimed against this Island.[185] The original intention was that if the garrison on the island surrendered after bombardment, a party of the Armed Police from Karwar should be landed on the island for its occupation. It was felt during discussions in a meeting of **Joint Operations Committee (JOC)** that it might not be desirable to use Police Forces for this purpose, for two reasons:-

(a) Armed opposition may be offered by the garrison; and

(b) The use of Police in Portuguese territory before a Civil Administrator had officially taken over in Goa might have political implications.

The Chiefs of Staff later decided that the landing party should be from one of the Services. The final orders for ANGEDIV were: "it is necessary that full naval control is established on Angediv Island as quickly as possible after H hour, by physical occupation of the island by naval personnel. The island is to remain under naval control until otherwise ordered by Naval Headquarters."

For the performance of naval tasks, a Naval Task force was to be created of which the **FOCIF, Rear-Admiral B.S.Soman**, was to be the commander. This Task Force was to be initially organized in two Groups, namely: **Surface Action Group** and the **Carrier Task Group**.

The **Surface Action Group** was to consist of one cruiser **(Mysore)** and three frigates (**Betwa, Beas and Trishul**); and the **Carrier Task Group** of the aircraft carrier (**Vikrant**), one cruiser (**Delhi**), three frigates (**Khukri, Kuthar and Kirpan**) and the destroyer **Rajput.**

A **mine sweeping force** comprising IN Ships **Karwar, Cannanore** and **Bimlipattam** of the 149th Mine-sweeping Squadron was kept in readiness for minesweeping operations if required.

ORGANISATION CHART [186]

of the operation

Duties of the two Groups[187]

The **Surface Action Group** was to operate off the Portuguese territory of Goa and Angediv Island. The earlier orders for this Group were that, as far as possible, it was to engage Angediv Island at first light on D-Day, effect a landing on the island and simultaneously engage the coastal batteries on Goan territory.

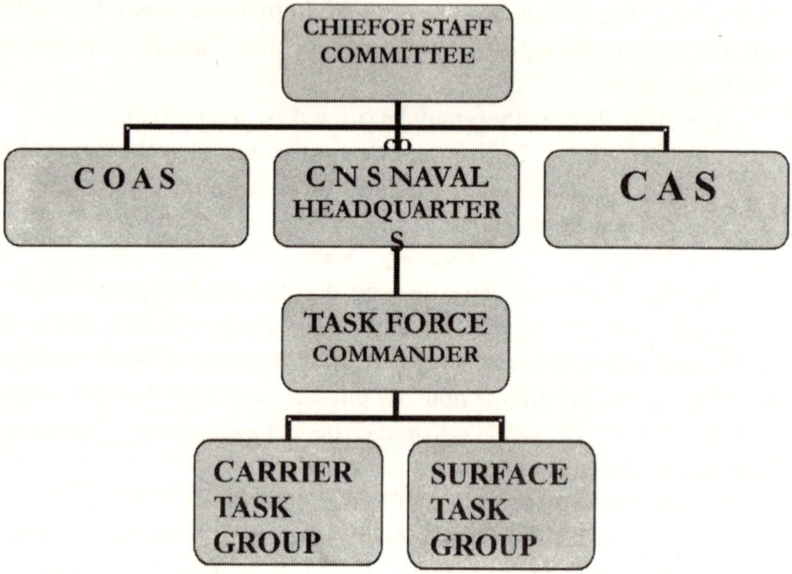

This group was also to enforce the blockade of Goa except for the egress of merchant ships. These tasks were later modified in so far as engaging the coastal batteries were concerned.

The **Carrier Task Group** was to operate initially between the latitudes of Bombay and northern limit of Goa at a distance of not less than 80 kilometres from the coast. It was to provide air support for naval operations as directed by the Task Force Commander, and also prevent any Portuguese warships from attempting to interfere in Marmagoa-Panjim area or from reaching within gun range of Bombay. This Task Group moved within a radius of 80 to 193 kilometres from Marmagoa–Goa from the midnight of 17/18 December, but in the event had no opportunity to join action.

However, it kept aircraft ready to fly out in support if called upon, and maintained air patrols for its own protection round the clock).

All Portuguese naval ships taking hostile action were to be neutralised or preferably captured and brought to the nearest Indian port without undue delay. The term 'hostile action' for this purpose would, of course, include situations when an enemy ship was found to be steering a course, which might adversely affect carrying out tasks assigned to the Indian Fleet.

Later, by the 14th of December, certain changes had taken place in the conception of the operations as envisaged on 4th and 5th December. One of these was that in addition to the occupation of Goa with utmost speed, the army would also occupy the Portuguese territories of Daman and Diu simultaneously. As a natural consequence of this change, it was decided that the Navy should assist the land forces if necessary, and the **INS Delhi** from Carrier Group was to be made available off Diu at H-Hour on D-Day as a show of force and if necessary, to support the land operations on the island by naval gunfire. Liaison officers were attached from one service to another to facilitate co-operation between the Army, Navy and Air Force. Apart from enforcing the blockade, which no Portuguese ship tried to ' run' ships of the Indian Fleet were engaged in action at three places, namely (1) at Angediv (2) off Goa and (3) off Diu.

CAPTURE of ANGEDIV

In November 1961, the Portuguese authorities in Angediv Island took it into their heads to indulge in some provocative acts, which precipitated India's decision to take military action for the liberation of the Portuguese enclaves by a combined operation of the three Services: the Army, Navy and Air Force.[188] Although there was excellent co-ordination and co-operation between these Services, it so turned out that the occupation of Goa was mainly an army affair, the air force was the deciding factor in Daman and Diu, and the capture of Angediv was purely a naval operation.

Naval Head Quarters however commented that the final success at Diu was mainly due to the bombardment by ***INS Delhi.*** It is true that the Portuguese resistance collapsed and white flags were raised only after bombardment of the citadel by ***INS Delhi.*** The task of establishing full control over the island by physical occupation, as quickly as possible after H Hour, was assigned to ***INS Mysore*** and ***INS Trishul*** The plan was that while ***INS Mysore*** was to provide covering fire, ***INS Trishul*** was to land a party on the island for its capture. In the event a party from Mysore was also landed on the island. On the night of 17th /18th December, the *Mysore* in company with ***INS Trishul*** proceeded on course to reach the island by first light on the 18th. This was done at 06:00 hours on the 18th, and ***INS Trishul*** was released to go and perform her task. She was directed to wait till there was sufficient daylight to have a clear view of the northern part of the island before landing the assault party. While *Mysore* remained at some distance, ***INS Trishul*** went ahead and rounded the North point. There it noticed that no flags were flying from either of the two flagstaffs in the island. At about 7 o'clock, she arrived eastward of the Round islet, where she lowered her boats in which two sections of the assault party were embarked. At this time Bofors were fired on the island in the vicinity of '*FOXTROT*' beach. Meanwhile ***INS Mysore*** had arrived at some point in between the mainland and the island and had also opened fire with her Bofors at suspected pillboxes at various points on the island from a range of approximately 2743 metres.

By about 07:15 the first wave of the assault party from ***INS Trishul*** called "*RUSTUM*" was underway and heading for **Beach Foxtrot (Beach F).** This party landed successfully without any opposition and having established themselves at the beach commenced to advance bit by bit. The landing operations were successfully carried out under Lieutenant Arun Auditto who was officer in charge of naval Landing Party. Lt Auditto as Commander, commanded later on Submarine INS Kursura during 1971 war against Pakistan.

At about 07:46 hours the second wave also left ***INS Trishul*** and headed towards the beach in boats. Ship's fire cover could not be given to this wave as the first wave had already landed and were moving forward. **When the second wave was about 137 metres from the beach the Portuguese hoisted a white flag at the flagstaff in front of a church near ' Beach Lima' Within a minute or so of the white flag being seen fire was opened on boards of the second wave from Portuguese gun-posts near a pillbox on the south hill-top causing casualties.**[189] However the boats pressed on and beached, and whoever was still fit landed, including Officer Noel Kelman who was in charge of this wave and who was wounded in both thighs. The boats, though holed by bullets managed to bring back some of the wounded to the ship. The treachery of hoisting a white flag followed up by firing was no doubt a bitter experience for our sailors. A little later some white troops were seen digging in near the white flag. ***INS Trishul*** opened fire with Bofors around this point. This incident was also being observed from command ship ***INS Mysore.***

One participant's account says that no prompt covering fire was given by ***INS Mysore*** at this crucial moment. Rear-Admiral Soman commanding the ship refused to fire the Bofors saying that the orders were "**to carry out indirect bombardment and after firing broadside, to wait and observe results to avoid unnecessary loss of life and property**". Listening to this comment other officers on board bundled him into his cabin despite his threats of a Court Martial and opened Bofors, saving the lives of remaining landing personnel.

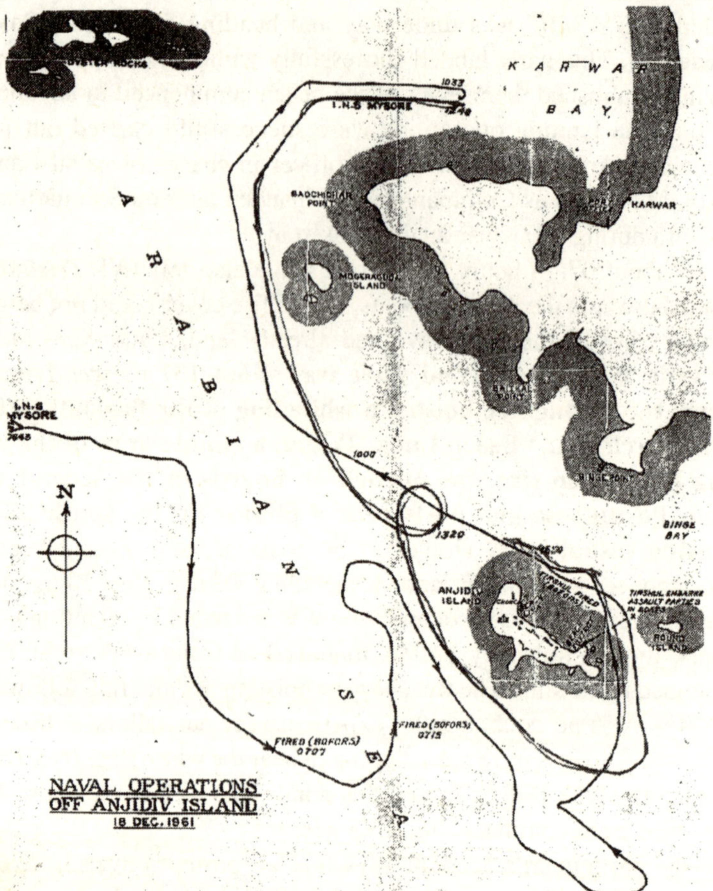

Naval Operations Off Anjidiv Island
18th Dec. 1961

I. N. S. Mysore

I. N. S. Trishul

By now ***INS Mysore*** also sent her landing party with orders to proceed round the island and take further orders from ***INS Trishul***. This party also landed at **'F beach'** and proceeded to support the main party and assist in establishing communications, which were not satisfactory.

These casualties and some others evacuated by Mysore's pinnace were all, finally, brought to ***INS Mysore***, which took them to Karwar for treatment. While leaving for Karwar it fired a few parting shots at southern end of the island. After landing the casualties, ***INS Mysore*** returned to action area to take part and guide the battle.

Meanwhile, "*RUSTUM*" was making steady progress and by 08:19 hrs had reached the pillbox on top of the southern hill. Then they advanced to the north on the western slopes. Contact with these troops was now lost due to failure of radio-telephony and so ***INS Trishul*** decided to move north-eastwards and from there to the western side hoping to re-establish communications This attempt was not successful but the men could be seen advancing along point **Romeo**, and a fair amount of exchange of fire could be heard. Meanwhile a party under Commander A.F. Collaco was sent ashore under orders of the **FOCIF** to obtain information on the progress of landing parties. This party working as a link was soon able to establish contact with "*Rustum*" and the ship ***INS Trishul***.

It was now learnt from "*Rustum*" that though the Southern position of the island had been easily over-run, the party in the northern sector had been kept at bay by strong opposition and needed fire support. Thereupon ***INS Trishul*** fired some salvoes at north point, taking particular care not to hit the church situated in that area. On receiving clear directions from "*Rustum*" regarding points to be fired at, ***INS Trishul*** went over and plastered the northern hill. Then it went over west and bombarded Hill 212 and its slopes.

At 12:40 hrs Commander A.F.Collaco's team advanced to the eastern side towards the wireless transmitter station with a view to taking it over. On nearing a church at the southern end of the F Beach, this party was fired upon from the church, fatally injuring a sailor. It is a pity that while the Indian Armed Forces scrupulously avoided causing any damage to churches and other places of worship the Portuguese used these as ammunition dumps and defensive posts. As no further progress could be made without damaging the church, the party withdrew to **F Beach**. Other parties were also asked to withdraw to **F Beach**. The landing parties had been instructed "to use their weapons in extreme necessity only" [190]

A plan was now agreed upon to bombard, after all our parties had withdrawn to F Beach, the northern area of the island. This was to be done by ***INS Mysore*** from the southwest and ***INS Trishul*** from the southeast. Just as this was to be put into effect, nine white Portuguese were spotted under the white flag in front of the flagstaff at 14:00 hrs. They all had their hands over their heads, except one who was waiving a white cloth.

The first landing party ("*Rustum*") was instructed by ***INS Trishul*** to take charge of the prisoners. This looked, after all, like real surrender. Officers and crews in motorboats were sent to take charge of the prisoners on other beaches as well, and bring them from the shore to ***INS Mysore.*** Although some white soldiers did surrender on that day, it was known that some other Portuguese soldiers were still to be captured and some pockets of resistance cleared. This was done the next day. All areas were thoroughly combed, some more prisoners (both civilians and soldiers) were taken and the **national flag hoisted on top of the flagstaff at 14:25 hours on 19th December.** [191]

The Indian Navy has built memorials at ANGEDIV Island and at INS Gomantak —Goa in memory of seamen killed in the action

"In memory of those who laid down their lives on 19th December, 1961 for the liberation of Angediv Island during Operation Vijay"

IN MEMORY OF THOSE WHO LAID DOWN THEIR
LIVES ON 19 TH DECEMBER 1961 FOR
THE LIBERATION OF ANJADIV ISLAND
DURING "OPERATION VIJAY"

NARENDRA NATH SENGUPTA	ABLE SEAMAN	N 47127
DURGESH CHANDRA TARAFDAR	ABLE SEAMAN	N 64231
SHAMBU SINGH	ORDINARY SEAMAN	86291
VIJENDRA PAL SINGH TOMAR	ORDINARY SEAMAN	66901
BACHAN SINGH	ORDINARY SEAMAN	66315
SAMUEL JAYASALAM MOHANDAS	ORDINARY SEAMAN	66395
BACHAN SINGH	ORDINARY SEAMAN	67103

The memorial honouring the seamen who died at Angediv

CASUALTIES at ANGEDIV[192]

INDIAN

	Officers	Sailors
Killed	-	7
Wounded	2	17
Total	2	24

Killed:

Narendra Nath Sengupta	Able Seaman	N 47127
Durgesh Chandra Tarafdar	Able Seaman	N 64231
Shambu Singh	Ord. Seaman	86291
Vijendra Pal Singh Tomar	Ord. Seaman	66901
Bachan Singh	Ord.Seaman	66315
Samuel Jayasalan Mohandas	Ord. Seaman	86395
Bachan Singh	Ord. Seaman	67103

PORTUGUESE

	Officers	Soldiers
Killed	1	6
Wounded	-	4
Total	1	10

PRISONERS

White	15
Goans	8
Total	23

ACTION by PORTUGUESE GARRISON
(Portuguese Version)

(This report[193] is based on interviews with the personnel present at Angediv during the Naval Operation and taken subsequently as prisoners. They were shifted later on to Prisoner's Camp at PONDA)

THE DAY 18th DECEMBER

NUCLEO A—Posto do Altinho [194]

This post consisted of a Cabo (Corporal) and three soldiers. It was armed with a Light Machine Gun.

At 06:45 hrs the soldiers of this post saw the warship Frigate TRISHUL located near the island of Round. It opened an intense bombardment in the Southeast zone of the island. The bombardment lasted about fifteen minutes. As soon as it stopped two landing crafts carrying troops left the frigate and started in the direction of "Praia Pequena"(Small Beach). Cabo Nelson Braganca posted at the "Post do Altinho" opened fire with his Bren gun and in the process wounded several people who were in the crafts. The Frigate located our gun and opened fire for a few minutes in order to silence it. However, it did not cause any casualties.

After landing of troops at Praia Pequena the crafts returned to the ship with the wounded and dead, and returned again with a new contingent. Once again Cabo Braganca opened fire with his gun, as it was easy to aim at people who could not move in that small craft. There were many casualties.

Meanwhile, Cabo Braganca was forced to stop firing as he was short of ammunition and also his gun had started malfunctioning due to over-heating.

Due to this fact the elements of this post had to withdraw. Two left to an unknown place, another left to the "Posto de Fonte" and Cabo Braganca went to "Posto de Diligencia" to bring more ammunition. When he returned to the "Posto de Fonte" with a view to joining the troops manning that post he saw the Indian Troops already at the post. With great difficulty he managed to reach the other spring situated in the west of the island. He remained there alone till nineteenth.

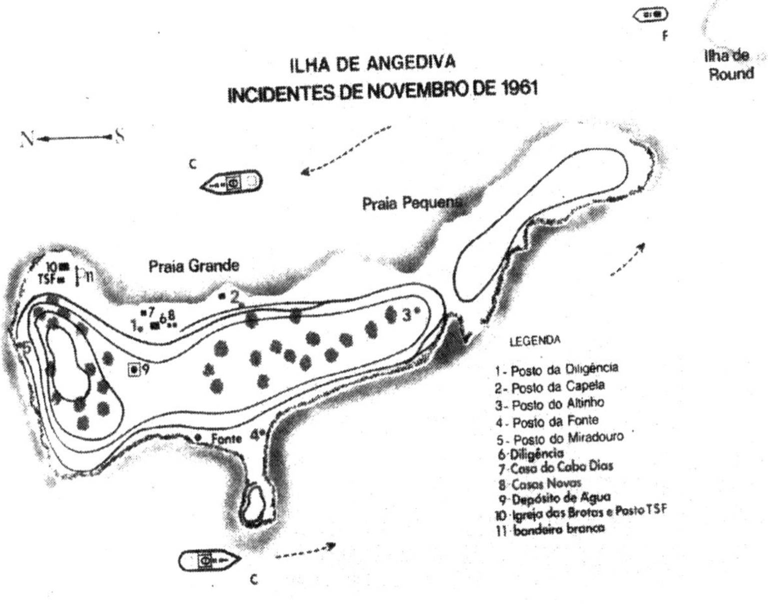

Incidents Occured In November 1961

NUCLEO B—Posto do Fonte (Post of spring)

It had identical manpower and weapons as in the post described earlier.

"The personnel saw around 06:30, to the west of island and at a short distance the Indian Cruiser"MYSORE". After some time they saw the firing of Very Light Signal from this ship which indicated the beginning of the attack on the island. Soon after, they heard the bombardment by the Frigate, which has been described earlier, and

the Bren gun fire from the "Posto de Altinho".The Cruiser then left in a Southerly direction.

After some time the soldier who had withdrawn from the "Posto de Altinho" appeared at this post and narrated what had happened there.

Around 09:30 the first enemy troops appeared at the South of the island.

As the place where they were situated could be easily zeroed, it was decided to leave and regroup near" ***Depo'sito de A'gua"*** *(Water Storage Tank). Meanwhile, the soldier Damuno Vassu Canencar slowed down in his movements and was fired at by Indian troops, which caused his death.*

After reaching the "Depo'sito de A'gua" and mounting the machine gun in a proper place, its operator Armando Teixeira as well as other soldiers opened fire stopping the advance of the enemy and causing some casualties. After the heavy shoot-out and noticing that they would be surrounded, they were compelled to withdraw in the direction of the (Diligencia) command post.

Meanwhile, the ammunition stock ran out during this encounter Cabo Antonio Jesus Costa was wounded. In order to help him they went searching for the medical orderly who normally was stationed in the command post, but he could not be located.

As it was not possible to continue fighting they decided to join the civilians who were employed in the construction of two houses near the military post. At this location they stayed awaiting the news. They surrendered to the Indian troops at 16:30 hrs without having any news about incidents taking place at other places in the island. The personnel from the "Posto de Capela also surrendered together with them." They were also forced to withdraw to this post.

NUCLEO C -Posto de Capela [196]

Its strength was equal to those of other posts described earlier but had over and above the anti-tank grenade launching weapon PIAT.

The post spotted at 06:30 hrs an Indian frigate near the island of Round. At 07:00 they witnessed the bombarding in the zone of Praia Pequena and heard machine gun firing from "Posto de Altinho".

Though they could see the landing crafts coming in the direction of the land, they did not have any weapons to effectively stop the enemy. After some time the cruiser appeared from the south and stayed in front of Praia Grande. It bombarded the area around "Posto Radio". It was not possible to know the result of this attack but one could presume that it must have created losses to our troops. The Cruiser moved thereafter to the north but returned to the same position later on.

The Indian troops, after having landed on the" Praia Pequena" entered the forest area and taking advantage of the cover from the same, approached the vicinity of "Posto de Capela" without much difficulty. After a small exchange of fire our soldiers withdrew in order to avoid encirclement. They reached the houses where there were other persons who had earlier withdrawn from "Posto de Fonte", as well as civilian workers.

They surrendered to the Indian forces together with others around 16:30 hrs.

NUCLEO D—Diligencia e Posto Radio [197]

This Nucleus was subdivided into two.

The commander of the garrison of Angediv 2nd Lt. (miliciano) Abel dos Santos Rito Ribeiro, the 2nd Sergeants Costa Chiu e Ramiro da Fonseca and six soldiers were stationed in the "Diligencia"-the Command Post. It had a Light Machine Gun. The 2nd Sergeant Gonsalves and two soldiers were stationed in the "Posto Radio" near "Igreja das Brotas"-the Church.

The 2nd Sergeant spotted at 06:30, near the island of Round, an Indian Frigate. Immediately he sent a message to "Quartel General" informing it about the matter and also about the attack, which the warship executed in the zone of "Praia Pequena".

After some time 2nd Lt. Ribeiro and others from the command Post appeared before "Posto de Radio." As there was heavy bombardment from the Indian warship the Garrison Commander wanted to know the opinion of his subordinates regarding the action to be taken, as the means at their disposal were not sufficient to offer an efficient resistance. There were conflicting opinions but after some moments someone who could not be identified hoisted a white flag on the pole adjacent to "Posto do Radio".

Meanwhile, the bombardment to the South of the island could be heard. At 08:00 hrs. the cruiser, which was stationed opposite "Praia Grande", opened a heavy barrage with its guns on the area where our people were standing. In the process the building of "Posto de Radio" was partially destroyed.

Some moments earlier 2nd Lt Ribeiro, Sergeant Ramiro da Fonseca and medical orderly Cabo Antonio Baptista Xavier had moved in the direction of the forest zone in the neighborhood of Radio Post. This place had received heavy fire from the Indian Cruiser.

One may believe that these three military men died in that place, as they never appeared alive thereafter.

Three landing crafts from the Cruiser and two others from the frigate left in the direction of "Praia Pequena".

However, our soldiers who had taken position behind the wall in front of the Radio Post opened fire on the landing crafts. In view of this fact, the warships resumed the attack on areas of "Praia Pequena" and "Posto Radio," resulting in big fire in the area where our people were stationed. The people hurriedly left for the North of the island. Moment's thereafter two violent explosions signalled the destruction of the ammunition dumps, which were located near "Igreja das Brotas". The Indian Cruiser, as a reprisal, turned around the island several times, bombarding the North zone non-stop, without inflicting however significant losses. Thereafter it went in the direction of Karwar and returned later, taking once again its original position.

Our military men were without ammunition and were awaiting developments.

The Cruiser restarted the attack on Angediv Island despite any provocation from our forces. It lasted till 15:30 hrs.

Our troops which had moved to the North-West direction in order to avoid fire from the cruiser were forced to retreat in the direction of "Posto do Radio, "as they could hear automatic arms fire coming from the area of "Alto da Bandeira". They signalled to the Indian Warship their surrender. From this ship they were directed to move to the Praia Grande and this order was promptly obeyed. Around 16:30 hrs. these military men joined the others who had already surrendered near the houses, as referred to earlier.

NUCLEO E—"Posto do Miradouro" [198]

This post had a Cabo and three other soldiers. It had a Light Machine Gun in its armament. This post was interconnected with "Nucleo D" and participated as such in its actions.

On 18th December at 16:30 hours there were three prisoners' groups in "Praia Grande": the first consisting of eight elements of Nuclei D and E; the second of thirteen of Nuclei A, B and C; and the third one consisting of nine civilians engaged in building work.

During the counting of the prisoners seven military men were found absent. Of these three were- 2nd Lt Ribeiro, the Sergeant Ramiro and Cabo Xavier- who were presumed to have died during the bombardment by the Indian Cruiser; the other was the soldier Canencar, who had died during the shootout while retreating from "Posto de Fonte". The other three whose whereabouts were not known were: Cabo Nelson Braganca, Cabo Valdemar Marques and the soldier Manuel dos Santos Caetano who were hiding in the interior of the island.

After noting down the details, the Portuguese prisoners embarked on a launch. There were also many wounded and dead from the Indian Navy.

On board of the cruiser the prisoners were interrogated as to why they continued firing even after raising the white flag; on the total strength of the personnel in the island and in Goa; locations of probable underground positions in Angediv; the existence of African troops; the whereabouts of the garrison commander and many other questions.

The reasons given for opening fire even after raising the white flag were: [199]

- Not all of them knew about the raising of the white flag,
- As there was no accord about the decision, those with a contrary opinion may have decided about continuing the combat;
- As radio communication between the different nuclei was not reliable there was no co-ordination about happenings in other parts of the island.

The prisoners reached Karwar in the evening, where they were lodged in the prisons. The European soldiers were segregated from the Goans.

So, during the night of eighteenth to nineteenth there remained on the island, **Cabo Braganca** near the spring, the **Soldier Manuel Caetano** hiding in the rocks in the neighbourhood of "Alto da Bandeira" and **Cabo Marques** near the same place, each unaware of the existence of the other.

Around 22:00 hrs. Cabo Marques cautiously went to the command post where he drank water and searched for food, returning thereafter to his hideout. On the way he collected some hand-grenades found in the command post and other areas occupied earlier by our troops.

THE DAY 19th DECEMBER

At KARWAR[200]

The Portuguese prisoners heard during the morning heavy bombardment, which they understood was executed by Indian warships on Angediv Island. They were interrogated again.

Around 21:00 hrs there appeared in the prison accompanied by the Indian Police one of the two old ladies who lived on the island. She had come to confirm if the commander of the garrison was amongst the prisoners. The prisoners were asked again and again if that officer was the same one commanding the garrison during the incidents which had taken place on 17th and 24th November.

At ANGEDIV[201]

(Information on the three soldiers in hiding in the interior of the island)

Cabo Braganca went to the command post around 04:00 in order to find some food but could not get any. Around mid-day he surrendered to the Indian troops who had disembarked at that time. He was forced to accompany them throughout the island in search of our soldiers whom the Indians felt sure they would find. By 3 o'clock in the evening, he saw the body of his colleague Damuno Canencar who had died in combat the previous day.

During the night of nineteen to twenty, he was taken on board the warship. He was put into prison at Karwar on the twentieth in a cell, separate from the other prisoners

At 05:00 **Cabo Valdemar Marques** decided to abandon the place where he had taken shelter in order to go to the nearby pond where he could drink some water. He took with him the grenades that he had collected the previous day. He was surprised to hear the enemy's presence near the pond. He threw the hand-grenades and tried to reach his hideout. However, he was captured and taken to "Praia Grande".

From there he was taken on board the Cruiser ***MYSORE***. After interrogation he was put into the prison in Karwar.

In the early hours of the 19th, **Soldier Manuel Caetano** heard the heavy bombardment from the Indian Warships while rounding the island. Around 21:00 hours he went to the water spring in the west of the island and jumped into the sea to reach a fishing craft lying at a short distance. However, he had to give up half way as searchlights from the ships moving round the island intercepted him. By 05.00 of the twentieth he reached the extreme south of Angediv. He stayed there during the daytime. He drank water and had mussels which he managed to pull out from the rocks.

By nightfall once again he jumped into the sea and swam in the direction of the island of Round. He reached the island and stayed there throughout the twenty-first in order to take some rest. Again, he had mussels to feed on. The next day at nightfall he tried to reach the Indian coast. He arrived there early in the morning. Completely exhausted, he reached a fisherman's hut where he was fed and taken care of.

As advised by the fishermen he handed himself over to the police, and then finally reached the prison at Karwar. He was hospitalized for some time, as he was completely exhausted. Thereafter he was taken on board the warship where he remained for eight days. Thrice he was taken to the island of Angediv to spot any remaining Portuguese troops.

During the last visit he was taken to the neibougherhood of "Igreja das Brotas" where the dead bodies of Portuguese soldiers were buried. He was overcome by the foul smell of the bodies in decomposition and was sure they belonged to his colleagues.

On board he was shown the badges of the medical orderly Cabo Xavier and the hunting knife of Sergeant Ramiro, which confirmed their death. On 8th January he was taken to Canacona and from there to the Prisoner's Camp at Ponda

The Portuguese Government decorated the following soldiers/units:

—**The garrison of the Island of Angediv**

— **1º Cabo Valdemar Marques**-*Medalha de cobre de valor militar.*

—**1º Cabo Nelson Braganca** – Louvor (citation)[202]*(Cabo Braganc No38/59 was a Goan)*

—**Soldado Manuel Caetano** –Louvor (citation)

ACTION AGAINST PORTUGUESE WARSHIP *AFONSO DE ALBUQUERQUE*

Since 1st December, 1961 Indian Naval vessels were maintaining a linear patrol, 13 kilometres off Goa. This patrol observed and reported the usual traffic of merchant ships of various countries entering and leaving the harbour. The airfield at Dabolim was also under observation and beyond normal commercial flights no unusual activity was observed. It was noticed that the only Portuguese warship in the area "*Aviso* ***AFONSO de ALBUQUERQUE***" kept moving between Angediv and Marmagoa, probably carrying supplies and reinforcements for the Angediv garrison [203].

When dawn broke on 18th December, ***BETWA*** *and* ***BEAS*** were on patrol 13 kilometres off the shore. ***AFONSO de ALBUQUERQUE*** was seen lying at anchor in Marmagoa harbour. It was firing away vigorously at the IAF aircraft overhead. Though her anti-aircraft fire appeared ineffective so far, it was obviously a danger and a nuisance. Moreover the four 4'. 7" guns mounted on the ***ALBUQUERQUE*** would pose a serious threat to Indian troops when they entered Goa town. At the request of the army and the air force, it was therefore, decided to silence ***ALBUQUERQUE.*** A little later the Task Force Commander

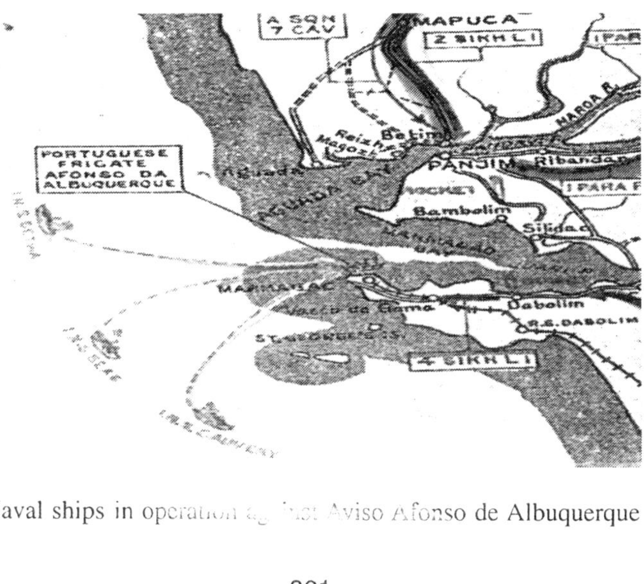

Naval ships in operation against Aviso Afonso de Albuquerque

received direct orders from New Delhi to try to capture the Portuguese frigate intact.

Soon after 12:15 hours on 18th December, 1961, ***BETWA*** and ***BEAS*** accordingly closed t range and fired warning shots. ***BETWA*** also signaled to ***ALBUQUERQUE*** to surrender. The Portuguese ship replied with gunfire. The action of ***BETWA*** and ***BEAS*** was hindered by the presence of a large number of merchant ships in Marmagoa harbour, and the danger of some of them being accidentally hit by the fire directed at ***ALBUQUERQUE.*** Ignoring these humanitarian considerations, ***ALBUQUERQUE*** continued firing furiously and even appeared to be trying to move further inside the harbour.

The Indian frigates soon secured direct hits on ***ALBUQUERQUE***. Fire and smoke was observed coming out of her at two or three places. For a time, however, her firing continued unabated. Shells whistled over the Indian ships, and fell all around them. At about 13.15 hrs ***ALBUQUERQUE*** suddenly seemed to go out of control and beached herself on the northern shores of Marmagoa bay at 13.20 hrs. A white flag was now hoisted on the stricken ship and her crew was seen jumping over-board and wading ashore.

During the later stages of this action, ***INS CAUVERY*** also arrived on the scene and took part in the engagement.

When all was over a party of Indian naval officers and men boarded the Albuquerque. They found that the Portuguese in their hurry to abandon the ship had left behind one of their dead comrade The dead body was given a proper sea burial. Captain Antonio da Cunha Aragao, the Commanding Officer of Albuquerque, had been wounded by a piece of shrapnel and was visited in the Panjim hospital by the Commanding Officers of **Betwa** and **Beas** who presented him chocolates and dry fruits.[204]

Shri Shivkumar who participated in the action says: "*When the Indian Navy took on the Portuguese forces on 18th December, 1961. I was on the naval frigate* ***INS BETWA****. We were accompanied by* ***INS BEAS*** *and also by* ***INS CAUVERY****.*

*"****INS BETWA*** *sent a signal to the Portuguese ship* ***ALBUQUERQUE*** *anchored at* ***DONA PAULA*** *bay and told its*

*officers to surrender who immediately raised a white flag. However, when we came within its range, they lowered the flag and began firing. Nevertheless they could not stand our counterfiring. . **ALBUQUERQUE** was badly damaged and everything was over by the same evening. Subsequently our Captain sent me along with the landing party on the Portuguese ship. When we reached their ship the Portuguese Naval Officers and men started running away.*" [205]

ALBUQUERQUE was repaired, refloated and renamed as **SARAVASTI** and taken to Bombay on 10th March, 1962.

Battle of Marmagoa Bay

I. N. S. Betwa

I. N. S. Beas

I. N. S. Cauvery (Painting)

ACTION OF AVISO AFONSO DE ALBUQUERQUE

(Portuguese version) [206]

Since 8th December "Aviso Afonso de Albuquerque" was in the action station. Interestingly no one amongst the crew knew about the radio-message received from Lisbon, and sent by "Presidente do Conselho" the Prime Minister Dr Salazar. The message conveyed the failure of our diplomatic initiatives to dissuade India from taking military action against "India Portuguesa"and hence the inevitable invasion was expected any moment.

The Operation Plan prepared by the Naval Command in GOA was sent to "Afonso de Albuquerque" at the end of 16th December. Due to the late dispatch of such an important document there was no time left for the Captain to call a meeting of subordinate officers for detailed action plan to be discussed and thrashed out.

The "Plano de Operacoes"or Operations Plan addressed to the Navy "(Afonso de Albuquerque" and patrol boat "Sirius") determined the main objectives as: the Defence of Mormugao Port and stoppage of landing of Indian forces on the adjoining beaches.

"Afonso de Albuquerque" was entrusted with the 2nd plan from Naval Command, which ordered:

I-Naval action against Indian Naval Forces as there were no great differences between the two;

II-Beaching the ship at a previously selected spot in case of damage in combat with resultant danger of sinking;.

III-Use of artillery as coastal battery defending access to Marmagoa port

IV-Destruction of ship when

-There is no ammunition left;

-The artillery is not in to state of being used

-Invading forces are threatening Panjim.

V-Inclusion of garrison in the defense nucleus concentrated in Mormugao.

The place chosen for beaching the ship as mentioned in number II was the beach in front of DONA PAULA.[207]

As there was some contradiction in the contents of the Operations Plan which merely said that the ship should be beached and the message received a few days earlier from Naval Headquarters which referred to the sinking of ship in case it was not possible to continue the fight, the Captain decided to consult the Chief of Engine Room. The fastest way of destroying the ship was found out. It was agreed that the engines and the boilers could be destroyed even when they were working. This was to be done on getting a proper order.

On 18th December "Afonso de Albuquerque" was anchored in Mormugao fully ready at third degree of alert. It was ready with armaments charged and explosive magazines loaded. The warship was ready to plunge into action awaiting the lifting of anchor.

Around 04:00 hours the radio officer heard the "EMISSORA de GOA" transmitting news that the Indian troops have started attacking our territory. The Naval Command in Goa however sent the message to the ship only at 06:40 hours informing that India has started the invasion.

The crew took positions of combat at 06:55 hours. The Indian Air Force began the bombardment of Dabolim Airport at 07:00 hours. Soon afterwards the Naval Radio Station at Bambolim was also bombarded. Immediately the Station ceased functioning.

Thereafter, the enemy planes started overflying the ship at high altitude beyond the range of our anti-aircraft guns. They did not attack our ship.

At 07:30 hours 'Afonso de Albuquerque' succeeded in communicating with Lisbon. This continued till 10.30 hours. During this period there were messages from Naval Headquarters asking the ship's position and from the Ministry of National Defense for 'Comandante Chefe' asking for ground information. The required answers were transmitted.

At 08.30 hours there was a communication from Naval Command in Goa informing that it was situated in Dona Paula.

Around 09.00 hours, three Indian frigates appeared near Mormugao port at a distance of 6 to 14 miles. The crew took combat positions.

At 11.00 hours the enemy jets overflew Marmagoa port at high altitude and carried out bombardment of the airport once again.

At 12.00 hours the Indian frigates seen earlier came in the direction of the port travelling at high speed. After some time they opened their artillery fire. The sound of approaching shells was heard followed by loud explosions.

"Capitao de Mar e Guerra" Antonio da Cunha Aragao without worrying about his inferior position immediately ordered the raising of the anchor, and to open fire and leave the port in order to engage with the Indian warships.

He then sent the following message to Naval Radio station in ALGES in Portugal:

"We are being attacked. We are answering."

At that moment there were five merchant ships, two of them very close to our war ship. The enemy fire hit one of these named "RANGER," an ore carrier. Great quantities of ore started gushing out.

The Indian frigates, meanwhile, were continuously transmitting signals in Morse. Due to nervousness and excitement during combat, it was not possible to immediately identify the transmitted signals. Captain Aragao ordered a halt to the firing in order to understand the contents of the message. However, due to noise from the explosions the order could not be heard and hence not followed. Seconds thereafter the message was understood. It was simply one word: - ***"SURRENDER"***[208]

Without waiting for all the letters to be understood the Captain ordered the resumption of firing.

One of the frigates was hit and it withdrew. An anti-submarine ship substituted it. During the combat the enemy ships moved in north- south direction outside the port and used their full artillery.

Meanwhile, Afonso de Albuquerque suffered a hit. A search-light was hit and its splinters fell on the command tower."

Due to the direction it was following, its guns Nos 3 and 4 situated in the rear were ineffective and the ship was being struck by enemy fire. The Captain ordered a change in direction and not to leave the port.

When 'Afonso de Albuquerque' was moving sharply to its larboard (left) to avoid the merchant ship anchored in the port, it was shaken violently by an explosion. There was a direct hit on the command tower. The 1°' Grummete telegrafista' 12970, Jose' Manuel Rosario da Piedade was dead and Captain Aragao was seriously wounded. He had fallen to the ground and was bleeding in the chest. He was injured near the heart by shrapnel. He told '2° Tenente Jose' Augusto de Morais Sarmento Gouveia the Chief Navigator, who was also slightly hurt and happened to be with him right from the beginning that the 2nd in Command should take over and that there should not be any surrender. [209]

The time was 12.20 hours of 18th December.

2° Tenente (medico) Francisco Alcada Cardoso gave all the possible medical help to the Captain. The news of the wounding of the Captain spread rapidly and considerably affected the morale of the crew.

Another enemy frigate was hit at the rear end and it withdrew. It was tilting at the starboard and emitting big clouds of smoke. It was replaced by another unit in the line of command.

2°Tenente Sarmento Gouveia immediately searched for the 2nd in command Capitao-de-Fragata Jose' Maria Caldas Frazao Pinto da Cruz in order to transmit the Captain's order to him. It was difficult to find him, but he appeared after some time

The 2nd in command went down to the engine room and ordered beaching of the ship as the machinery and the boilers were prematurely destroyed and it was not possible to reach the previously chosen place for beaching. This was done around 12.35 and thus 'Afonso de Albuquerque' was motion-less in front of Bambolim beach, one hundred and fifty metres away from the right side of the Zuari River

The Captain of the ship had instructed the Chief of the Machinery- 'Capitao Tenente Enginheiro Maquinista Naval Joao Valentim Soares Felner, to destroy the machinery and the boilers before beaching the ship. However, this operation was to be conducted only after the receipt of the proper order. Though the order was not given, the Chief of the Machinery conducted the operation after getting the information from an officer. The order of 2IC was to open the bottom valves and inundate the rear ammunition magazine but the Chief thought that the machines should be destroyed before beaching [210]

Meanwhile, 2° Tenente Sarmento Goveia found that a white flag had been raised on the signal mast. When he questioned the signalman,he was told that he was ordered to fly the flag by Sergeant (Signals). He in turn named the officer who had ordered him to do so. This meant that it was not ordered by 2IC.

However, it was presumed that enemy warships might have not noticed this white flag, as it was engulfed in a multitude of signal flags. They tried several times to remove this flag but it turned out to be very difficult. Ultimately the flag mast broke and the flag was removed and destroyed by 1°Tenente Francisco Martins Gonsalves. [211]

Meanwhile, the command tower was not functioning, the electric circuits were out of order, the loading system of the forearm was out action and the 3rd gun damaged. Soon afterwards the 4th gun too stopped firing.

According to calculations the ship must have fired during the combat 350 to 400 shots. At 12:50 hours the personnel in the boiler room were ordered to leave the ship. A few used the small crafts and others started swimming. The enemy fire, which had stopped for some time, had resumed once again.

There was some disorientation on board the ship due to the sudden turn of events. However, the National Flag continued to fly.

NRP AFONSO DE ALBUQUERQUE - F470
Classe AVISO - 1934 - 18/12/1961
Lost in combat near Marmagoa with Indian Naval Forces

Capitao Aragao being decorated by Contra Almirante Quintanilha (Ex- Governor General of Goa) and Minister for Navy of Portugal

Around 12:55 hours it was the turn of the other personnel to abandon the ship. They were instructed to reassemble at Dona Paula. Those who were leaving by boats were supplied with personal weapons.

By 13:10 hours the majority of officers and the 2 IC had left "Afonso de Albuquerque". The dead body of 1° Grumete Rosario de Piedade remained on board.

The Captain was evacuated in a boat accompanied by the doctor and Tenente ***Cervaens Rodrigues****. They reached the beach after some time without any problem. In trickles all members of the crew reached the beach.*[212]

The enemy warships continued their fire with full intensity, not only on the ship but also around it in order to hit the personnel trying to leave the ship.

The Captain was accompanied at a protected place on the beach by Doctor Tenente Alcada Cardoso, the tenentes Baptista Coelho and Sarmento Gouveia Sergeant Secundino Alves Pinto and a sailor.

To take the Captain up to Dona Paula in such a serious state and through difficult terrain subjected to heavy firing, more help was necessary. There was a request for more volunteers. Sergeant Joao Duarte Pinto, sailor Branquinho and Grumete Armenio joined the group.

The doctor was using pain-killing injections but the Captain insisted that he should be left alone and that they should try to save themselves. He asked about what had happened after he was injured.

As it was difficult to transport him by land, it was thought of searching for a motor craft, which would enable to take the wounded to Mormugao by sea. Thus Tenentes ***Baptista Coelho*** *and* ***Sarmento Gouveia****, Sergeant* ***Duarte Pinto*** *and the sailors* ***Branquinho*** *and* ***Ferreira*** *and Grumete* ***Armenio*** *went again to "Afonso de Albuquerque" after using a craft abandoned in the bay. They saw that the ship was completely damaged and the command tower destroyed and full of debris. At many places there was fire and heavy smoke. The enemy firing had started anew.*

There was no possibility of finding any motor craft and so they decided to return by the same small craft they had used earlier to come to the ship. The journey was carried out under fire and when they reached the beach it was again bombarded by enemy artillery.

The groups under Capitao Tenente ***Felner*** *and* ***1º*** *Tenente* ***Mendes Rebelo*** *met Comandante* ***Abel Oliveira*** *who had rushed in search of crew of 'Afonso de Albuquerque'. He indicated that the place for assembly was"Clube Militar Naval" situated at Caranzalem. The naval command was not now in Dona Paula. It was not possible now to reach Mormugao using the two launches abandoned in that locality. The Indian warships were covering with fire the entrance to the port and the estuary of Zuari.*

The patrol craft ***"SIRIUS"*** *was found beached at Dona Paula with its engines running. This ship was neither attacked nor was it threatened but had beached prematurely without firing a single round. In the quay there was some abandoned baggage, vehicles and the body of 1º Sergeant Antonio Duarte Santa Rita, victim of the bombardment in that area.*

Comandante ***Abel de Oliveira*** *accompanied by two of his officials met the other groups in order to direct them to safer places. Meanwhile* ***1º*** *Tenente* ***Mendes Rebelo*** *tried to evacuate the wounded, after using a vehicle. Finally he evacuated Comandante* ***Aragao*** *to the Medical School Hospital at Panjim around 17:00 hours.*

The ship's personnel stayed at Caranzalem awaiting instructions from Naval Command. However, due to some reason or other, there were no instructions. In the morning of the 19th the Indian Command, already in control of Panjim, was informed that the garrison of ***"Afonso de Albuquerque"*** *was in Caranzalem. The personnel were imprisoned by 13:00 hours, when the Indian Army Commander had gone to the Medical School Hospital to visit and enquire about the condition of Comandante Aragao and other wounded naval personnel.*[213]

The wounded included besides Comandante ***Aragao,*** *the Tenentes* ***Marques Pedroso, Sarmento Gouveia*** *and* ***Alcada Cardoso***, *2nd Sergeant* ***Joaquim Matias***, *Sailor* ***Valdemar Vieira Simoes*** *and Grumetes* ***Antonio Araujo*** *and* ***Henrique Lourenco da Costa***.

Thus, the action of the garrison of Aviso ***"Afonso de Albuquerque"*** *ended. It had confronted the Indian Fleet which was considerably superior in numbers and firepower.*

In the beginning of January 1962 the ship was towed and moored to a buoy in Marmagoa port, in front of "Campo de Alparqueiros"

On 27th December all the personnel of ***'Afonso de Albuquerque'*** *were transferred to the Prisoner's Camp at Ponda*

Gen.Carlos Azaredo who was a Captain during this period has these comments to make about this incident:

"Due to lack of communications equipment I had to go by car to the Commander–in-chief "some two kilometres behind". During one of these incursions, when I had reached a high position, I witnessed the combat between "Afonso de Albuquerque" and the Indian Navy –three frigates and two torpedo boats. "Our vessel was in anchorage at Dona Paula, the other side of river Zuari. By around midday, on being targeted, it left its moorings and manoeuvred with the intention of taking to the high seas. The enemy artillery was using anti – personnel shrapnel bombs; one could distinctively hear the explosions and see the clouds they left. One of them exploded directly above the ship", killing a cabin boy and seriously injuring the commander Cunha Aragao. The ship then "swerved 180 degrees and ran aground by the bows on Bambolim beach. The official version, maintained for years, would exalt the heroic stand of "Afonso de Albuquerque"-to the extent of stating that it was sunk. "All tales! I state with the authority of one who directly witnessed the hostilities".

The ship "Afonso de Albuquerque" was renamed as SARAVASTI and taken to Bombay. Its canons were preserved in the Naval War museum, and the hull sold as scrap.

The following persons were given awards/ penalties by the Portuguese Government: [214]

DISMISSED: *2º Tenente* **Manuel Jose' Marques da Silva** *and 1º Sergeant* **Carlos Sao Marcos da Piedade** (Both for having ordered the raising of the white flag)

COMPULSORY RETIREMENT:
Commodore **Raul Viegas Ventura** (*Lack of leadership*)

SUSPENDED for six months: *Capitao Tenente* (*Engenheiro maquinista naval*) **Joao Valentim Soares Felner** (for having destroyed the machines without proper order of the commander)

AWARDS: *Capitao de Mar e Guerra* **Antonio da Cunha Aragao** *Commander of Aviso Afonso de Albuquerque promoted to the post of* **Commodore.** 1° Tenentes **Francisco Manuel Martins Gonsalves, Luis de Sa Machado Rebelo, Jose' Augusto de Morais Sarmento Goveia, Vitor Marques Pedroso** –Silver medals for distinguished service; 1° Grumete Radio- telegrafista **Jose' Manuel Rosario da Piedade** (posthumous) – promoted to the next post; 1° Sergeant de manobra **Francisco da Lima** Copper medal for distinguished service.

SPECIAL ORDERS for *DELHI*
(OPERATING OFF DIU.)

The object of **DELHI** *operating off* ***DIU*** *was that*[215] *by her presence the local garrison would be forced to surrender quickly.*

(a) To prevent any Portuguese warship interfering with the smooth conduct of the operations.

(b) To provide gunfire support to our Army Units if required and called for.

2- At H-hour ***DELHI*** is to probe as close inshore as possible and silence any shore batteries that may engage her. Great caution in opening fire is to be exercised, as it is likely that our own Army Units may be operating in very close vicinity of the shore targets.

3-An Army Liaison /Signal Unit consisting of one Officer and four Jawans will be placed on board before departure for the operations. The unit will carry their own portable wireless set for communications with the Army Forces operating from Diu.

4-If encountered by a Portuguese Warship ***DELHI*** to close in just outside the gun range, open fire, at the same time signal her to surrender. If fire is returned necessary retaliatory action is to be taken by ***DELHI***

5-**Surrender**—In the event of the Portuguese Warship surrendering

- a boarding party is to be sent to the warship,
- The boarding party should immediately immobilize the armament,
- Post sentries to prevent scuttling and damage to machinery.

The Warship is to be escorted to Bombay and handed over to the Flag Officer, Bombay after completion of the task at **DIU** or after H-5 whichever is later.

Naval Operation Off Diu [216]

When the army could not enter the island of Diu in the morning of the 18th December the air force and the navy were both sent into action. ***INS DELHI*** was detailed to be off **Diu** to support the land operations.

On 18th December at 04:30 hours ***DELHI*** was some 16 kilometres off **Diu** when she detected two small vessels on her radar. ***DELHI*** approached them and illuminated one of them and found that it was a seaward patrol craft. On being called to surrender, the hostile vessel started speeding towards the harbour at high speed. The ***INS DELHI*** therefore opened fire and sank her within minutes. The second hostile craft had in the meantime managed to escape inside the harbour.

At 10:15 hours on 18th December, ***DELHI*** opened fire at the citadel situated on the eastern tip of **Diu** Island. At 12:00 hours, a large white flag appeared near the position of the mast inside the citadel. Soon there were numerous white flags fluttering all along the foreshores of the island. The island however was still resisting at places and at about 14:00 hours, ***DELHI*** opened fire at the control tower of the **Diu** airfield on a request received from the army.

To assist the army in crossing over to the island, a naval platoon and boats were provided by **DELHI** on the morning of 19th December.

The platoon had the honour of hoisting the Indian flag in Diu, and it also participated in the surrender ceremony.

NAVAL OPERATIONS OFF DIU
(The Portuguese Version)

The Portuguese did not have any big warship around Diu. It had a patrol boat named "VEGA" and two Customs Launches –DIU and FOLQUE.

Action of Patrol Boat Vega

The patrol boat ***VEGA*** [217] *was a small naval unit of 18ton displacement. It was 17 metres in length with a 20mm machine gun. It had a garrison of eight men.*

The patrol boat ***VEGA*** *patrolling the waters in the District of Diu was not a part of* ***'Agrupamento Antonio de Silveira'.***

Nevertheless it participated in the violent actions of the Indian Air force.

As its commander 'Segundo Tenente' ***Jorge Manuel Catalao de Oliveira e Carmo*** *died in combat the description of events was collected from the surviving crew members.*

The ship left Diu on 17th December by 21:40 hours for patrolling in the direction of ***Nagoa*** *where it anchored at 22:00 hours.*

On the 18th around 01:40 hours machine gun fire as well as isolated gun fire coming from land could be heard. When the commander was informed of this he immediately ordered the lifting of the anchor and sailing in the direction of the sea.

The radar was in operation and it was showing the presence of a ship anchored near the beach of ***'Brancawara'*** *in our waters. When the radar was set to 24 miles the eco showed a ship of a big size that was navigating with its lights off. The patrol boat continued moving in the direction of Diu.*

When we crossed the area near the fort we heard loud detonations coming from artillery fire from the ***Fort,*** *towards the region of the border of Gogola'. The commander rapidly maneuvered the craft and returned to the sea. Once again the echo of unknown ship was captured. Its distance was calculated to be 12 miles from the coast.*

The commander ordered to navigate closer to the land and in the zone of the fort at slow speed. He wanted to give some time for the crafts ***FOLQUE*** *and* ***DIU*** *to come out to the sea and accompany the patrol craft* ***VEGA****.* ***FOLQUE*** *left as per the orders at 02:40 hours. It met* ***VEGA*** *at 03:00 hours in the coastal area of* ***'Podamo'****. At this point of time it was also observed that the approaching enemy ship was at an approximate distance of 12 miles.*

The commander ordered to take the direction of the bay of ***Nagoa****.* ***FOLQUE*** *followed* ***VEGA****. At 03:45 hours the radar saw the clear approach of the ship and its capturing of all the movements of* ***VEGA*** *maintaining a distance of 1..5 miles. At 03:55 hours* ***VEGA*** *left* ***FOLQUE*** *behind and went in the direction of the unknown ship for better identification.*

At 04:00 hours the commander managed to identify that the ship was of heavy tonnage and noticed on its eastern side some luminous signals "T N T" to which the commandant ordered that no reply should be given. He suspected its intentions and returned rapidly to meet ***FOLQUE****. He met the launch and embarked all the persons in it. Meanwhile, the enemy ship illuminated both the crafts in order to locate and destroy them. The commander decided to leave* ***FOLQUE*** *at once with its engine running and ordered the* ***VEGA*** *to run at high speed in the direction of* ***DIU.*** *It anchored between Fortim do Mar and the Fort at 05:00 hours. Meanwhile, the cruiser had aimed and fired its heavy machine gun and managed to destroy* ***FOLQUE****.*

At 06:15 hours the commander ordered to lift the anchor in order to identify completely the cruiser and recover ***FOLQUE*** *if possible or destroy it if necessary. He saw in front of* ***VEGA*** *at a distance of 2 miles a cruiser with a 'fire' flag on its mast and the Indian flag at the rear mast.*

At 07:00 hours the fighter jets were seen strafing ***'PASSO SECO'****. A siren was sounded by the launch to alert the persons in the FORTALEZA. At 07:30 hours the aerial attack on the* ***Fortaleza*** *had started. Two planes appeared above the launch before strafing the Fortaleza. The anchor was lifted in order to reach the harbour. However, the planes returned to attack the launch. They attacked* *from both sides. Artillery sailor Ferreira was killed and the commander's legs were totally cut at the thighs.*

There was a fire, which engulfed the engine room and then the command post .The resistance of the small launch VEGA ended as fuel supply lines were cut in the strafing. The remaining persons tried to extricate themselves and transfer the badly wounded commander to a safer place. There was fresh bombardment in which the commander was mortally wounded in the chest. Others too were badly hurt.[217]

The patrol boat VEGA was destroyed and sunk around 09:00 hours by the Indian Air force. The bodies of the commander 2o Tenente ***Carmo*** *and Sailor* ***Antonio Ferreira*** *went down with the ship.*

In this action there were the following casualties: [218]

DEAD:

-Commander 2^0 Tenente **Jorge Manuel Catalao de Oliveira e Carmo**

-Artillery sailor no 10030—**Antonio Ferreira**

-Artillery Sailor no10519—**Anibal dos Santos Fernandes Jardim.**

WOUNDED:

-Sailor (Telegraphy)—no 11027— **Antonio Costa Bagoim**

-Grumete (Artillery) No 13032—**Venancio dos Ramos**

UNHARMED:

-Sailor No 5645—**Armando Cardoso da Silva**

-Sailor (Electrician) No 5353—**Francisco Mendes da Freitas**

-Sailor N0 6788 –**Antonio da Silva Nobre**

The Portuguese Government rewarded the following personnel from this patrol boat:

2^0 Tenente **Jorge Manuel Catalao Oliveira e Carmo** promoted to the post of Capitao- Tenente (Posthumous)

-Sailors—**Antonio Ferreira** and **Anibal dos Santos Fernandes Jardim** (both posthumous) to the next post, Sailors—**Armando Cardoso da Silva, Francisco Mendes Freitas, Joao de Lopes** da **Costa Bagoim**, 1o Grumete **Venancio dos Ramos** and Sailor **Antonio da Silva Nobre** all decorated with Medal of Cross (4th class).

It is seen from the records that the launch **FOLQUE** was sunk by **INS DELHI** while the patrol boat **VEGA** was destroyed and sunk by **IAF planes**.

Refrences

191—P.N.Khera-Op. Vijay—p120
192—Ibid-p-121
193—C.A.Morais—Queda da India—p-152
194—Ibid-p-152
195—Ibid-p-153
196—Ibid-p-154
197—Ibid-p-155
198—Ibid-p-158
199—Ibid-p-159
200—Ibid-p-159
201—Ibid-p-160
202—Detenus list-Page 10 –Sl No 654—Goan 38/59
203—P.N.Khera-Op Vijay-p-121
204—Ibid-p-122
205—Interview of Ex.Naval Rating Shiv Shankar in Navhind Times-Goa
206—C. A. Morais-Queda-p-163
207—Ibid-p-164
208—Ibid-p-167
209—Ibid-p-167
210—Ibid-p-168
211—Ibid-p-168
212—Ibid-p-169
213—Ibid-p-171
214—Ibid-p-386-387, 389
215—P.N.Khera-Op Vijay-Appendix E –p-232
216—Ibid-p-122
217—C.A.Morais-Queda da India –p-245
218—Ibid-p-249

CHAPTER XIV

THE AIR FORCE IN OPERATION VIJAY

When the Government ordered the Chiefs of Staff on 30th November, 1961 to prepare for and liberate the Portuguese possessions in India, it was made clear that the operation was to be conducted with the utmost speed and with the minimum use of force.

To ensure speed it became necessary to employ all the three services: Army, Navy and Air Force. The Chiefs of Staff therefore appointed three theatre Commanders-one for each Service. Lt. Gen. Chaudhuri was the Theatre Land Force commander and Rear Admiral Soman the theatre Naval Commander. The Theatre Air Commander was Air Vice Marshal E. W. Pinto (Rosario).

The task[218] given to the Air Force was:

(a) To deny to the Portuguese the use of their airfields, the Dabolim airfield in Goa to be rendered unserviceable by bombing of the runway, and the airfields in Daman and Diu to be kept under observation.

(b) To provide offensive air support to the land forces engaged in the operation.

(c) To provide required support to the naval forces.

(d) To undertake anti-shipping operations in the event of Portuguese Naval forces attacking Bombay/ Jamnagar sectors.

(e) To provide adequate air transport support to the forces taking part in the operation.

(f) To provide photo-cover.

In addition to the units in the operational command under Air Vice Marshal Pinto, a section of four Mysteres, a squadron of Toofanis (Ouragans) and a signal unit from Eastern Command were also placed under him for this operation.

To conform to the plan of the army, the theatre of air operations was divided into three sectors viz Goa, Daman and Diu, and responsibility for air operations in these sectors was assigned to various units stationed at three different places, namely Poona for Goa sector, Santa Cruz (Bombay) for Daman and Jamnagar for Diu.

The tactical Headquarters of the Theatre air commander was set up at Poona, but after the move of the land forces, tactical Headquarters also moved forward to Sambre (Belgaum) with a Wing Commander in charge. Thus there were actually four stations involved in air operations and the functions performed by each of them might be summarised as follows:

The Theatre Air Commander's headquarters being in Poona, air operations in all the three sectors were under the overall control of A. V. M. Pinto from Poona. The planning and execution of air tasks in the Daman and Diu sectors was controlled directly from Poona, while the Goa air operations were controlled from Poona through the advance tactical element at Belgaum.

No 2T A C under Air Commodore Shiv Dev Singh controlled tactical air operations in the Goa sector with headquarters alongside the 17th Infantry Division. In the Daman sector they were conducted by O C No 2 Wing, Group Captain S. J. Dastur and in Diu by O C, A T W. Group Captain R. B. Godkhindi on an ***"on call"*** basis through ***"cab-ranks"*** controlled by ACT.

Air Marshal A. M. Engineer,
Chief of Air Staff in 1961

AVM E. W. Pinto,
Theatre Air Commander

TOOFANI (OURAGAN) used in
DIU operations

MYSTERE used in
DAMAN operations

CAB RANK METHOD OF ATTACK

In the ordinary course, when advancing ground forces make a demand for an air- strike, considerable time is likely to elapse before the attack from the air can materialize on the suggested target. This delay is due to the fact that air squadrons have to study maps and photographs, then take off, reach and bombard the exact position. In order to shorten this period between the demands made by the advancing ground forces and the air attack the system of '**cab rank**'[219] is followed. In this system, two or more aircraft take to the air simultaneously with the move of the ground forces. These aircraft remain high up in the sky and are available at call, always ready to come down and attack a target.

They are of course constantly in touch with the forward troops through radiotelephone, which is operated on the ground until relieved by a fresh **'cab-rank'** flight. This method is no doubt uneconomical in terms of aircraft and fuel, but is perhaps the only way of providing constant and immediate close support to an advancing army.

AIR SUPPORT TO NAVY

The air operations in support of the Navy[220] were conducted under the control of the 'Maritime Operations Room' located at Bombay. Group Captain J.S. Virk who was the principal coordinating authority for maritime reconnaissance effort commanded the air force element of the Joint Headquarters. Liaison officers were placed aboard IN ships **MYSORE** and **DELHI** for advice, control and direction of IAF strikes against maritime targets in the Goa and Diu sectors.

It was considered that Poona was too far to the rear for tactical support aircraft to be brought to bear either in the sectors of Goa and Daman. For this reason, two new air stations were established, namely **SAMBRE** and **SANTA CRUZ**. This also helped in doing away with concentrating aircraft in a confined area at Poona. It would have made them an easy target for possible raids by enemy aircraft. The dispersal of the aircraft in different areas widely separated from each other proved in practice to be well conceived. During the two days of fighting, no difficulty was experienced in bringing the aircraft to strike with maximum firepower, at the right place, and importantly at the right time.

ROLE AND DEPLOYMENT OF THE AIR FORCE IN OPERATION VIJAY

The Air Force was deployed[221] at

(a) BOMBAY

(i) Four aircraft of No 1 Squadron to be employed in anti-shipping role and for fighter sweeps.

(ii) Two **Packet aircraft** of No 12 Squadron for transport support duties.

(iii) Four aircraft of No 20(**HUNTER**) Squadron for air defence of Greater Bombay.

(iv) One **Mi 4 Helicopter** of No 109 Helicopter flight for air sea rescue operations.

(b) POONA

(i) Nos 16 and 35 B.58 squadrons (**CANBERRA**) to be employed for tactical bombing.

(ii) No 17 (**HUNTER**) Squadron (less one section) for air defence of Poona-Bombay and for fighter escort / fighter sweep duties.

(iii) No 6 (**LIBERATOR**) squadron (less detachment at Jamnagar) to be employed on M.R. duties.

(iv) No 37 Squadron for night fighter duties at Bombay.

(v) Four aircraft of No 45 (**VAMPIRE**) Squadron to constitute reserve.

(vi) Two **IL-14** aircraft of No1 communication Flight.

(c) SAMBRE

(i) Eight aircraft of No 45 Squadron for close support of the Army and interdiction.

(ii) Four aircraft of No 17 Squadron for air defence of Sambre area.

(iii) Two aircraft of No 122 (**HARWARD**) Flight for supporting target direction duties.

(iv) No 3 **A.O.P.** Flight.
(v) Two **OTTERS** of No 2 Communication Flight.
(vi) Three **Mi 4** Helicopters of No 109 helicopter Flight.
(vii)Three **VAMPIRE** aircraft of 108 F. R. flights for photoreconnaissance / Tact. R. Duties

PREPARATIONS

The build up of the air forces for **Operation Vijay** commenced on 2nd December [222] and the units were all geared up and completely ready for operations within a week. During this period, the establishment of a full-fledged air force station at SAMBRE as the main base for operations in the Goa sector, the establishment of a satellite wing at SANTA CRUZ for the Daman sector, movement and stockpiling of armament, stores, petrol, oil, spares, equipment, etc., for a possible period of ten days operation, setting up of "Operations Room" and establishment of wireless and land line communications were all completed. For this rapid deployment of forces and the dispatch of men and material to their respective locations, the maximum use was made of any type of transport aircraft that was available.

JAMNAGAR air station in full working condition was already available for the Diu sector.

For the proper co-ordination of air transport effort within the tactical area, an Air Movement Control Centre was established at Poona under the Tactical Headquarters of Air Vice Marshal Pinto. This organisation took over complete responsibility for air movement into and out of the tactical area and was in sole charge of distribution of loads and personnel for airlift to their destinations and for reception of aircraft from the rear airfields. The whole arrangement worked smoothly. All these arrangements for achieving readiness in the short available time were satisfactory except for a little disjointedness in the beginning.

ASSESSMENT OF PORTUGUESE FORCES

After having done the necessary arrangements, the next step before D-Day was to make accurate assessment of the Portuguese forces on land, air and sea.[223] For this purpose, photo and maritime reconnaissance of three sectors was necessary to get an idea of the deployment of enemy forces.

Fighters therefore probed the areas near the borders and light bombers on 8th and 9th December in order to force the Portuguese air arm to react and thereby disclose its strength. Orders were given that the territorial borders were not to be infringed, and that enemy air opposition was to be engaged only after drawing it over Indian territory.

The Portuguese, however, did not react to these probing activities and it seemed that either they had no air defence organisation or were not ready to come to grips with our forces. A strategic photoreconnaissance mission was thereupon sent on the 9th, and it accomplished its task without meeting any opposition. Within the next few days probes were made near Daman and Diu borders and intensive maritime reconnaissance was also made to see what type of shipping was entering or leaving Portuguese harbours. These would serve as a pointer to the volume of reinforcements and build up of the Portuguese garrisons. On no occasion was any enemy aircraft encountered. All these missions were flown during daytime.

On 17 December, a tactical reconnaissance flight conducted by Sqn Ldr I S Loughran in a Vampire NF.54 Night Fighter over Dabolim Airport in Goa was met with 5 rounds fired from a ground anti aircraft gun. The aircraft took evasive action by drastically dropping altitude and escaping out to sea. The anti aircraft gun was later recovered near the ATC building with a round jammed in its breech.

Reports of Portuguese air activity by night at the airfields of Daman and Dabolim were however, continuing to come in. Night missions of Canberra aircraft were therefore sent out to report on the activity at these airfields. From these and information received from other sources it was confirmed that the traffic was of commercial or transport type. Actually the Portuguese were evacuating families of their armed forces personnel to Lisbon by way of Karachi.

From 14th December, the intensity of air probes by day and night was stepped up and aircraft were now briefed to fly at a lower height in a determined attempt to "invite" the Portuguese air defence system to react. But as before "the invitation remained unaccepted". "Invitation" and probing missions were also flown from Santa Cruz to Daman and from Jamnagar to Diu but the Portuguese did not react. It was clear now that the Portuguese had no air defence system. A close watch was also kept by day and night on Portuguese shipping. Some sorties for assessing weather and light conditions were also flown and on the 17th, the final strategic photo-reconnaissance of the Portuguese airfields was made.

AIR OPERATIONS

When the final date and the orders for **OPERATION VIJAY** were conveyed by the Chief of the Air Staff—**Air Marshal A. M. Engineer**—to the Theatre Air Commander, he was told to carry out the following tasks[224] with effect from first light of 18th December:

(a) The runway at DABOLIM airport in Goa was to be bombed and made unserviceable. It should, however, be ensured that the adjoining hangars and the terminal buildings are not attacked.

(b) The wireless station at BAMBOLIM in Goa is to be attacked and put out of use.

(c) Provision of close support to the land forces operating in Operation VIJAY in the Portuguese enclaves of Goa, Daman and Diu.

(d) Use of airfields at Diu and Daman are to be denied to the Portuguese by fighter patrols. These airfields are not to be bombed without my prior approval.

He was further told that although the objective was to eliminate all opposition as soon as possible, he should ensure that the minimum force was used and that the "civil population is not attacked under any circumstances"

The aim of the air operations as originally envisaged, was firstly to neutralise the Portuguese air arm in the three territories on the first day of operations and secondly, to provide air support to ground forces in the field. Since it became evident from the probing and photo reconnaissance sorties from 8th to 17th December, that the Portuguese had little or no air opposition to offer, the first aim (of neutralizing the Portuguese air force) was changed to isolating the three territories from reinforcement by air while the land battle was in progress. To prevent reinforcement by sea the navy was to maintain a blockade of the ports of Goa, Daman and Diu.

In keeping with the altered aim of air operations, strategic action was to be taken against the three main targets on first light on the 18th, namely the airfield at Dabolim and the wireless stations at Bambolim (in Goa) and Diu. The airfields at Daman and Diu were to be kept under surveillance by fighter swoops. The tactical task remained the same. As planned, the strategic targets were engaged successfully on the 18th:

i) **Dabolim airfield in Goa**: On the morning of 18th December, twelve bombers escorted by four fighters and led by **Wing Commander N.B.Menon, OC No 35 Squadron** raided the airfield. Sixty-three bombs (each of 1000 lbs) were dropped and several direct hits were scored on the main runway. The standard of bombing was of such a high order that there was no spill over of bombs into surrounding built-up areas and into the airfield dispersal area where one Super Constellation and one DC-6 aircraft were parked on the apron. The intention was not to damage these aircraft but only to make it impossible for them to take off by making the runway unserviceable.

(ii) A second raid by 8 Canberras led by **Wing Commander, Surinder Singh, OC No 16 Squadron**, was made over the target at 11:20 hours on the same day when 4,800 lbs of bombs were dropped, some of which again registered direct hits on the main runway. The Portuguese aircraft were again left untouched. By this time, it was assumed that the airfield was rendered unserviceable and these aircraft could be captured intact as they had nowhere to go. However the Portuguese pilots of these aircraft proved to be both foolhardy and brave! The same night, information was received that both Portuguese airliners parked on the apron had made a desperate getaway from a clear portion of the airfields which was evidently just enough for such a foolhardy but nevertheless courageous and successful take off" [225]

(iii) **Bambolim wireless station: -** A force of 6 Hunter aircraft led by **Squadron Leader Jayant Singh** and armed with rockets and rounds of 30 mm ammunition, left Sambre and was brought to bear on Bambolim wireless station at 07:10 hours. So many direct hits were scored that in a short time; the target was a smoldering wreck. After the successful raid the Hunters landed at Poona.[226]

(iv) **Diu airfield–wireless station:** The directive for Diu had clearly laid down that no offensive action was to be taken without direction of the air control team (ACT). As contact with the

Canberras used in bombing of DABOLIM airport

Hunters used in bombing of BAMBOLIM Transmission Centre

Bambolim Wireless Station burning after air strike

BAMBOLIM WIRELESS STATION DAY AFTER THE STRIKE

Diu ACT could not be established in the morning, the first raid, which was scheduled for the morning, took place at 14:00 hours when two Toofanis dropped 1000 lb bombs at the intersection of the two runways scoring direct hits. More attacks were made after this, by fighter/ bomber aircraft against the airfield installations and the wireless station. Within one hour, the airfield control tower, meteorological office and wireless station were completely destroyed. A wave of 4 Toofanis sent earlier at 11:00 hours had returned without bombing the target on seeing white flags being waved from the area around the airfield. It seems the 'flags' were probably Dhobi's laundry!

Another raid, this time a bigger one, by 16 Canberras in two waves of 8 each, was planned on orders from Delhi, but was called off on learning that the ground forces were attacking in that area and it would be unsafe to carry out a full-scale bombing attack. Moreover, it was also learnt that the airfield had already been put out of commission.[227]

Four Vampires flying from Jamnagar over the sea near Diu, noticed a Fast Patrol Boat travelling out of the Diu harbour. Upon closer observation, the Vampires were fired at by the boat. Fg. Off. P.M. Ramachandran –the lead pilot –immediately engaged with gunfire and rockets and sank the patrol boat. For this feat he received the Shaurya Chakra.

Flight of Portuguese Planes of Tap and Taip

"At 10 o' Clock of 18th December, **Tenente-Coronel (Lt. Colonel) Solano de Almeida**, *Director of TAIP (Transportes Aereos da India Portuguesa) informed the P. C. (Posto do Comando) that the General Commanding Chief had authorized him to fly out with the aircrafts belonging to TAIP as well as TAP (Transportes Aereos Portugueses) which had arrived at dawn of the18th. He requested* **Major Cardeira da Silva** *to take necessary measures so that the only anti-aircraft gun in operation at the Mormugao Plateau would not aim at these two planes while taking off."*

"The two planes were not damaged after the bombardment of the airport. Around 16:00 the crew of TAIP contacted the Governor General, personally, requesting him to permit the plane to take off. They argued that the crew and the plane were civilian in nature. The permission was granted. At 1800 the permission was extended to both the planes allowing them also to transport the civilians who wished to leave.

"During the night the debris and splinters caused by the bombardment which were causing problem for take-off were removed. This was done by using vehicles side by side and with their lights off so that the enemy would not detect the projected operation."

The first aircraft to leave was the TAP Constellation commanded by Manuel Correia Reis, which took off using only 700 metres; the debris from the runway damaged the fuselage with 25 holes and a flat tyre. In order to take off in the short distance, the TAP pilots had jettisoned all the extra seats and other unwanted equipment so that they could do a 'short take-off'.

The second to leave was the TAIP DC-4, piloted by TAIP Director Ten. Coronel Solano de Almeida. *It had as* Co-Pilot Jose' Tinoco *and as* Navigator Capitao Manuel Chorao Vinhas Both aircraft used the cover of night and a very low altitude to break through Indian aerial patrols and escape to Karachi, Pakistan.

"Around 23.30 the plane of TAP piloted by **Commander Reis** *took off. It was followed by the plane of TAIP piloted by* **Ten. Coronel Solano de Almeida**.

"After the departure of the first plane and due to the noise so created the artillery of the Indian warships fired in the zone of airport but there was no damage. These planes did not follow the normal route along the coast, but went far off in the direction of the sea to make its detection difficult. On reaching Karachi in sound condition the crew was given an ovation for having conducted such a daring mission" [228]

Tactical Air Operations

Tactical air operations[229] in support of ground forces were successful in Goa, Daman and Diu except for two minor mishaps, and no casualties to own personnel or aircraft were suffered as a result of air action. Of the two mishaps, one occurred to a Harvard aircraft in the Goa sector when it was fired upon by our own ground troops. This aircraft had been sent on a message dropping mission to the 50th Para brigade Headquarters with whom all contact was lost on the 18th on account of the rapidity of the advance resulting in the failure of communications.

As this aircraft had no roundels painted on the under surface, our own ground forces had no means of identifying it. So as it flew above them they fired at it with small arms and the aircraft received two bullet holes with the compliments of 2 Sikh light Infantry! The damage was not serious and the plane returned safely to Sambre, where air force roundels were immediately painted on the under surface.

Another incident of mistaken identity of the opposite nature also occurred in Goa, when four of our aircraft which had gone out to attack enemy tank concentrations, attacked the wrong target. Fortunately no casualties were inflicted on our own positions on the ground. This had happened as there was no smoke or ATC (air target controller) available to indicate the target area to the aircraft.

In all 23 sorties were flown in the Goa sector. 14 were flown in Daman and 35 in Diu on D-Day, and a few more on D+1 Day. These were for missions of various kinds, such as recce, strike, photo reconnaissance, message dropping, and providing air cover to ground troops, close support and so on.

Miscellaneous Air Support

In addition to the above there were numerous[230] other flights for transport support, logistic air support and for communications duties and search in which Otters and helicopters played an important part.

In Diu, the army had lost a major portion of their armament in their unsuccessful attempt to cross the creek on the morning of

the 18th. To replenish them 15,000 lbs of urgently required armament stores were also airlifted from Ahmedabad to the front. This was not envisaged earlier at any stage of planning, but the stores were delivered within three hours of the call for help. This 'immediate transport operation' was indeed a creditable performance!

Maritime reconnaissance was maintained throughout the 18th and 19th, in addition to which special anti-submarine sea reconnaissance patrols were carried out during strategic air strikes. Liberator aircraft used to drop flares by night to assist in identification of coastal traffic at the approaches to Diu and Daman and also to assist the mopping up operations by the army near Mormugao shortly before the surrender on the 19th.

Liberator aircraft were also used on the 18th in the Goa sector to drop leaflets, publicising the intentions of the armed action and warning the people not to let the Portuguese destroy places of public utility.

The leaflets[231] said:

"The defence forces that are now with you are for your protection. It is their task to defend the honour and the security of the motherland from which you have been separated for too long and which you largely by your own efforts, again made your own. They will take every step to ensure your safety and uphold your dignity and honour, whatever the cost

"At this critical moment, however, Goans must remain watchful. The Portuguese will do everything to leave Goa in ruin and the Goan people in misery. They do not care what happens to Goa now. For they must and will depart. They have nothing to lose *by sowing destruction in the land. Their Portugal is at a safe distance. They will try to destroy our bridges, our railways, our temples and churches, our schools and public buildings, and the fine and God-given harbour.*

"Crores of rupees and immense human endeavour will have to be spent to rebuild all that is destroyed."

"Goans cannot, and must not, allow this to happen at any cost.

"Be calm and brave. Rejoice in your freedom and help to safeguard it."

One can see that all air operations were conducted in almost ideal conditions of air supremacy and good weather. This, however, does not and should not detract from the high standard of efficiency shown by all concerned. These qualities were amply reflected in the results. The role of air operations in the achievement of the aim of armed intervention was almost decisive in Daman and Diu, where the Portuguese did offer stubborn resistance to the ground forces. In Goa also the co-operation offered by the air force was very valuable, and even in those cases where no ammunition was expended from the aircraft, their mere presence overhead had a demoralizing effect on the Portuguese soldiers and raised the morale of Indian troops in the area.

References:

218—P.N.Khera—Op.Vijay-p124
219—Ibid-p-125
220—Ibid-p-126
221—Ibid-AppendixV-p-182
222—Ibid-p-126
223—Ibid-p-127
224—Ibid-p-128
225—Ibid-p-129-130
226—Op.Vijay-p-130
227—Op.Vijay-p-130
228—Queda-p-145-146
229—Ibid-p-131
230—Ibid-p-131
231—R.P.Rao-Portuguese rule in Goa-p-163-164

CHAPTER XV

COLLAPSE OF SALAZARIST POLICY

The Salazarist policy was based on the support he expected from Great Britain and countries of NATO

Article 1 of the Anglo-Portuguese Treaty of 29th January, 1641 said: "None of the said most Serene Sovereigns, their heirs or successors, shall do or attempt anything, or through others, against one another, their kingdoms on land or sea, nor shall consent or adhere to any war, council or treaties to the detriment of the other."[232]

The last Article of the treaty of 23rd June, 1661 confirmed that "Over and above all and singular, agreed and concluded, it is by this article concluded and accorded that His Majesty of Great Britain...shall promise and oblige himself, as by this present article he doth, to defend and protect all conquests or colonies belonging to the crown of Portugal, against all enemies, as well future as present."[233]

The Anglo-Portuguese declaration of 14th October, 1899 expressly confirmed the article 1 of the Treaty of 29th January, 1641 as well as the last article of the Treaty of 23rd June, 1661[234]

It is interesting to note that, a quarter century earlier, this 'oldest ally of Britain' i.e. Portugal had not honoured her five-and–a half centuries old friendship. It had continued to help Germany by supplying her with wolfram or tungsten, an important war material. It was in June 1944 when an Allied victory seemed reasonably certain, that she stopped sending wolfram to Germany. It also did not allow Britain to use her ports and airfields during the Battle of Atlantic. Now the clock had turned full circle and it was now the turn of Portugal to remind her 'oldest ally'! [235]

As for the North Atlantic treaty of 4th April, 1949, its articles 5 and 6 defined an Atlantic Zone of guarantee and immediate action, which evidently did not cover India. The Portuguese Government

had formally communicated this to the Indian Union on 20th April, 1953. The treaty however had Article 4, which said: "The parties will consult together, whenever, in the opinion of any one of them, the territorial integrity, political independence or security of any of the parties is threatened."[236] This was the article Salazar was banking on to get help from NATO countries!

Goa or the Beginning of the End

Operation Vijay lasted just 40 hours.[237] The Portuguese came to Indian shores in 1498. They conquered the Island of Goa in 1510. They ruled the seas around India for more than a century till the Dutch and British dislodged them. The Marathas ousted them from Bassaim and Chaul and threw them out from their Northern Territories. However they continued to stay on Indian soil till they were thrown out on 19th December, 1961 by our Armed Forces.

How the Portuguese managed to stay in India for 14 long years after Independence of the country is worth an indepth study. The Portuguese policy concerning their Colonial Empire in Asia and Africa after the Second World War requires to be understood. The first thing they did was to change its name to Portugal Ultramarino or "Ultramar Portugues". Portugal refused to follow the decolonising example of the big European Colonial powers. It called their action, privately as well as publicly as irresponsible and cowardly.[238]

The political answer to the decolonising danger that began in Asia and rapidly progressed to Africa was thought possible by making some legal-constitutional adjustments in 1951. It revoked the Colonial Act of 1930 and included it with some minor changes in the new chapter VII of the Constitution.[239]

When Portugal joined the United Nations, in December 1955, the Secretary General had written the usual letter asking her to list the territories under her control and cover by Article 73 on decolonisation. Portugal's reply was that none of the Portuguese territories came within the scope of Article 73, because Portugal, by her Constitution, was a unitary state of which all her territories in the homeland and overseas were provinces- a pluricontinental state. None of them could thus be regarded as non-self-governing.

On 1st July, 1955 it published a new 'Estatuto'. With a magical legal manoeuvre it changed 'Colonias' into 'Provincias Ultramarinas' and the empire 'Imperio' into 'Ultramar'. So a 'pluricontinental' nation was born and Portugal tried to wriggle itself out from the requirements of the Charter of the United Nations according to which it had to furnish a report about the non-autonomous territories under its control.

In 1959, the General Assembly passed resolutions 1467(XIV), which set up a Special Committee of Six to study and enumerate the principles, which should guide members in determining whether or not an obligation existed to transmit the information called for in Article 73 of the Charter.[240]

At this session, the General assembly labelled Goa and other Portuguese "Provinces" as non-self-governing territories. At the same time Portugal was requested to provide information not only on the affairs of her colonies but on her efforts to assist them to independence. Almost a year later, the UN General Assembly's Trusteeship Council endorsed a thirty-three-nation move to condemn Portugal's refusal to transmit information about her overseas territories.

Three months after establishment of diplomatic relations (November 1949), the Government of India presented an 'Aide-Memoire' (27th February, 1950) by which it asked the Portuguese Government to start negotiations for the transfer of Indian Territories under Portuguese administration. The Portuguese Government refused even to accept the proposal claiming it to be against the constitutional provisions. It said that Goa was not a Portuguese Colony but an investment of Portugal in the East. It was a transplantation of the West in the lands of the East. [241]

The matter worsened due to the intransigence of the Portuguese Government. The Indian Government decided to close its legation in Lisbon. In 1954 the Goan freedom fighters occupied the enclaves of Dadra and Nagar Haveli. In 1955 unarmed Satyagrahis marched into

Goa. The Portuguese answer to this peaceful march was brutal. Many were shot point blank. Hundreds were wounded and maimed for life. The Indian Government cut diplomatic relations and closed its borders with the State of Goa.

Portugal launched a ferocious propaganda campaign in the Press and on the streets against India and against the personality of Mr. Nehru. Meanwhile on 22nd December, 1955 it lodged a complaint against India in the International Court of Justice at The Hague claiming that the access to the enclaves of Dadra and Nagar Haveli is being denied by India. The matter proceeded till 1960 when the Court decided that the Portuguese troops couldn't transit through Indian Territory without its authorisation. On 12th April, 1960, the regime celebrated as a decisive victory the **sentence of the International Court of Justice that recognised the Portuguese Sovereignty over the enclaves and its right of passage through the Indian Territory, except for the Portuguese troops for which it depended on Indian authorisation.**[242] This was an '**ineffective**' sentence for all practical purposes, and hastened further events.

On 11th August, 1961 the Indian parliament approved a legislation ordering the integration of Dadra and Nagar Haveli enclaves and guaranteeing Indian citizenship to its 5000 inhabitants.

The Indian parliament approved on 11th August, 1961 the law integrating these enclaves with India and granting Indian Citizenship to its inhabitants.[243]

Portugal had been claiming since 1947, that 'Estado da India' was Portuguese on the basis of its Constitution and moral order and that Goa was "Western, Christian, Luso-Tropical" and not a colony, but an extension of European Portugal in the East. [244]

The Failed Strategy

The Salazarist strategy[245] was based on three important points:

Firstly, military strategists accepted since 1954, that the territories were not militarily defensible in case of an Indian attack. From this point in mind a military strength was to be maintained just sufficient to dissuade India from launching a simple police action. It would be forced to launch a large-scale operation to occupy the territory militarily. This would create an International uproar and expose the contradiction of the so-called pacifist policy of Mr. Nehru. Dr. Salazar was convinced till the last, even after the Indian attack, that it would never succeed. Despite several requests from the last Governor-General, the Government in Lisbon had decided to maintain in Goa till the last, a military force of small size without an air force, anti-aircraft cover, anti-tank weapons, adequate ammunition and with obsolete armaments and an old warship in Marmagoa.

So, Salazar was convinced that India would not use military option, and believed that it would not be possible to face it, in case India decides to use this option. It is claimed that he decided intentionally to keep the territory under- armed and prepared for symbolic defence. In fact the armed forces had to be just sufficient to draw the military attack that would not take place due to the reasons cited above.

Secondly, Dr. Salazar as the head of Government had invested everything in diplomatic, political and legal battles to put pressure on the Indian Union and pin down Nehru under the contradiction between pacifism and military occupation. With this intent he reminded Great Britain about the Treaty of Alliance and its duty to help Portugal in case of attack on its colonies; it insisted with the United States and the NATO to interpret the Pact in a manner to get support from this organisation even for the territories in the southern hemisphere; it resorted to complaints to the International Court of Justice in order to entangle New Delhi in the web of the process and to the decision of the Hague; it conspired with Pakistan against India; it invited foreign and friendly journalists to visit 'India Portuguesa' and write about it; it subsidised publicity campaigns in the Western media and Pakistan; it promoted and supported study tours which in any form would give scientific explanation and support to the Portuguese presence in India.

Thirdly, when everything was seen to have been lost, an order was given on the eve of the attack by the Indian Union to a total sacrifice- ***"Sacrificio total"***. Salazer wrote in his dramatic telegram dated 14th December, sent to the last Governor General, General Vassalo e Silva, that he did not foresee possibility of truce, of Portuguese prisoners or ships surrendered. ***"I feel that there can be only soldiers and sailors***

***victorious or dead.*"** As the victory was beyond reach he was ordering them to die and offer a resistance of **"*minimum eight days*"**, so that it would enable the Government to hold up the attack through mobilisation of international institutions. [246]

On 17th August, 1961, Nehru said in the Indian Parliament "The steps to be taken for Liberation of Goa could be reviewed in order to include the use of the Indian Army at the appropriate time."

Salazar greatly worried, confided to his friends: **Yes, Nehru is a twisted hypocrite. I do not believe in his pacifism, and I also do not believe that he will make the mistake of attacking Goa. Hence one must not allow him any other alternative short of war. This is still the only policy which might save Goa."**[247]

Between August and December 1961 the Government of Lisbon fought a desperate and final diplomatic battle to avoid the military action by taking recourse to all possible diplomatic and political means that it could mobilise. At the last moment it tried to reinforce the military by the aerial route but this move did not concretise due to lack of transport and landing permissions from various countries.

All this turned out to be in vain: during the night of 17th / 18th, 40000 Indian soldiers, supported by tanks and heavy artillery, by Air Force and Naval Squadron, attacked Goa, Daman and Diu by land, air and sea. Within 24 hours after the beginning of the offensive the small and under-armed Portuguese Army and Police (just above 3000 men) surrendered by the middle of 19th December.

When Franco Nogueira, Foreign Affairs Minister of Salazar, landed in New York, on that day, to participate in the meeting of the Security Council of the United Nations, he got the astounding news that everything was over. Nothing could be done: the Soviet veto stalled the approval of the motion ordering the suspension of the conflict and retreating of the troops to the starting point. In fact, the foundation of the strategy of intransigence of Salazar, which had withstood for some time, had tumbled like the pack of cards, showing the **"*beco sem saida*"** or blind alley of the complete policy. [248]

The old dictator while building his policy on Goa had made a mistake in judging the adversary, with the assumption that he would not attack. Dr. Salazar did not believe that a young State just recently emerging out from British custody, over and above led by a disciple of Gandhi and his policy of non-violence, would dare to challenge the opposition of the United States and Britain and attack an 'old ally' of the latter and a member of 'NATO'.

It was true that the world had changed and he was mistaken.

Nehru was forced to attack when all attempts for peaceful transition were finished. He was forced by public opinion on the eve of the general elections. He was under pressure from the African anti-colonialists, especially from the African nationalists. (*During October 1961, there was a Seminar on Portuguese colonies in New Delhi when the Angolan and other African nationalist delegates put strong pressure on the Indian Government to take action against Portuguese possessions in India.)* [249]

Salazar also made mistake regarding the loyalty of the allies and the efficacy of the alliances. The colonialist Portugal discovered in 1961 that it was vulnerable, isolated internationally and without true outside support for its policies. The previous sympathetic show towards the Portuguese political policy, from the earlier Republican Administration in the United States belonged to the past. With the new Kennedy Administration, the Americans, trying to invest strongly with relations with India, limited themselves to putting some diplomatic pressure to hold up the attack and offer some pious condemnation when it took place.

On being requested by Lisbon the old ally"**Velha aliada**" said in the midst of the crisis on 12th December, 1961, that it could provide only limited help in this dispute with another member of the **'Commonwealth'.** It informed that it was beyond doubt that there would not be any British participation in the military operations. It would intercede with New Delhi like the United States and other countries of NATO, to avoid the Indian attack and let its criticism known when it happened. These were pious words!

The Salazarist Government discovered that the ***"Velha Alianca"*** the old alliance had turned out to be a useless relic in the post world-war world, and that it could no longer rely on the new alliances to which it belonged in the defence of its threatened ***"Imperio"*** empire.[250]

Finally, a victim of his own propaganda, Salazar made the mistake about the sacrificial capacity of the troops on the ground, and the "P*ortuguesismo*' of the Goans. In reality the order for total sacrifice was a cruel one, given the fact that the military was left without means to take defensive measures, precisely as it was decided that no military defence was possible. In these conditions, he ordered them to offer resistance for at least eight days. Naturally, the order was not followed except for the resistance offered by **'Aviso Afonso de Albuquerque'** in the port of Marmagoa and by a few garrisons in Daman. The majority of troops and the Police after a nominal initial resistance, surrendered en masse before the crushing superiority of the adversary, making ineffective the plan of last point of defence in Vasco da Gama.

To escape the massacre, General Vassalo e Silva and his General Staff, citing ***"Razoes de Consciencia"***(reasons of conscience), decided not to follow the orders of Salazar and offered to surrender.[251]

Salazar had suspected Goans and was not ready to rely on their '***Portuguesismo***' in the defence of ***'Roma do Oriente'***. The Hindu majority was clearly supportive of integration in the Indian Union. The Christian minority, with the exception of a nucleus of '***Descendentes***' and a small ***mestico*** community in Daman was predominantly hostile to the Portuguese colonizer and desired an association with India. Some however desired autonomy for preserving the Goan uniqueness. The fact remains that the majority of Goans celebrated the Indian military action as **Liberation.** It was evident that the fall of the so called Estado Portugues da India was foreseen with the hope that would really be: **The beginning of the end of the last European Colonial Empire.** [252]

As a result of the emotional shock caused by the events, Dr. Salazar could not deliver his address in person. It was read on his behalf in the National Assembly on 3-1-62 by Mr. Mario Figueiredo, the then president of the National Assembly.

The address said:

"In my last message sent to the Governor-General, written God alone knows with such bitterness in my soul, I was telling that we had full knowledge of our modest forces, and that the Indian Union could always multiply the attacking forces with any arbitrary factor.

Finally it did reveal a great disproportion. The policy of the Government had been always based on the inpossibility of ensuring an efficient defence of Goa by maintaining armed forces. It wanted to maintain forces in Goa just to compel Indian Union to launch a large-scale military operation that would scandalise the world, and it would not trust the success of its claim of a simple police action. The facts corroborated the first mission. The second mission consisted in not dispersing the forces against the terrorist agents masquerading as freedom fighters, but to organise the defence in the best possible way so as to bring out the valour of our men befitting the old tradition in India.

It was a horrible situation for me to think that this would mean a "sacrificio total" a total sacrifice, but I was recommending it and hoping that this sacrifice as the greatest service one could render to the Nation".[253]

Upon receiving news of the fall of Goa, the Portuguese government formally severed all diplomatic links with India and refused to recognise the incorporation of the seized territories into the Indian Republic. An offer of Portuguese citizenship was instead made to all Goan natives who wished to immigrate to Portugal than remain under Indian rule. This was amended in 2006 to include only those who had been born before 19 December 1961.

Later, in a show of defiance, Salazar's government offered a reward of US $10,000, for the capture of Brigadier Sagat Singh, the commander of the maroon berets of India's parachute regiment who were first troops to enter Panjim, Goa's capital.

On receiving news of the fall of Portuguese India, Lisbon went virtually in mourning, and Christmas celebrations were extremely muted. The U.S.embassy placed a curtain in front of its Christmas display in the ground floor window of the U.S. Information Office. Cinemas and theatres shut down as tens of thousands of Portuguese marched in a silent parade from Lisbon's city hall to the cathedral, escorting the relics of St. Francis Xavier.

Portugal was sure that it was going to lose Goa. However, if it had accepted any other solution to the problem, it would have affected its other colonies as well, and then its grip on these colonies would have collapsed. It wanted India to use the military to occupy it. In fact it could be said that it had kept a symbolic army in Goa in order to defend Angola, Mozambique and Guine. Accordingly it never accepted the Liberation of Goa till the regime was ousted in 1974.[254]

As expected and persistently emphasised by the African delegates, the Portuguese Colonial Empire in Africa collapsed once Goa was freed from its hold and the subsequent downfall of the dictatorial regime.

The Portuguese African colonies became free one after another. Guine –Bissau became free on 12th September, 1974, Mozambique on 15th June, 1975 and Angola on 11th November, 1975.

Portugal conquered the island of Goa on 25th November, 1510 and was ousted on 19th December, 1961. One shudders to think that but for the much belated **Operation Vijay** executed in lightning speed by our valiant Armed Forces the Portuguese would have continued to stay firmly on our sacred soil forever!

Internment and repatriation of POWs

Following their surrender, the Portuguese soldiers were interned by the Indian Army at their own military camps at Navelim, Aguada, Ponda and Alparqueiros

By January 1962, most POWs had been transferred to the newly established camp at Ponda. The captivity lasted for six months. The Portuguese Government insisted that the POWs be repatriated by Portuguese aircraft - a demand that was rejected by the Indian Government who instead insisted on aircraft from a neutral country. The negotiations were delayed even further when Salazar ordered the detention of 1200 Indians in Mozambique allegedly as a bargaining chip in exchange for Portuguese POWs.

By May 1962, most of the POWs had been repatriated—being first flown to Karachi, in chartered French aircraft, and then sent off to Lisbon by three ships: *Vera Cruz*, *Pátria* and *Moçambique*.

On arrival at Tejo in Portugal, returning Portuguese servicemen were taken into custody by military police at gunpoint and without immediate access to their families who had arrived to receive them. Following intense questioning and interrogations, the officers were charged with direct insubordination on having refused to comply with directives not to surrender to the Indians. On 22 March 1963, the Governor General, the military commander, his chief of staff, one naval captain, six majors, a sub lieutenant and a sergeant were cashiered by the council of ministers for cowardice and expelled from military service. Four captains, four lieutenants and a lieutenant commander were suspended for six months.

The Liberation of the Portuguese enclaves took place on 19th December, 1961 and soon within ten months there was the border war with China in October 1962. The western countries notably the USA and the Great Britain supported India during this period. However, these countries had earlier supported Portugal in the international fora and one could presume that they would have pressurised India to abandon the military option to liberate these enclaves, had they not been liberated the previous year in 1961!

In fact the last Portuguese Governor General, Gen. Vassalo e Silva during his visit to Goa in 1982 did express in an interview that had Chinese attacked India a year earlier i.e. in October 1961, the whole picture would have been different!

Relations between India and Portugal thawed only in 1974, when following an anti-colonial military coup d'etat and the fall of authoritarian rule in Lisbon. Goa was finally recognised as part of India and steps were taken to re-establish diplomatic relations with India. In 1992, Portuguese President Mario Soares became the first Portuguese head of state to visit Goa after its annexation by India. This followed Indian President R. Venkataraman's visit to Portugal in 1990.

MESSAGES OF CONGRATULATIONS

Personal Message from Prime Minister to Maj.Gen. K.P.Kandeth[255] "Received full report of operation. You and the officers and men serving under you in the Goa operation have my warm congratulations on the splendid way all of you carried out the task allotted to you with efficiency, courtesy and humanity."

Jai hind.

'Jawaharlal Nehru'

Message From COAS [256]

Special order received from COAS (.) quote (.) you were given a delicate and difficult task, which you have completed with great speed and competence (.) your conduct during the operation has been exemplary and worthy of the high traditions of our army (.) I therefore send you on this occasion my personal congratulations and my appreciation for the high sense of duty and discipline you have displayed (.) unquote (.) into all tps (.) this will be read out to all ranks.

Gen. J.N.CHAUDHURI, G.O.C.-in-C. Southern Command [257]

From Lt. Gen. CHAUDHURI (.) quote (.) my warmest personal thanks and congratulations for your brilliant execution of the operation plan (.) I always knew you could do it quickly but you did it even quicker than I thought (.) I have sent thanks on behalf of us all to the Navy and Air Force whose active co-operation made our task so much easier (.) unquote (.) into all tps (.) this will be read out to all ranks.

Jawaharlal Nehru's letter to Chandrakant Keni, written just two days after Goa's Liberation.

प्रधान मंत्री भवन
PRIME MINISTER'S HOUSE
NEW DELHI

No. 2481-PMH/61

December 21, 1961

Dear Shri Keni,

I have your letter of December 20. I needhardly tell you how happy I am at the freedom that has come to Goa. It may be said that with the freedom of Goa, India herself is more free. Thus far India's freedom was incomplete.

Freedom is a great blessing, but it also brings responsibilities. Only those who can shoulder these responsibilities worthily profit by that freedom or can maintain it. I earnestly hope that the people of Goa will rise above petty disputes and conflicts and work together for the advancement of Goa and of India.

Yours sincerely,

Jawaharlal Nehru

Shri Chandrakant Keni,
Hon. Secretary, Goa Information Centre,
'Sannidhi', Rajghat,
New Delhi 1.

Personal message from Maj. Gen. K.P.Candeth to all units of task force.[258]

Personal msg from Maj.Gen. KP CANDETH to all units of TASK FORCE (.) To be read out to all ranks (.) quote (.) in liberating GOA and ending PORTUGUESE OCCUPATION of Indian Territory in 42 hours you have made history (.) I congratulate all of you for determination speed and courage with which you have overcome every obstacle (.) this is in the finest traditions of the Indian Army (.) I am sure that you will undertake the reconstruction of Goa with the same determination (.) well done (.) JAI HIND (.) all info.

Jawaharlal Nehru

Good bye to the last Portuguese G.G. of Goa, Daman and Diu

Epilogue

OPERATION VIJAY was the ultimate solution India had to pursue to free our Motherland from the shackles holding her in bondage. We Indians were at last free from the rule of foreigners on our sacred soil!

Vandé Mataram

References:

232—Article I of Anglo-Port.Treaty of1641
233—Last article of the Treaty of 23 rd June 1661
234—Anglo-Port. Declaration of 14 Oct 1899
235—S.N.Roskill, Britain's Official Naval Historian
236—North Atlantic Treaty of 4 th April 1949
237—Fernando Rosas-Goa ou Principio do Fim-p-111-114
238—Ibid-p-11
239—Ibid-p-12
240—Article 73 of UN Charter on Decolonisation
241—Fernando Rosas-Goa ou o principio-p-15
242—Ibid-p-19
243—Ibid-p-19
244—Ibid-p-17
245—Ibid-p-17
246—Ibid-p-19
247—Franco Nogueira-Salazar-p-223
248—Fern. Rosas-Goa ou-p-20
249—Ibid-p-20
250—Ibid-p-21
251—Ibid-p-22
252—Ibid-p-22
253—Cunha Leal-Patria em Perigo-p-253
254—V.N.Maencar-Maza Kala Vijanwas-p-103
255—Congratulary Message from Prime Minister to Maj.Gen. Kandeth-p-212
256—Message from COAS-p-212
257—Message from Lt.Gen. Chaudhuri-p-212
258—Message from Maj.Gen. Candeth to all units of Task Force

Manuscripts

1— **HAG—Directiva Geral para a Defesa da India, Damao e Diu—General Paulo Benard Guedes—Military Records—file No. 119.**

2— **HAG—Plano de Contra Ataque—Coronel Tirocinado Liborio Monteiro—Military Records—file No. 627.**

3— **HAG—Nominal Roll of Detenus in Goa—Military Records—file No. 91.**

Bibliography

1. **Action in Goa**—-Dr. Ram Manohar Lohia
2. **A India Portuguesa**—-Lopes Mendes
3. **A Patria em Perigo** —Cunha Leal
4. **A Queda da India Portuguesa**--Carlos Alexandre Morais
5. **Dossier Goa— Vassalo e Silva** Ed—Botelho Simoes
6. **Goa, ou o Principio do Fim** — Prof. Fernando Rosas
7. **History of Gujarat Kingdom (1458—1537)** —J. Chaube
8. **India's Use of force in Goa** — Arthur G. Rubinoff
9. **Jawaharlal Nehru's Speeches Vol III** — The Publication Division
10. **Mahatma Gandhi**- Pyarelal —Navjivan Press
11. **Mahatma—Vol. VII** —D. G. Tendulkar
12. **Maza Kala Vijanvas** -- Dr. Vinayak N. Mayencar
13. **Nagar Havelicha Mukti Sangram ani Mim**—Prabhakar Vaidya
14. **Netaji** —V. S.Valimbe'
15. **Operation Vijay** — P. N.Khera (Historical Division Ministry of Defence) GOI
16. **Passagem para a India** - Gen. Carlos Azeredo
17. **O fim do Estado Português da India** - Gen. Franscisco Cabral Couto
18. **Portuguese rule in Goa**—R.P.Rao
19. **The Liberation of GOA**——Dr. P.D. Gaitonde
20. **Vinte Anos de Defesa do Estado Portugues da India** Volumes I, II, III and IV Ministerio dos Negocios Estrangeiros De Portugal.
